SOCIAL WORK

Past, Present and Future

Edited by
Terry Bamford and Keith Bilton

GW00585610

P

First published in Great Britain in 2020 by

Policy Press
University of Bristol
1-9 Old Park Hill
Bristol
BS2 8BB
UK
t: +44 (0)117 954 5940
pp-info@bristol.ac.uk
www.policypress.co.uk

British Library Cataloguing in Publication Data
A catalogue record for this book is available from the British Library

ISBN 978-1-4473-5653-0 hardback
ISBN 978-1-4473-5654-7 paperback
ISBN 978-1-4473-5655-4 ePdf
ISBN 978-1-4473-5656-1 ePub

The rights of Terry Bamford and Keith Bilton to be identified as editors of this work has been asserted by them in accordance with the Copyright, Designs and Patents Act 1988.

Cover design by Gareth @ Qube
Front cover image: iStock-901997260

For Terry Bamford OBE

8 August 1942 – 9 February 2020

Contents

Terry Bamford

Terry and I had just got this book completed and into production, and he and his wife Margaret had left for a well-earned holiday in Morocco. Then on 28 January came news that Terry had fallen down a flight of stone steps and suffered a catastrophic head injury. He was flown back to England in an air ambulance and died on 9 February without regaining consciousness.

Terry worked for BASW as Assistant General Secretary and later served as Chair of the Association. He was a Director of Social Services in Northern Ireland in the 1980s and Executive Director of Housing and Social Services in Kensington and Chelsea throughout the 1990s. He chaired a Primary Care Trust for five years and was Director of the Social Perspectives Network for Modern Mental Health. He has written four books on social work. He was, until his untimely death, Chair of the Social Work History Network. He was also very active in the International Federation of Social Workers, serving *inter alia* as Secretary of its Human Rights Commission for ten years, taking up cases of social workers imprisoned or persecuted for their professional activities in different countries. As a Director of Social Services, he was probably unique in retaining a close involvement not only with social work practice, both in this country and internationally, but also with social work teaching and research.

Keith Bilton

Acknowledgements

No book is produced without the involvement and support of many people. Our first debt is to our contributors, who accepted our invitation to write a chapter, tolerated our badgering about the importance of keeping to the agreed time-scales and produced some excellent and thought-provoking pieces. They even cheerfully accepted our pleas to reduce the word count to bring it in line with that agreed with Policy Press. And they did deliver on time, as we were under pressure to have a book coming out to coincide with the British Association of Social Workers' (BASW) 50th birthday, the 50th anniversary of the 1970 Local Authority Social Services Act and the establishment of a unified training for social work agreed in 1970.

Our colleagues at Policy Press have been unfailingly supportive and encouraging throughout. We are particularly grateful to Sarah Bird, Commissioning Editor, Jo Morton, Editorial Project Manager, and Amelia Watts-Jones, Editorial Assistant, for their assistance.

The Social Work History Network, where the concept of the book germinated, has been a fertile source of ideas and support. The British Library is a wonderful resource and has provided assistance in finding references, however obscure.

Finally, we wish to thank our wives, both named Margaret, who have tolerated the hours spent beavering over the book, provided invaluable comments and offered gentle criticism when required. Without their constant support this book would not have seen the light of day.

Terry Bamford

Notes on contributors

Terry Bamford OBE – see p vii.

Peter Beresford OBE is Professor of Citizen Participation at the University of Essex, Co-Chair of Shaping Our Lives, the national disabled people's and service users' organisation and network, and Emeritus Professor of Social Policy at Brunel University London. He is a long-term user of mental health services and has a long-standing background of involvement in issues of participation as a writer, researcher, activist and teacher. His latest book is *Madness, Violence and Power* (Toronto University Press, 2019).

Keith Bilton qualified as a child care officer in 1963 and worked as a child and family social worker until 1966, when he was appointed General Secretary of the Association of Child Care Officers (ACCO). ACCO was dissolved in June 1970 and he joined the staff of the newly formed BASW as an Assistant General Secretary, leaving this post in February 1973 to take up a managerial post in a social services department. In 2000, with Joan Baraclough and David Jones, he set up the Social Work History Network.

Suzy Croft worked for 30 years as a palliative care social work practitioner and ran the social work department of St John's Hospice, the Hospice for Central London. She played an active role in social work as a commentator, writer, trustee of social work and related organisations and a practice educator. She is currently working as a welfare rights worker with older people. She received the Lifetime Achievement Award for Social Work in the 2016 Social Worker of the Year Awards.

Emma Gant worked as a medical secretary before training as a social worker at Anglia Ruskin University. After qualifying with a first class honours degree she worked in children and families social work for a local authority. After working for a mental health charity as a social worker and project manager she has now returned to local authority social work.

David N. Jones qualified as a social worker in 1974. He worked in a local authority and then in a National Society for the Prevention of Cruelty to Children specialist team. He was General Secretary of

BASW and subsequently played an active role in international social work. A former President of the International Federation of Social Workers, he now leads on the Global Agenda for Social Work and Social Development. In a varied career he has worked for the Central Council for the Education and Training of Social Workers and the Office for Standards in Education, and as an Independent Chair of both Adult and Children's Safeguarding Boards. He is Chair of Northamptonshire Healthwatch. An author of numerous articles and books, he coordinates the Commonwealth Organisation for Social Work.

Dr Ray Jones is Emeritus Professor of Social Work at Kingston University and St George's, University of London, and a registered social worker. From 1992 to 2006 he was Director of Social Services in Wiltshire. He was the first Chief Executive of the Social Care Institute for Excellence, and has been Deputy Chair and Chair of BASW. From 2008 to 2016 he was Professor of Social Work at Kingston University and St George's, University of London. He has been a visiting professor at the University of Exeter and at the University of Bath and is an honorary fellow of the University of Gloucestershire. He has led inquiries following the deaths of children and adults; from 2009 to 2013 he was chair of Bristol's Safeguarding Children Board; and from 2010 until 2016 he oversaw children's services improvement in Salford, Torbay, the Isle of Wight, Sandwell and Devon. He is the author of seven books, including *The Story of Baby P: Setting the Record Straight* (2014; 2nd edn 2017) and *In Whose Interest? The Privatisation of Child Protection and Social Work* (2018). He is now completing 'A History of the Personal Social Services'. A frequent media commentator and columnist, in 2017 he was awarded the Outstanding Contribution to Social Work Award at the Social Worker of the Year Awards.

Malcolm Jordan's career commenced with six years of community work in a London overspill town and a brief spell in the Borstal service. He was a psychiatric social worker based in two large hospitals for seven years, followed by a similar period responsible for a radical CQSW course in Maidstone and three years in the Social Work Service of the DHSS. He moved to Lancashire as Deputy Director of Social Services for nine years, then entered the private sector as director of a school and community homes for children with severe learning difficulties and challenging behaviours. He was a Board Member of the GSCC. He is currently a volunteer with young offenders and on the executive of SWU and the SWU/BASW Austerity Action Group.

He enjoys a full family life, has a continuing interest in the cinema (including a long campaign to have social work recognised) and is a member of XR – Extinction Rebellion. His book *Social Work and Proud* will be published in the autumn of 2020.

Karen Lyons, PhD, CQSW is Emeritus Professor at London Metropolitan University, UK. Following experience in practice, she taught social work at the University of East London, including award-bearing courses in international social work. Her doctoral research (British social work education), plus experience in a European network, on the board of the International Association of Schools of Social Work and as the Editor of *International Social Work*, resulted in contributions to social work education in a variety of countries in Europe and beyond. Apart from supervision and examining of doctoral students she continues with some writing projects, most recently on international labour mobility and transnational social work.

Guy Shennan qualified as a social worker in 1989, having gained pre-course experience in mental health. He worked as a generic social worker and then with children and families. He trained in solution-focused practice in 1995 and now specialises in this approach as an independent practitioner, trainer and consultant. Guy was Chair of BASW from 2014 to 2018, during which time he campaigned for social justice, leading the Boot Out Austerity initiative. He has co-founded the Solution-Focused Collective with a view to using this approach for the purposes of social change.

June Thoburn CBE, LittD is Emeritus Professor of Social Work at the University of East Anglia (UEA), UK. She was a generalist and child and family specialist social worker in England and Canada before taking up a joint appointment with UEA and Norfolk Social Services Department in 1980. Her teaching focuses on social policy and child and family social work. Her research and publications have covered family support in the community and child placement services (including residential care, foster care and adoption). She was a founder member of the General Social Care Council and is a member of the BASW children and families policy and practice group.

Hilary Tompsett is Emeritus Professor of Social Work, Kingston University and St George's University of London. A registered social worker with experience over 16 years as a practitioner/manager in children and families, mental health, elderly care and renal work, and

23 years as an educator and researcher, Hilary is on BASW Council and has been involved in professional regulation and education with GSCC, the Health and Care Professions Council and, currently, the General Optical Council. Previously she was Chair of JUC-SWEC (the Joint University Council Social Work Education Committee), contributed to strategic government working parties, parliamentary select committees and national social work reforms. She has presented widely in the UK, Japan, Finland, Russia and South Korea on social work education, research and social care for older people.

Jane Tunstill is Emeritus Professor at Royal Holloway College, University of London, where she was responsible for professional and post-qualifying social work education as well as an extensive children's services research programme. She is also Visiting Professor and Children's Services Consultant at the Social Care Workforce Research Unit, King's College London. She has a long-standing practice, policy-campaigning and research record of seeking to highlight the importance of family support and early access to services. Her research output includes many government-commissioned evaluations of services for children in need, including the first study of the implementation of section 17 of the 1989 England and Wales Children Act; the National Evaluation of Sure Start, in which she directed the Implementation Module; centre-based services; and a range of voluntary sector service evaluations. She was a founder member of the national social care knowledge-dissemination project, Making Research Count.

List of abbreviations

ACCO	Association of Child Care Officers
ADSS	Association of Directors of Social Services
AGM	annual general meeting
APSW	Association of Psychiatric Social Workers
ASW	Association of Social Workers
ASYE	Assessed and Supported Year in Employment
BASW	British Association of Social Workers
CCETSW	Central Council for Education and Training in Social Work
CFAB	Children and Families Across Borders
CPD	continuous professional development
CQSW	Certificate of Qualification in Social Work
CRC	Community Rehabilitation Company
CSS	Certificate in Social Service
DfE	Department for Education
DH	Department of Health
DHSS	Department of Health and Social Security
DipSW	Diploma in Social Work
DOLS	Deprivation of Liberty Safeguards
Erasmus	European Region Action Scheme for the Mobility of University Students
FRG	Family Rights Group
FSU	Family Service Unit
GP	general practitioner
GSCC	General Social Care Council
HCPC	Health and Care Professions Council
IASSW	International Association of Schools of Social Work
IFSW	International Federation of Social Workers
IMSW	Institute of Medical Social Workers
IT	Intermediate Treatment
JRT	Joint Review Team
JUC-SWEC	Joint University Council Social Work Education Committee
LSE	London School of Economics
MOH	Medical Officer of Health
MoJ	Ministry of Justice
NAAS	National Assessment and Accreditation System
NAPO	National Association of Probation Officers
NHS	National Health Service

NISCC	Northern Ireland Social Care Council
NISW	National Institute for Social Work
NQSW	Newly Qualified Social Worker
Ofsted	Office for Standards in Education
PCF	Professional Capabilities Framework
SCOSW	Standing Conference of Organisations of Social Workers
SCW	Social Care Wales
SIAG	Seebohm Implementation Action Group
SSSC	Scottish Social Services Council
SWAN	Social Work Action Network
SWE	Social Work England
SWRB	Social Work Reform Board
SWTF	Social Work Task Force
SWU	Social Workers Union
TCSW	The College of Social Work

Introduction

Terry Bamford

The genesis of this book was a casual suggestion at a meeting of the Social Work History Network. Why don't we do something to mark 50 years since BASW was formed in 1970, the Local Authority Social Services Act was passed and a unified social work training was about to be introduced? And this book is the something.

Perhaps I should clarify what it is not. It is not an official history, nor even an unofficial history of the last 50 years. It presents different perspectives on the evolution of social work during that period and reflects the views and stances of individual contributors. It looks at current trends and what they mean for the future direction of social work. It is predominantly about England and Wales, which have been more subject to government intervention than the other countries of the UK, but marked divergence in Scotland and Northern Ireland is noted.

Austerity is a theme running through the contributions. Its impact on many social work clients has been dire both in financial terms, with benefits frozen, and in the reduction in public services as budget cuts have taken hold. But it would be naive to expect the 'New Jerusalem' to be round the corner, just as the hopes of 1970 were never fully realised.

Keith Bilton reminds us of the fragmentation of social work in the years leading up to 1970. His perspective is fascinating, as he was a participant in the discussions leading to the establishment of BASW and served as secretary of the Seebohm Implementation Action Group. His Chapter 1 is a salutary reminder of the tortuous negotiations that were eventually to make 1970 a landmark year in the development of social work.

Chapter 2, on social services departments, poses the question whether they were a success or failure. Certainly they put social services at the top table in local government and for a short period they grew very rapidly. The 1975 financial crisis put the brakes on, just as the 2008 financial crash led to the years of austerity. In terms of services, much was achieved, but in terms of the promotion of good social work practice, the verdict is mixed.

The many twists and turn in social work regulation are traced by David Jones in Chapter 3. The GSCC realised a long-held ambition for social work but it fell short of self-regulation for the profession. Changes since, including Social Work England, show that the profession has a long way to go to achieve full recognition. From best value through the three Es of economy, efficiency and effectiveness, regulators have sought to measure performance, but they have rarely focused on social work practice.

Where there has been substantial change in social work is in the development of its knowledge base. From the smattering of psychology and psychiatry that informed knowledge of human growth and development 50 years ago, in Chapter 4 June Thoburn identifies the many influences on social work knowledge, from government, employers, university-based research and clients. She cites the growth of social media as a fertile area for the interchange of ideas, while cautioning about the risks from dubious research in this space.

At a time when social work training is again in danger of fragmenting, with setting-specific training, as happened with probation in the 1990s, Hilary Tompsett in Chapter 5 reminds us why a unified training was introduced and considers key arguments affecting education decisions over 50 years. As apprenticeship models increase in number there are concerns about the influence that employers and government will exercise over training.

Social work practice has changed from professional practice to procedural practice, with a proliferation of checklists, assessment schedules and manuals. In Chapter 6 Guy Shennan laments the dominance of child protection in children's services and of the assessment function in adult services. He argues that social workers, through BASW or elsewhere, have to find the 'moral courage' to rely on ethical practice, including challenges to their employers if necessary.

The two personal views by Malcolm Jordan and Emma Gant in Chapter 7 are separated by more than 60 years of experience, yet have a striking symmetry. Malcolm remembers a world of professional judgement and autonomy animated by a radical conviction that social work could change the world. Now he sees a world of procedures and checklists and paper-bound bureaucracy limiting social workers' ability to interact with their clients. Emma found her commitment to relationship-based social work impossible in a local authority context. They raise important issues about whether and how social work can flourish in a publicly accountable agency with fixed budgets.

Peter Beresford and Suzy Croft have long championed the importance of listening to service users and engaging them in co-production. The gains made are now under threat from a neoliberal emphasis on individual responsibility that downplays the impact of inequality and disadvantage. In Chapter 8 they call for an empowering and liberatory social work based on co-production with service users in practice and policy. Social work should be a universal service, not a marginal one working with marginalised people.

Looking back, the 1989 Children Act can be viewed as a model for crafting legislation. It was based on evidence. It involved key stakeholders. It was carefully drafted, building on the work of the Law Commission. It sought to balance parents' rights and children's needs. In Chapter 9 June Thoburn and Jane Tunstill trace the evolution of the Act and ask whether its vision of partnership working has been realised. They see piecemeal interventions from successive governments as weakening the framework laid down in the legislation. Too often governments ignore the existing knowledge base. Yet, despite this, the Act stands as the basis for both promoting and safeguarding the welfare of children.

The probation service abandoned its link with social work training in 1995. The focus has shifted from the traditional model of 'advise, assist and befriend' to one of risk management and surveillance. By contrast, services to young offenders have retained rehabilitation at their core. The 20 years since 2000 have seen a national probation service, integrated management with the National Offender Management Service and, most recently, a disastrous part privatisation. Chapter 10 argues that if reoffending is to be addressed effectively, the remodelled service will need to look at the social factors – housing, employment, income – and their impact on the offender.

In Chapter 11 Ray Jones challenges the widely held view that scandals drive policy change. From the 1948 Children Act following the Curtis Committee report after the death of Dennis O'Neill, through to the 1975 Children Act following the death of Maria Colwell, he shows that the reforms were under discussion prior to the inquiries and the publicity they generated. Similarly the 1989 Children Act had a long gestation process as described by Thoburn and Tunstill in Chapter 9, and was not a response to the Cleveland Inquiry. The Climbié Inquiry did not precipitate the 2004 Children Act, which went further than Laming's recommendations in his inquiry report. The chapter is a salutary warning that policy making through legislation is a long and complex process. What scandals provide is an opportunity to secure priority in the parliamentary timetable.

One of the significant changes in the last 50 years is a greater awareness of social work in other countries. In part this is because there are many social workers from other European countries and elsewhere in the world practising in the UK. They come with different training and different cultures. In part too it is because UK-born social workers are now better travelled and some bring work experience from elsewhere. Karen Lyons' Chapter 12 looks at the increasing emphasis on international work with the wider use of the International Definition of Social Work. She raises the question of the relatively narrow construction of social work in the UK as a local authority role – a theme that echoes those of other contributors.

1

Social work in 1970

Keith Bilton

Social work in 1970 was practised in many settings. In the public sector there were social welfare officers, mental welfare officers and child care officers, based, respectively, in local authority welfare, health and children's departments. Education departments employed social workers in child guidance clinics, and also education welfare officers and youth and community workers. The National Health Service (NHS) employed social workers in its hospitals. Probation officers serving the courts were also social workers. The Church of England had moral welfare workers, and many social workers worked for a large number of voluntary organisations of various kinds. 'Independent' social workers were virtually unknown. Others worked in central government inspectorates, or as social work teachers in universities and colleges, their courses, or specialist options within courses, being validated by two central government councils, by one statutory council and by two of the many different associations of social workers.

Two events in 1970 brought significant changes. The British Association of Social Workers (BASW) was established on 24 April and the Local Authority Social Services Act became law on 29 May. This Act, which implemented some of the recommendations of the Seebohm Report (Seebohm, 1968), required counties, county boroughs and London boroughs in England and Wales to establish Social Services Committees, to appoint Directors of Social Services and, in effect, to set up social services departments. It also established the Central Council for Education and Training in Social Work (CCETSW). These two dates, 24 April and 29 May, may be misleading. BASW had in effect been operating for some time before its official inauguration, but the part of the 1970 Act applying to local authorities came into force only on 1 April 1971, and CCETSW was not set up until 1 October 1971. The two events may appear now, and indeed seemed then, to form part of the same unifying process, but they sprang from different concerns and the effects on BASW and, indeed, on social workers themselves of the setting up of social services departments were not what they had expected. This chapter considers the origins of the two events and examines that relationship.

The development of the idea of social work as a profession, and of training for social work

For Clement Attlee, writing in 1920, the social worker is usually a volunteer, although he mentions hospital almoners and probation officers. Attlee saw social workers as being defined more by their values than by their field of work. Their engagement in social service 'has arisen out of a deep discontent with society as at present constituted' and 'is the expression of the desire for social justice' (Attlee, 1920, p 2). The social worker has 'this conception of his duty as a member of a civilised society to make his contribution to the well being of his fellows' (Attlee, 1920, p 27). Attlee sought to distinguish social service, which he saw as an egalitarian concern to address social injustices, from philanthropy, which he associated with condescension. 'It is, I think, clear,' he wrote (Attlee, 1920, p 110), 'that the specialist should be a paid official, the nurse, the doctor, the teacher and the midwife are all professional people.' There was at this time no concept of social work as a separate profession, although Attlee does record (Attlee, 1920, p 145) that 'the Universities have taken up the work of training men and women for social service, London, Bristol, Birmingham, Leeds, Liverpool, Edinburgh and Glasgow having departments of social science and administration. Certificates or diplomas are awarded to those passing the examination.'

Degrees, diplomas or certificates in social science or social studies came to be regarded as an appropriate academic preparation for a broad range of occupations generally accepted as constituting social work. In 1934 a British Federation of Social Workers (BFSW) was established. Its six founder members were the Association of Mental Health Workers, the Women Public Health Officers Association, the Public Health section of the College of Nursing, the London County Council Children's Care Committee Organisers, the Association of Psychiatric Social Workers (APSW) and the National Association of Probation Officers (NAPO). Significantly, the Hospital Almoners Association, one of two precursors of the Institute of Medical Social Workers (IMSW) – the other being the Institute of Hospital Almoners – declined to join because they considered the implied definition of social work to be too wide. In 1951 the BFSW was transformed into the Association of Social Workers (ASW), an individual membership association. Its membership continued to be broader than would now be considered appropriate, and in 1953 included eight housing managers and six health visitors (Sackville, 1987).

Already in 1929 a course for which a degree or diploma in social science was an entry requirement, and which focused more specifically on social casework, had been established at the London School of Economics (LSE). This was the one-year mental health course for the training of psychiatric social workers. Further such courses were established in Edinburgh in 1944 and in Manchester in 1947. APSW was consulted on the development of these courses and recognised them for the purposes of its membership. The Institute of Almoners had for some time been running its own training course, which until 1954 was the only means of qualifying. In that year the Institute approved courses at Edinburgh University and LSE for the issue of its certificate. The course at LSE was the first 'generic' applied social studies course in the UK (Sackville, 1987).

While the Institute of Almoners and the APSW controlled the approval of qualifying courses, for the probation service it was the Home Office which, having in 1936 assumed formal responsibility for the service, took the lead in developing training, by which time NAPO had existed for more than 20 years. The history of the probation service and of the service provided by hospital almoners (as medical social workers were known until 1965) is one of evolution, but the child care service was planned from the beginning. In 1946 the Curtis Committee recommended that local authorities should be required to establish Children's Committees and appoint Children's Officers to take responsibility for looking after children deprived of a normal life (Curtis, 1946). These recommendations were enacted in the 1948 Children Act, which was implemented in July of that year. In an interim report the Curtis Committee had recommended that the Home Office should organise training for the staff of the new departments, and, in response, the Home Office created the Central Training Council in Child Care (CTC), which in 1947 approved six courses for 'boarding-out officers' at the universities of Birmingham, Wales (Cardiff), Leeds, Liverpool, London (LSE) and Nottingham. The Association of Child Care Officers (ACCO) was established in 1949 by graduates of these courses (Sackville, 1988).

By 1959 it seemed that a pattern of training for social work had developed, based on a degree in the social sciences or, for graduates in other subjects, a postgraduate social studies diploma, followed by a one-year applied course, either specialising in medical social work, mental health, probation or child care, or generic with specialist fieldwork placements, including the specialism of family casework. Missing from these specialisms was anything specially designed to meet the needs of social workers in local authority health and welfare departments, although some health departments attempted, sometimes successfully, to recruit psychiatric social workers to work as mental welfare officers.

In 1959 the Working Party on Social Workers in the Local Authority Health and Welfare Services reported, and came to this conclusion about initial training requirements:

> The content of the case loads of social workers throughout the health and welfare services can broadly be divided into the following categories: (a) people with straightforward or obvious needs who require material help, some simple service, or a periodic visit; (b) people with more complex problems, who require systematic help from trained social workers; (c) people with problems of special difficulty requiring skilled help by professionally trained and experienced social workers. (Younghusband, 1959, p 7)

The Working Party considered that the first group could be served by welfare assistants, and the third by social workers trained on one-year applied social science courses for holders of university social science degrees or diplomas. For the second group they recommended 'a general training in social work equivalent to two years full-time training' (Younghusband, 1959, p 8). The Working Party clearly intended the two types of training to be at different levels, and reserved the epithet 'professional' to the higher level. The recommendations therefore appeared consistent with the pattern of professional training in social casework that was developing, and the Council for Training in Social Work (CTSW) was set up in 1962 to develop two-year, non-graduate Certificate in Social Work courses. Already in 1960, however, the CTC had begun to sponsor two-year, non-graduate courses outside the universities for mature students (aged 23 and over) and to award the same Letter of Recognition to students qualifying from both postgraduate and non-graduate courses. Local authority health, welfare and children's departments did not distinguish non-graduate from postgraduate courses for salary purposes. Thus, Younghusband's recommendation of two levels of social work qualification went by the board, and in 1968 the Seebohm Report commented: 'We would deplore a pattern which envisaged a rigid division between those who had received university education and others who had been educated at colleges that are not universities' (Seebohm, 1968, p 178). CCETSW confirmed this situation by awarding the same Certificate of Qualification in Social Work to students successfully completing courses at academic levels ranging from a two-year, non-graduate course to a Master's degree.

Reactions to the Seebohm Report's recommendations for social work training

The Seebohm Report (Seebohm, 1968) recommended that

> there should be one central body to be responsible for promoting the training of the staff of the personal social services. The single new advisory council should have a standing committee on training, and the responsibilities of the standing committee should include training for the probation and aftercare service ... A central government department ... should be responsible for ... planning training. (Seebohm, 1968, p 232)

This would have replicated the Home Office's arrangements for overseeing and promoting training for the probation and child care services. It led to a major disagreement within the Standing Conference of Organisations of Social Workers (SCOSW). APSW and IMSW wanted an education and training council independent of ministers. ACCO and NAPO supported the Seebohm recommendations. In effect, they wanted what they were used to having. APSW and IMSW were prepared to surrender their control over training, but only to an independent council with adequate social work representation. Little attention was paid to the difference between a social work training council and a council for 'the training of the staff of the personal social services'. In recommending a training council accountable to ministers, the Seebohm Committee may have had in mind the information they published about the numbers of social workers, by specialism, qualifying in 1967 (Seebohm, 1968, p 337). This showed:

probation	216
child care	326
CTSW Certificate in Social Work courses	300
medical social work (MSW)	80
psychiatric social work (PSW)	75.

The probation, child care and CTSW numbers are for England and Wales; the MSW and PSW numbers are for the UK.

The Local Authority Social Services Act modelled CCETSW on the CTSW, which was statutorily accountable not to ministers but to the Privy Council. CCETSW began its life on 1 October 1971, with the appearance of independence, and with a membership of 60, eight of whom were nominated by BASW, representing the various interests of workers, employers, educators and others, but not those of service users, and with central government observers. Hall (1976, p 89) states that the model of 'an autonomous Council for Social Work Education' was adopted, and that was the prevailing view of informed social work opinion at the time, but CCETSW was to become increasingly subject to government influence and, indeed, control.

Unifying social work: the professional associations

Writing about the early 1960s, Terry Bamford observes that 'all the social work professions were expanding rapidly, but the generic base to training that had developed in universities became a driving force towards unity in the professions. The Standing Conference of Organisations of Social Workers ... was established in 1963 to give effect to that sense of unity' (Bamford, 2015, p 17). SCOSW's stated aim was to establish a unified association of *trained* social workers.

Initially, SCOSW had seven member associations. They included the five already mentioned (ACCO, APSW, ASW, IMSW and NAPO), together with two smaller associations, the Association of Family Caseworkers and the Moral Welfare Workers' Association (MWWA). An eighth association, the Society of Mental Welfare Officers (SMWO), joined in March 1964. Applications from the National Association of Home Teachers of the Blind, the Institute of Welfare Officers and the Institute of Social Welfare were rejected (Sackville, 1987). These rejections meant that SCOSW had no member association representing social workers in local authority welfare departments. The relevance of this became apparent when social services departments were established in 1971.

The associations had different characteristics. Men were predominant in NAPO and SMWO; women in IMSW and MWWA. The ASW was generic in character, as to a certain extent was the APSW, reflecting a time when mental health courses had been regarded as a more advanced form of training for practice in any field of social work. NAPO, SMWO and ACCO were, on the other hand, strongly identified with the services in which their members worked. Probation officers and mental welfare officers were statutory officers, but child care officers were not,[1] and ACCO's members included social workers in voluntary children's societies and in the Home Office Inspectorate. NAPO was alone in being registered with the Registrar of Friendly Societies as a trade union, and formed the staff side of the Probation Service's negotiating machinery. APSW and IMSW controlled the recognition of qualifications for membership and, in the NHS, for salary purposes. NAPO admitted all serving probation officers to full membership, irrespective of qualification; APSW and IMSW limited membership to qualified social workers; and ACCO and SMWO admitted unqualified practitioners to associate membership. The nature of decision making also varied. For NAPO and ACCO annual general meetings (AGMs) were the supreme decision-making body, and debates were often vigorous. In IMSW it was the Institute's Council, and AGMs were ceremonial events.

By 1967 discussions in SCOSW had reached the point at which the Standing Conference was able to resolve 'to proceed immediately with negotiations for the formation of one unified association of trained social workers with the aim of agreeing a constitution by 1st July 1968'. Work on the drafting of a constitution began. One of the perceived advantages of a unified association was that, with its larger membership, it would be able to operate at a more local level. It was therefore agreed that local branches should be an important part of the new Association's structure, and also, after some discussion, that they should have some ability to influence decisions taken at national level. Direct representation of the branches on the Council was rejected as entailing an excessively large central body in which proper discussion would not be possible. Thirteen regions were therefore devised as groupings of branches, each of which would have one representative on the Council. It is interesting now to note the acceptance that Scotland, Northern Ireland and Wales could be treated as regions alongside ten English regions. It was also agreed that members would join one of four sections of the Association, representing the specialisms of General Health, Mental Health, Family and Child Care and Treatment of Offenders, each having its own committee with a representative on the Council. Also represented on the Association's Council would be six standing committees.[2]

Eligibility for membership proved more contentious, but agreement was reached that members of the existing associations and associate members of ACCO and SMWO should be eligible to be members of BASW and that in future unqualified social workers should be eligible to be associates, with voting rights at branch but not at national level. The wording of the constitution here is significant. People not qualified in social work were eligible to be not Associate *Members*, but

Associates, people not really belonging to the Association but merely associated with it, and were referred to not as social workers but as people in posts in which it would be appropriate to employ a qualified social worker. This suggests that SCOSW had not entirely given up on its wish to restrict the title 'social worker' to qualified people.

This somewhat unwieldy constitution should be seen not as a blueprint for the efficient running of an association but as a treaty setting out the safeguards that its negotiators required before recommending the members of the existing associations to vote to dissolve them.

Seven associations did indeed vote at general meetings to dissolve themselves, and to recommend their members to apply for membership of BASW, but NAPO decided to continue in being. However, 775 NAPO members did join BASW, forming the core of its Treatment of Offenders Section (Sackville, 1987). There were various reasons for NAPO's decision. The decision to establish BASW as a company limited by guarantee would debar it from registering as a trade union and, while this would not debar it from inheriting NAPO's negotiating rights, without trade union immunities its bargaining power would be weakened. Probation officers tended, with some justification, to the view that the service offered an environment particularly suited to a professional approach to social work practice. Their service had a higher proportion of professionally qualified staff than local authority health, welfare and children's departments did. They had the valued casework facility of an individual office, and good secretarial support. Once confirmed in their appointment by the Home Office, their employment by Magistrates' Probation Committees protected their independence as officers of the court, and created organisational distance between their service and the Home Office and local authorities, who paid for it. The legal requirement on the courts to place all probationers under the supervision of a named probation officer, who was then answerable directly to the court, gave them some protection from unwanted managerial direction. The high value that the service placed on independence was also reflected in a view that professionals should seek consultation when they felt they needed it, but should not be required to accept supervision of their casework by a senior officer. Probation officers' statutory duty to advise, assist and befriend was consonant with social work values.

The main reason, however, for NAPO's decision was the perception that there were threats to the independence of the Probation Service, and that the Association needed to continue in being in order to defend against them. The 1968 Social Work (Scotland) Act had abolished probation services north of the border, integrating their work into the duties of newly formed local authority departments of social work. NAPO had strongly resisted this change, which had, however, been vigorously and effectively supported by the other seven SCOSW members (Hiddleston, 2013). Probation officers' fears that the government might make local authorities in England and Wales responsible for all social work services to the courts were hardly surprising. In Scotland, the process of change began with the Kilbrandon Committee's proposal to give a new local authority department responsibility for serving the juvenile justice system (Kilbrandon, 1964). In England, there had been similar proposals in White Papers (*The Child, the Family and the Young Offender* and *Children in Trouble* (Home Office, 1965, 1968) and in the Seebohm Report (Seebohm, 1968). Those in the second White Paper were largely enacted, although many were not implemented, in the 1969 Children and Young Persons Act. Might England and Wales go further, and follow the Scottish model? Although these fears were to prove unjustified, they were not unreasonable.

Unifying social work: social services departments

The process of unifying the local authority personal social services in England and Wales was very different from the smooth pattern of Scotland's bolder changes. A process that took seven years in Scotland, from the setting up of the Kilbrandon Committee in 1961 to the passing of the Act, took twice as long for England and Wales. It was in October 1956 that the Home Secretary set up the Ingleby Committee (Ingleby, 1960), asking it to consider whether local authorities should 'be given new powers and duties to prevent or forestall the suffering of children through neglect in their own homes'. The Committee reported in October 1960, and one of its recommendations urged 'the importance of further study by the Government and the local interests concerned of the reorganisation of the various services concerned with the family'. The Committee considered that to combine them into a single, unified family service might well be the best long-term solution. No action was taken until, in August 1965, the Labour government, which had taken office the year before, announced in its White Paper *The Child, the Family and the Young Offender* the setting up of a small interdepartmental committee.

The Seebohm Committee was appointed on 20 December of that year 'to review the organisation and responsibilities of the local authority personal social services in England and Wales, and to consider what changes are desirable to secure an effective family service'. The Committee reported in July 1968. The local authority departments that were its primary concern were the health and welfare departments, represented in central government by the Ministry of Health, and the children's departments, overseen in a rather more interventionist manner by the Home Office. The Committee's terms of reference spoke of an effective *family* service, and appeared to envisage recommendations for an enlarged children's department, which would take over various child and family welfare functions from welfare, health and education departments. This line of thought had support in the Home Office and in the child care service. It aroused concern, however, among those social workers and social policy academics who were concerned for the development of services for people who did not belong to families with children. An ad hoc group representing these interests was set up in 1964. Its members were Geraldine Aves, David M. Jones, Robin Huws Jones, Professor Jerry Morris, Timothy Raison, Barbara Rodgers, Margery Taylor, Richard Titmuss and Lewis Waddilove. This was an extremely distinguished group. Geraldine Aves was from 1941 to 1963 the Chief Welfare Officer at the Ministry of Health. Robin Huws Jones became in 1961 the first Principal of the National Institute for Social Work Training. Jerry Morris was an epidemiologist who led the Social Medicine Research Unit and was later, like Huws Jones, a member of the Seebohm Committee. Timothy Raison, a progressive Conservative of a kind it is now difficult to imagine, had been since 1962 the founding editor of *New Society*. Richard Titmuss was Professor of Social Administration, an academic discipline which he more or less founded, at LSE. Lewis Waddilove was director of the Joseph Rowntree Memorial Trust. The ad hoc group mobilised the concern of the Ministry of Health. (Hall, 1976, p 142, gives the text of the ad hoc group's memorandum.) Thus, in 1965 two social work and social policy interest groups, the ad hoc group on the one hand and, on the other, a group of representatives of the Children's Officers and ACCO, each with different views as to how the local authority personal social services should be developed, found themselves allied with two different ministries, each with an interest in assuming responsibility for the resultant local services.

The Seebohm Report opted for the more extensive changes recommended by the ad hoc group. It proposed social *service* departments rather than the social *services* departments set up under the 1970 Act, emphasising the abstract and unifying notion of service rather than a collection of concrete services, but nevertheless listed the services that the Committee wished them to deliver. These were the child care service, welfare services provided under the 1948 National Assistance Act, education welfare, child guidance, home help services, adult training centres, day nurseries, mental health and other social work services provided by health departments and the social welfare work then undertaken by some housing departments (Seebohm, 1968, p 11). The Report also recommended, however, that the new departments should have 'responsibilities extending well beyond those of existing local authority departments' (Seebohm, 1968, p 51). The Committee's proposals should be seen 'as embodying a wider conception of social service, directed to the well-being of the whole of the community, ... encouraging and assisting the development of community identity and mutual aid' (Seebohm, 1968, pp 147 and 148). 'Above all, the development of citizen participation should reduce the rigid distinction between the givers and the takers of social services' (Seebohm, 1968, p 151).

With the exception, discussed above, of the proposal of a training council accountable to ministers, social workers and their associations were quick to agree on the goal of full implementation of the Seebohm Report. There were two main issues. First, would the government implement only an administrative reorganisation of services, or would it introduce legislation promoting the Seebohm Committee's wider vision and extending local authorities' responsibilities by including a general duty to promote social welfare, as in Scotland? Second, would the Report be implemented at all? Non-implementation of the Report seemed a distinct possibility. The Report was published in a climate favourable to local government. There was a sense that local authorities had come of age, and they were looking for more freedom from central government, particularly freedom to decide how to manage themselves. This had been advocated in the Maud Report (Maud, 1967), and the Seebohm Committee's recommendation that each local authority should be required to appoint a Director of Social Service and a Social Service Committee, with strictly defined functions, and that the Director's appointment should require, at least during the first 12 months, confirmation by the Secretary of State, was the kind of central control from which authorities were seeking to be freed. Also, a Royal Commission on Local Government was sitting. It reported in 1969 (Redcliffe-Maud, 1969), and it was argued that reorganisation of the personal social services should await that report's implementation, or least the government's decisions on it. Within local authorities there was particular opposition from most Medical Officers of Health (MOH), for whom the Seebohm proposals would have involved a significant reduction of responsibilities, and they were largely, though not universally, supported in their opposition by the medical profession. Richard Crossman, who at the time of the Report's publication was Lord President of the Council, with responsibility for coordinating the social services, and who later that year became Secretary of State for Social Services, in charge of the newly formed Department of Health and Social Security (DHSS), later told Phoebe Hall that he found the Report 'both boring and unconvincing' (Hall, 1976, p 83).

A particular problem was posed by decisions by a number of local authorities, particularly in London, to merge their health, welfare and children's departments under the direction of the MOH. These reorganisations usually amounted to little more than subordinating the Children's Officer to the MOH. (In many authorities the Chief Welfare Officer already reported to the MOH within a combined health and welfare department.) However, they were presented as improving on Seebohm by going beyond it. Ministers had deprecated in Parliament this practice of 'pre-empting Seebohm', but they also warned privately that if too many authorities followed this course the government would not do battle with them by implementing the Seebohm Report.

Faced with these adversities, SCOSW was not in a strong position to lead or coordinate pressure from social workers for implementation of the Report. It was, as its name implies, primarily a meeting ground for its eight member associations, and had few resources of its own. It had not been in the habit of obtaining general permissive mandates from the associations and acting on them. It did, however, campaign for the introduction of legislation, a campaign which included a very successful mass lobby of Parliament by social workers from many constituencies, and the Home Secretary and the Social Services Secretary jointly received a SCOSW deputation. At the suggestion of Tom White, and with SCOSW's approval, the Seebohm Implementation Action Group (SIAG) was formed to add further weight to this campaigning. Tom White was a past President of the Association of Child Care Officers and one of ACCO's representatives on SCOSW. It would be difficult to overestimate his influence and effectiveness in the campaign to secure implementation of the Seebohm Report. At that time Deputy Children's Officer for Lancashire, he had been much involved in the Labour Party, having been chair of the National Association of Labour Student Organisations and a parliamentary candidate. He chaired the SIAG, and nearly all of the ideas that it attempted to put into effect were his. SIAG brought together the SCOSW member organisations most closely concerned, the Institute of Social Welfare and three chief officers' groups: the Association of Children's Officers, the Association of Directors of Welfare Services and the Society of County Welfare Officers. It organised a range of pressure group activities, including a deputation to Home Secretary James Callaghan, a set of 'speakers' notes' on Seebohm and numerous contacts between social workers and their MPs. Hall (1976, p 147) reproduces as Appendix Four a SIAG publicity handout.

Opposition to local 'pre-emptions' of Seebohm was led by ACCO, whose 1969 AGM had authorised its Executive Committee to 'blacklist' any local authority that combined its health, welfare and children's departments. As a result, there were discussions with about half a dozen authorities that had either carried out or were proposing such amalgamations. In only one, the London Borough of Sutton, was a boycott actually organised. This action appears to have been sufficient to stem the tide until February 1970, when the government introduced the Local Authority Social Services Bill. In Sutton there was committed support for the action from social workers who were prepared to resign their posts; action in other authorities might well have proved ineffectual, and substantiated the view expressed by some radical social workers that ACCO was a paper tiger. BASW continued this work. 'The Secretariat of BASW was active up and down the country to ensure that the intentions were not defeated, and they intervened in some 29 local areas by visits, phone calls or correspondence' (Sackville, 1988).

Joan Cooper, who was until 1971 Chief Inspector in the Home Office Children's Department, and then Director of the Social Work Service in the DHSS, gave this assessment of SIAG's achievements (Cooper, 1983).

> It is not easy to assess the influence of SIAG in the whole tide of events. It was vitally informative to MPs, to the many occupational groups employed in social services, and it raised and maintained the alert over the perils of delay … It became clear that other agencies could not count on the compliant resignation of social workers to whatever organisational bases were invented, and that local authorities could not assume that they could ride roughshod over the Seebohm proposals. SIAG came near to overplaying its hand once the legislative strategy was settled for by this stage 'time was of the essence', and pressure for the Seebohm programme rather than the Bill's restricted organisational aims risked delay for which the parliamentary timetable did not allow.

The Local Authority Social Services Bill implemented only the machinery-of-local-government recommendations of the Seebohm Report, requiring local authorities to establish a Social Services Committee, to appoint, with the Secretary of State's approval, a Director of Social Services and to provide the Director with sufficient supporting staff. It also listed the statutory functions that were to 'stand referred' to the Social Services Committee. The Bill made no attempt to translate into legislative terms the Report's recommendation that the new departments should have responsibilities extending well beyond those of existing local authority departments, nor to implement its insistence that social services departments should promote the well-being of the whole community. The response of the social work associations was to press, unsuccessfully, for the inclusion in the Bill of a general duty to promote social welfare. Such a duty had already been laid on Scottish social work departments by the far more ambitious 1968 Social Work (Scotland) Act. As time went on, it became clear that Parliament would soon be dissolved, and this might cause the Bill to be lost. In the end 'the Bill became law just before Parliament was dissolved' (Cooper, 1983, p 119).

At a late stage Margaret Dobie, General Secretary of APSW, and I, as General Secretary of ACCO, went to see Martin Russell, an Assistant Secretary in the Home Office who was leading the Interdepartmental Social Work Group (Cooper, 1983, p 113), to press again for the inclusion of a general duty to promote social welfare. He drew our attention to the two-paragraph Conclusions of the Seebohm Report, which read in part:

> The first necessity is to establish a unified social service department within each major local authority; and we urge the Government to introduce the necessary legislation at the earliest possible date. In our opinion, this legislation should not wait for the report of the Royal Commission on Local Government in England and any reorganisation which may follow it, or for the reports of other enquiries that may be in progress. (Seebohm, 1968, p 218)

This, he said, meant: 'We need a *Bill*; we need a *machinery* Bill; we need a machinery Bill *quickly*.' And that, he said, is what you are going to get. And that is what we got. Nevertheless, there was confidence that the personal social services in England and Wales were about to follow Scotland in establishing themselves as the fifth social service, alongside education, health, social security and housing, and that social work values would permeate them.

In April 1970 Peter Leonard, a member of the Seebohm Committee, wrote:

> As it stands, the Bill provides only the skeletal framework for a new social service in line with the aspirations expressed in the Seebohm Report. The legislation itself could lead to the development of services as bureaucratic and remote as ever and the ghost of the Poor Law might never be laid. Whether or not a really *new* social service is created depends on the extent to which the organisational framework can be seen as the means for mobilising community resources so as to enable radical change to take place (Leonard, 1970).

Notes

1 Probation officers and mental welfare officers had duties laid directly on them as individuals by statute. In children's departments all decisions on cases were taken under powers delegated by the employing local authority.

2 They were: Education and Training, International Relations, Membership, Professional Development and Practice, Parliamentary and Public Relations and Salaries and Service Conditions.

References

Attlee, C.R. (1920) *The Social Worker*, London: G. Bell and Sons, Ltd (republished, 2012, Forgotten Books).

Bamford, T.D. (2015) *A Contemporary History of Social Work: Learning from the Past*, Bristol: Policy Press.

Cooper, J.D. (1983) *The Creation of the British Personal Social Services: 1962–74*, London: Heinemann Educational Books.

Curtis, M. (1946) *The Care of Children*, Cmd 6922, London: HMSO.

Hall, P. (1976) *Reforming the Welfare: The Politics of Change in the Personal Social Services*, London: Heinemann.

Hiddleston, V. (2013) 'The Social Work (Scotland) Act 1968', *Bulletin of the Social Work History Network*, vol 6, no 1, pp 21–4 (online journal, kcl.ac.uk/scwru/swhn) (paper given in 2006, published posthumously).

Home Office (1965) *The Child, the Family and the Young Offender*, Cmnd 2742, London: HMSO.

Home Office (1968) *Children in Trouble*, Cmnd 3601, London: HMSO.

Ingleby, Viscount (1960) *Report of the Committee on Children and Young Persons*, Cmnd 1191, London: HMSO.

Kilbrandon, Lord (1964) *Children and Young Persons in Scotland*, Cmnd 2306, Edinburgh: HMSO.

Leonard, P. (1970) 'Comment – a new social service?', *Social Work*, vol 27, no 2, pp 3–6.

Maud, J. (1967) *Report of the Committee on the Management of Local Government*, London: HMSO.

Redcliffe-Maud, Lord (1969) *Report of the Royal Commission on Local Government in England*, Cmnd 4040, London: HMSO.

Sackville, A. (1987) 'The Association of Social Workers and moves towards a unified association, 1951–1970', Professional Associations and Social Work WP14, https://www.kcl.ac.uk/scwru/swhn/2013/sackville-wp14-association-of-social-workers-1951-1970.pdf

Sackville, A. (1988) 'The British Association of Social Workers 1970–1988', Professional Associations and Social Work WP15, https://www.kcl.ac.uk/scwru/swhn/2013/sackville-wp15-british-association-of-social-workers-1970-1988.pdf

Seebohm, F. (1968) *Report of the Committee on Local Authority and Allied Personal Social Services*, Cmnd 3703, London: HMSO.

Younghusband, E. (1959) *Report of the Working Party on Social Workers in the Local Authority Health and Welfare Services*, London: HMSO.

2

Social services departments: success or failure?

Terry Bamford

Four important pieces of legislation span the life of social services departments. Established by the 1970 Local Authority Social Services Act, they were given a new brief by the 1989 Children Act and the 1990 NHS and Community Care Act, and then terminated by the 2004 Children Act. Their demise was not greatly mourned. Although they were long lived as compared with most local government departments, their reputation had been tarnished by a succession of professional failures in adult care and in the care of children. They were viewed as toxic in some deprived areas because of their readiness to remove children from their families. Their ability to deliver high-quality services was compromised by the unremitting pressure on local government resources.

The 1970 Local Authority Social Services Act

The Act established a single social services department in each local authority. The departments were based on the principles set out in the Seebohm Report (1968). This had emphasised the need for a coordinated and comprehensive approach to social care that would support families, detect need and encourage people to seek help. The new departments were to be responsible for domiciliary help, residential care, registration of independent residential homes and social work support. This was a huge remit.

Local authorities were required to establish a Social Services Committee, and the Act listed those functions which were the task of the Committee. It also required the appointment of a Director of Social Services subject to the approval of the Secretary of State. That approval was not a formality, and in a number of instances the power was used to disqualify the preferred candidates of local authorities – often where the authority had sought to appoint the existing Medical Officer of Health to the position.

The process of appointment was chaotic:

> Sometimes the children's officer and the chief welfare officer
> were competing in their own authority for appointment ...
> or else trying their luck elsewhere as directors or deputies,
> sometimes by choice or sometimes *faute de mieux*. This was
> a harsh game of musical chairs for some who were left out
> altogether ... Conversely some people applied for and were
> appointed to a succession of more lucrative posts before
> they actually started work. (Younghusband, 1978, p 240)

The hope of those campaigning for the implementation of the
Seebohm recommendations was that the new departments would
be headed by social workers. In practice, the backgrounds of those
appointed were more diverse. Of the 174 Directors appointed, 79
were welfare officers, 58 were children's officers, 10 were from
central government departments, 8 were from Scottish social work
departments; 5 were medical practitioners, 4 were local authority
deputy or assistant clerks, 3 were social work teachers, 3 were from
voluntary organisations, 2 were probation officers and 2 were mental
welfare officers (Smith, 1971).

The proportion of professionally qualified staff was much higher
in Children's Departments than in Health and Welfare Departments.
Qualified staff often accelerated up the managerial hierarchy, leaving
front-line practice in the hands of inexperienced or unqualified staff.
In addition to the turmoil of reorganising several departments into
one, the new departments had to cope with attempting to implement
the concept of the generic social worker.

Genericism and specialisation

The first task facing newly appointed Directors was to decide how
to organise their departments. Seebohm had advocated area teams
based on populations of 50,000 to 100,000, and most departments
established devolved offices on this basis. There were two shortcomings
to this model. First, the size of the area offices meant that it was
difficult to establish close links with key players in the neighbourhood
– schools, general practitioners (GPs), voluntary groups – and even
more so to engage service users in the work of the offices. Second,
NHS community services and social security offices – key partners
in the delivery of social welfare – were organised on a different basis.

Most of those appointed as Directors were familiar with social work decisions on individual cases. They were now responsible for extensive domiciliary, day care and residential services, which presented different managerial challenges. Some chose to organise departments with a separate division responsible for these services and one responsible for fieldwork services. Others, particularly in large counties, organised on a geographical basis.

Within fieldwork services there were social workers struggling with unfamiliar problems and legislation. The Seebohm recommendation that, as far as possible, families should have to deal with just one worker so as to avoid multiple visits to the household was interpreted by some as meaning that all workers should be able to deal with all problems coming to the department. This led some authorities to lump all social workers together in generic teams, with staff obliged to deal with problems of mental health, child care and disability – tasks for which they were poorly equipped. Hall suggests that this was a misreading of Seebohm and that the Report was instead 'a plea that one social worker should take primary responsibility for each case, not that every social worker should be able to deal with every eventuality' (Hall, 1976).

It was early in the life of the new departments that specialisations began to re-emerge as a way of handling workload pressures. Children's services were the first to identify a specialism in fostering and adoption. Child protection became a specialism as a response to the Colwell case, discussed below, and subsequent child care tragedies. Gradually, specialisations developed in relation to adult care groups, including those with mental health problems, disabilities and older people.

A succession of measures increased the pressures of demand on the fledgling departments. The 1968 Health Services and Public Health Act required local authorities to 'promote the welfare of older people'. The 1970 Chronically Sick and Disabled Persons Act required all local authorities to register disabled people and publicise services. It encouraged, but did not require or adequately fund, expanded community-based services such as home helps and day centres. As a result, departments faced an explosion of referrals. For the beleaguered workers on the front line this felt like 'bombardment'. Continuity of care – a key principle of practice – was subordinated to managing demand pressures. Intake teams were devised as a means of handling referrals and identifying those cases requiring long-term work. The bold vision set out in Seebohm of detecting need and encouraging people to seek help was abandoned.

This was a long way from the 'New Jerusalem' that the reforms had anticipated. Social work professionals found themselves at the bottom of a hierarchical structure, reporting to a senior social worker, an area officer, an assistant director, a deputy director and a director (often with additional layers interposed). In the first four years after the establishment of the new Social Services Departments in 1971 expenditure in constant prices increased by 74% (Evandrou and Falkingham, 1998). This was a period of political turbulence encompassing the three-day week and inflation that peaked at 25%. It was matched by growing discontent in the workforce. Simpkin described social services departments as 'Seebohm Factories', in a powerful critique of the new social work role as 'processing clients and applying technical solutions to problems which were of a moral and political order' (Simpkin, 1979).

Colwell and Crosland

The initial hopes invested in social services departments were hit by two severe blows that were to shape the future – one professional and one political.

The publicity given to the public inquiry into the death of Maria Colwell, a seven-year-old child beaten to death by her stepfather, was a rude awakening for the profession. (This is considered in detail in Chapter 11.) Professor Olive Stevenson's dissenting note to the Colwell Inquiry, with its ringing phrase, 'There, but for the grace of God, go I' (Colwell, 1974), resonated with social workers, who recognised that it was the social worker on the front line who would bear the brunt of media criticism.

At the same time, the pell-mell growth of social services came to a grinding halt. In 1973/74 real-terms growth was over 19%. The ten-year plans sought by Sir Keith Joseph when Secretary of State were based on a 10% per annum growth rate. They were put in reverse as growth assumptions were reined back to 2% and capital spending fell by 67% from 1974/75 to 1977/78. It was never to be 'glad confident morning again' as social services departments struggled to match resources to needs. Tony Crosland famously told local authorities in 1975 that the party was over. It was another 40 years before social care received priority in funding and above-inflation increases in resources through the Better Care Fund.

These two influences – professional failures and financial pressures – were to dominate social services departments. They spawned legislation addressing the perceived professional failures, and a range of patchwork solutions to the financial problems.

Child abuse inquiries and their impact are considered in Chapter 11. It is worth noting here the link between such inquiries and subsequent legislation. One of the elements in the Colwell case was the 'blood tie' between Maria and her mother. Social workers were felt to have attached too much weight to the rights of natural parents. Legislation to improve adoption law, the 1975 Children Act, was therefore presented as a response to Colwell.

Practice became more assertive, with a sharp increase in the number of place of safety orders. That assertiveness had a cost in public trust. In Rochdale in 1990 20 children were removed from their parents on suspicion of satanic ritual abuse. Similar suspicions led to nine children on the island of South Ronaldsay being removed from their parents. In Cleveland in 1987, following diagnosis by paediatricians of suspected sexual abuse, over 80 children were removed on place of safety orders.

While there was some evidence of abuse in a small minority of these cases, the heavy-handed approach of the local authorities and their readiness to act first, investigate later, led many households in deprived areas to become deeply suspicious of social services. That affected the readiness of the public to alert social services to their concerns.

Efficiency, economy and effectiveness

Social services departments have struggled since the International Monetary Fund required cuts in public expenditure as a condition of its support to the UK government in 1975. They had to cope with a far greater demand for services than had been anticipated – reflected in the pressure of referrals; there was pressure from government to assist the NHS by supporting speedy discharges from hospitals; and the overall reduction in local government spending affected social services, although local councillors have often sought to protect statutory services.

The political context changed in 1979 with the election of the Thatcher government, which brought a determined scepticism to public expenditure and, in particular, to the work of local government. It introduced compulsory competitive tendering for many local government services, based on a deeply held belief derived from the economist Friedrich Hayek and the apostles of neoliberalism that the private sector was superior to the public. It was more efficient and more cost-effective. That belief still has currency in 2020, despite the lack of evidence of the superiority of the private sector in welfare.

Residential care has seen debt-ridden companies collapse; scandals of inadequate and abusive care for people with disabilities; fraud in criminal justice, like the SERCO tagging scandals and poor standards in private prisons; and failures in probation supervision. Together, these constitute a dismal catalogue of private sector failures.

The cost of residential care to the taxpayer was a major pressure point. There was an explosive growth in private provision in the 1980s – more by accident than by design. A ruling by the Social Security Appeal Tribunal made it possible for social security to meet private residential care and nursing care fees, and the fee levels were higher than those in local authority residential care. Both the NHS and local authorities moved swiftly to divest themselves of nursing and residential care homes, transferring them to private providers or non-profit bodies created for that specific purpose. There was no assessment of need prior to admission to private care. The Audit Commission was scathing about the effect: 'Supplementary Benefit funding cannot be targeted towards those most in need of residential care, nor are homes judged on whether they are giving value for money within the category of care for which they are registered' (Audit Commission, 1986).

The lack of assessment of need or quality meant that the numbers of private nursing home places increased fourfold (Lieveley et al, 2011). Private sector providers became dominant in a sector where local authorities had previously provided over 60% of total places. The social security bill rose 'from a mere £10m in 1979 to £500m by early 1986, and to a mighty £2.5bn by 1992 ... The numbers covered rose from 11,000 in 1979 to more than a quarter of a million by 1992. Unwittingly, the Conservative government had created a new state-financed but privately and independently run industry' (Timmins, 2019).

The effect was not wholly negative. Many new homes were built to higher standards. En suite facilities became the norm.

The scale of expenditure prompted a re-examination of the funding of community care. The government appointed Sir Roy Griffiths (1988), who had previously undertaken a review of the NHS. He recommended that care should be delivered on social, not income, grounds and that local authorities should have responsibility for the assessment of need and the delivery of services to meet that need. After much deliberation in Whitehall (Timmins, 2017), which was dubious about giving more powers to local government, that recommendation was accepted, leading to the 1990 NHS and Community Care Act.

The 1990 NHS and Community Care Act

The Act gave social services the funding responsibility for residential care and the money to meet it. But there was a sting in the tail. The Government required 75% – later 85% – of the funding transferred from social security to be spent in the independent sector. This was consistent with Griffiths' view that local authorities should be the commissioners and enablers of services, rather than direct providers. This consolidated the mixed economy of welfare with an increasing share of services being delivered by the private sector.

Griffiths argued that a more plural welfare system would deliver choice, flexibility, innovation and competition. Social workers would be involved in assembling packages of care and support, using public, private and voluntary sector resources to build a service tailored to the needs of the individual. This was a fine vision, successfully tested in pilot studies (Davies et al, 1990; Davies, 1992). However, case management – sometimes called care management – failed to achieve what had been hoped for, as cash constraints bore heavily on the ability of staff to create a truly personalised service. Assessment manuals and checklists militated against creativity. As thresholds of eligibility were tightened, the need for assessment grew and that task came to dominate the social work role. The gatekeeping role of assessment resembled that used in the early 1970s to cope with 'bombardment'. Social workers were less involved in direct practice with adults, except with the most vulnerable.

One area where the social work role remained one of direct practice was in mental health. The 1983 Mental Health Act had greatly strengthened patients' rights. It required local social services authorities to appoint Approved Social Workers (ASWs), who, in deciding whether to apply for a person's compulsory admission to hospital, were required to seek the least restrictive alternative. The role was retained under the 2007 Mental Health Act with a designation of Approved Mental Health Professional. Few other professionals have joined social workers in that role. Specialist training was required prior to approval as an ASW. In mental health the delivery of community services was through multidisciplinary teams, although financial pressures meant that local authority commitment to partnership working was not always whole-hearted.

The move away from direct provision of services by local authority departments was also happening in residential child care. Overblown hopes that all troubled children could be supported through intensive foster care schemes led local authorities to move out of provision of residential care. Again, the gap was filled by the private sector. The same factors were in play in residential child care as in care of the elderly:

- a belief in the greater efficiency of the private sector;
- a readiness to try new approaches;
- a history of past abuse in local authority care – most notoriously in the Pindown scandal (Levy and Kahan, 1991).

The result was that by 2019 almost half of local authorities in England had no residential child care, 72% of children's homes were private 'for profit' and these were often located in areas with low property prices (Jones, 2019).

Modernising social services

The incoming Labour government in 1997 determined to modernise public services, including personal social services. The failures to secure adequate protection of children and vulnerable adults, the lack of coordination with health and housing services, the lack of agreed standards for services and the postcode lottery in care, with wide variance in the costs of services between different authorities, were among the issues addressed in *Modernising Social Services* (DH, 1998). This was followed by Implementation Guidance and a Modernisation Fund.

The local authority role under New Labour remained that of an enabler of services rather than a provider. Central government saw its role as setting a national framework, requiring action within defined time-scales and leading a consultative process involving service users.

In children's services the government launched Quality Protects, an initiative backed by earmarked funding. This had six strands: increasing placement choice for looked after children; increasing support for children leaving public care; developing management information systems; improving assessment, care planning and recordkeeping; developing effective quality assurance systems; and establishing or improving arrangements for listening to young people. The programme emphasised the importance of working across boundaries with housing, health, education and social security. It was backed by a review of the regulatory framework for social services and the creation of a National Care Standards Commission to set and monitor standards. The Commission was succeeded in 2004 by the Commission for Social Care Inspection, which in turn was succeeded in 2009 by the Care Quality Commission as regulation assumed greater importance.

Links with health

A theme throughout the life of social services departments was the desirability of closer links with health. In 1974 the responsibility for employing social workers in hospitals moved from the NHS to local authorities. Many moved the service from a hospital setting to community-based teams. It was not a happy move. Many medical social workers felt that their skills and expertise were not recognised. Many hospital staff felt that they were losing vital access to social work staff who understood the medical setting. It made the task of joint planning more difficult, even when joint finance was introduced in 1976 as a means of using NHS resources for local authority spending where this was likely to be of greater benefit in terms of total care.

Joint finance was an ingenious mechanism, which was to be echoed 40 years later by the Better Care Fund as a means of transferring NHS funds to social services. Plans had to be approved through the cumbrous machinery of joint planning. The attraction for local authorities was a long revenue tail, which meant that the full cost of schemes was met by health in the first year, and did not have to be met in full by the local authority for at least five years.

The schemes supported by joint finance were predominantly those for older people, designed to achieve early and safe discharges from hospital, and those providing community services for individuals with a learning disability, particularly following the Jay Report (Jay, 1979). The progress made was acknowledged in the 1989 White Paper on Community Care (DH, 1989), which emphasised the need for social services care assessments prior to discharge from hospitals, coordination of purchaser–provider arrangements and formal planning agreements between the NHS and local authorities.

This would have been easier to achieve if the budgetary cycles had been aligned and if the resources available had grown at the same rate. In practice, however, the NHS – partly because of its totemic significance in electoral terms – grew more rapidly under Conservative and Labour governments alike than did its partners in local government. This meant that local authorities became increasingly resistant to using joint finance because of the revenue consequences after the initial period of 'free' money.

In an attempt to bring some new momentum into partnership working the 1999 Health Act introduced new flexibilities to the system. This made it possible for health and social services to pool budgets, to delegate responsibility from one to the other, to arrange secondments and transfers of staff and to create new organisational structures to deliver services. The flexibilities were most used in relation to learning disability, usually with social services leading, and mental health, usually with the NHS leading.

But it was the care of older people that was the source of most tension between the two statutory bodies. When older people were assessed as medically fit for discharge from hospital there was often a delay prior to discharge. Social services were blamed for this, when there could in fact be many reasons for the delay. Occupational therapists might not have assessed what aids and adaptations would be necessary to enable an individual to live safely at home; there might be no agreed package of care support; further non-acute hospital care might be needed. But facts were not allowed to get in the way of decisive action by government, which introduced the 2003 Community Care (Delayed Discharges) Act to allow fines on local authorities. Subsequent guidance clarified that hospitals must notify social services of patients needing further support on discharge, while social services had set time-scales (governed by complex rules, but often about three working days) in which to assess patient needs and find/fund appropriate community services. Where someone was delayed in hospital beyond this time for social care reasons only, the hospital could 'fine' social services £100 per day (£120 in London).

This was not the best means of promoting healthy partnership working! Subsequent research established that the majority of delayed discharges were due to the NHS, not to social services (Bate, 2017).

A solution to the continuing problems was sought in the shape of Care Trusts, proposed in the 2000 NHS Plan as a vehicle for delivering primary and community healthcare as well as social care. The then health minister, John Hutton, boldly predicted that 90% of social care would be delivered by Care Trusts by 2005. In reality, only 12 Care Trusts were established, and most dealt only with mental health and learning disability rather than with the full range of services. They could have been established using the Health Act flexibilities. The failure illustrated the danger of using organisational structures to pursue integration without addressing the basic problem that NHS services are free at the point of access and social care services are subject to a means test.

The lone sustained attempt at delivering integrated care was in Northern Ireland, where there were four Health and Social Services Boards after Direct Rule was imposed on the province in 1972. Significantly, the original decision was not informed by theoretical models of healthcare, but by an urgent need to reorganise the system of local government, which had become widely discredited. The governance arrangements for social services were slightly different from those for health services. There was initially a separate budget for social services, which facilitated a rapid build-up of community services. There was also a Director of Social Services. There were benefits in terms of joint planning, relatively easy transfer of resources between services and good links at primary care level.

Surprisingly, there has been relatively little qualitative research about the effectiveness of this integration. What is clear, however, is that Northern Ireland does not constitute a blueprint for successful integration. It has a higher proportion of patients in long-term care than other parts of the UK; community care has been neglected, under-developed and under funded (Heenan, 2013). A government-commissioned review noted the over-reliance on hospitals and noted the need to deliver care closer to home; evidence for this included a bed utilisation audit of 2011 that showed that, on the day in question, up to 42% of the in-patients reviewed should not have been in hospital (Heenan, 2013). Obviously there are a number of specific problems in Northern Ireland, but this suggests that structural integration alone will not deliver improved care. Yet the search for the 'Holy Grail' has continued. (The final section of this chapter reviews the current position against the government's stated intention to ensure that all health and social care is integrated by 2020, and considers what lessons can be drawn from the efforts over the past 50 years.)

As Care Trusts foundered another child care tragedy brought the failings of children's social services back into the headlines. The death of Victoria Climbié, a foster-child sent from the Ivory Coast to live with her great-aunt, who died after torture and cruelty at the hands of her aunt and her cohabitee, led to an inquiry that was scathing in its criticism of social services departments and their practice (Laming, 2003). The themes of poor inter-agency communication, staff vacancies, a lack of training and a lack of clear accountability echoed those of numerous previous inquiries. The report was most critical of management, with 'too many examples of those in senior positions attempting to justify their work in terms of bureaucratic activity rather than in outcomes for people' (Laming, 2003, para 1.28). They 'seemed to spend a lot of time and energy, devising ways of limiting access to services, and adopting mechanisms designed to reduce service demand' (Laming, 2003, para 1.52).

The inquiry identified 12 occasions when the local authority could and should have intervened. Lord Laming's recommendations were designed to strengthen accountability for children within social services, but they were overtaken by more radical reforms set out first in the 2003 Green Paper *Every Child Matters* and then in the 2004 Children Act. These set an agenda for children's services based on the five outcomes for children identified in the Green Paper: being healthy, staying safe, enjoying and achieving, making a positive contribution and achieving economic well-being. The Act required the appointment of a Director of Children's Services, thus separating adult from children's services; the creation of a Children's Trust; the development of a children's plan; and a new, multi-agency framework for safeguarding to replace area child protection committees.

Social services departments came to an end in 2005 with the new local authority structures introduced following the 2004 Children Act. But the changes ran into a period of unparalleled austerity for services. After an uncertain period, in which many of the early appointments as Director of Children's Services were from an education background, some local authorities sought again to bring adult and children's services together. This was rarely an issue of principle, but a pragmatic response to the financial costs of running two separate departments.

There are compelling arguments for some linkages at senior management level. First, children are brought up in families. Families will sometimes have elderly relatives, sometimes people with disabilities and sometimes people with mental health difficulties. Social workers need to have an understanding of these issues and their impact on children. Second, an arbitrary division runs the risk of one department seeking to shunt costs to the other department. Third, it makes the issues of transition from child to adult services more acute. A young person may have received intensive support from child and adolescent mental health services, but at age 18 their needs may not meet the threshold for support from adult mental health services.

Lessons for the future

Social care does not have a high political priority. Governments of both political persuasions have funded the NHS more generously than social care. Between 2003 and 2012 NHS expenditure went up by 66%. Social care expenditure went up by 14% (Health and Social Care Information Centre, 2013). While social care is administered and delivered by local authorities, central government can cheerfully evade responsibility and blame shortcomings on the failure of local authorities to spend their money wisely. Spokespersons for the government point to increases in expenditure – blurring cash and real-terms increases – and claim credit for additional funds like the Better Care Fund. But the collapse of services is not far distant as local authorities run down their reserves while delivering ever more limited services.

The Local Government Association (LGA, 2019) has warned that

- one in three councils fear they will run out of funding to provide for their legal duties by 2022/23;
- the number rises to almost two-thirds of councils by 2024/25 or later. The LGA estimates that councils face an overall funding gap of £8 billion by 2025;
- an unprecedented rise in demand means many councils are having to spend more than they planned for in adult social care, children's services and homelessness support. These overspends have seen councils forced to make in-year budget cuts to try to balance their books.

The crisis in adult social care has been recognised for over 20 years, with a Royal Commission reporting in 1999 (Royal Commission on Long Term Care, 1999) and subsequent reviews and reports identifying the problems of funding long-term care. The disastrous confusion of policy proposals at the time of the 2017 general election has caused a policy hiatus, with the promised Green Paper always due shortly but never appearing.

Children's services have seen an explosion in demand, with child protection assessments tending to crowd out preventative services. Although initial referrals to local authorities increased by only 7% over the period from 2010/11 to 2017/18, local authorities carried out 77% more child protection assessments (NAO, 2019). The proportion of spending on preventative services, such as children's centres, fell from 41% in 2010/11 to 25% in 2016/17. Spending on statutory activities rose from 59% to 75% over the same period. Add to these pressures the escalating cost of Education, Health and Care Plans introduced by the 2014 Children and Families Act, and greater awareness of the needs of children with mental health problems, and the strain on budgets is evident.

The Better Care Fund was introduced in 2014 and is the vehicle for transferring resources from the NHS to social services expenditure in cases where it will deliver improved NHS outcomes. This is usually in terms of shorter hospital stays or reduced hospital admissions. The National Audit Office was scathing in its initial review of the Better Care Fund, noting that 'the Fund has not achieved the expected value for money, in terms of savings, outcomes for patients or reduced hospital activity, from the £5.3 billion spent through the Fund in 2015–16'. Even worse, it failed on its two principal objectives: 'Compared with 2014–15, emergency admissions increased by 87,000 against a planned reduction of 106,000, costing £311 million more than planned. Furthermore, days lost to delayed transfers of care increased by 185,000, against a planned reduction of 293,000, costing £146 million more than planned' (NAO, 2017).

Integration as the standard model had initially been promised for 2018 (DH, 2013), but this had slipped to 2020 by the 2017/18 planning round. The conditions for the use of the Better Care Fund remain jointly agreed plans; the NHS contribution to adult social care to be maintained; investment in NHS-commissioned out-of-hospital services, which may include seven-days-a-week services and adult social care; and a clear plan for reducing delayed transfers of care. The Health and Wellbeing Board was the vehicle for signing off Better Care Fund submissions. But the simple vision of working together was obscured by bureaucratic requirements of great complexity that were incomprehensible to most members of Health and Wellbeing Boards.

What we can conclude is that central government departments are consistently over-optimistic about the savings that can be made from instruments like the Better Care Fund. They are over-sanguine about the low costs attached to new legislation (from the 1970 Chronically Sick and Disabled Persons Act through to the 2014 Children and Families Act, a pattern is evident of grotesque under-estimation of the costs involved in implementation). And they present unrealistic timetables for change.

The pattern has not changed significantly since the separation of adult and children's services. The cuts in day and domiciliary care have borne heavily on those with long-term conditions. As thresholds for support have been raised, along with steep increases in means-tested charges, the numbers getting help have reduced when they should be increasing in line with demographic change. The vision of the NHS and Community Care Act of tailored services to meet individual need still seems very distant.

Set against this picture, there have been some gains for the clients of social work services since 1970.

First, they have access to a much wider range of services, often as a result of legislation. The 1970 Chronically Sick and Disabled Persons Act greatly widened the opportunities for people with disabilities.

Second, they have rights to an assessment, which were not formerly written into statute.

Third, carers have rights to support and, in some instances, to financial allowances.

And, above all, clients now have a right to be consulted and to work in partnership. The best social workers may have done this before, but the advent of direct payments and the language of co-production have made that a necessity.

It is a tragedy that these gains have been accompanied by a period of austerity. The potential for preventive services has never been realised. If the integration agenda with the NHS is carried forward there remains a real risk that community services will be less persuasive in securing resources than will be the political muscle of the acute sector.

References

Audit Commission (1986) *Making a Reality of Community Care*, London: HMSO.

Bate, A. (2017) 'Delayed transfers of care in the NHS', Briefing Paper No 2415, June, London: House of Commons Library.

Colwell Report (1974) *Committee of Inquiry into the Care and Supervision provided in relation to Maria Colwell*, London: HMSO.

Davies, B. (1992) *Case Management, Equity and Efficiency*, Canterbury: Personal Social Services Research Unit, University of Kent.

Davies, B., Bebbington, A. and Charnley, K. (1990) *Resources Needs and Outcomes in Community-based Care*, London: Gower.

DH (Department of Health) (1989) *Caring for People: Community Care in the Next Decade and Beyond*, Cm 849, London: HMSO.

DH (1998) *Modernising Social Services: Promoting Independence, Improving Protection, Raising Standards*, Cmnd 4169, London: HMSO.

DH (2013) *Our Shared Commitment*, London: DH.

Evandrou, M. and Falkingham, J. (1998) 'The Personal Social Services', in H. Glennerster and J. Hills (eds) *The State of Welfare: The Economics of Social Spending*, Oxford: Oxford University Press, pp 189–295.

Griffiths, R. (1988) *Community Care: Agenda for Action*, London: HMSO.

Hall, P. (1976) *Reforming the Welfare*, London: Heinemann.

Health and Social Care Information Centre (2013) *Personal Social Services Expenditure and Unit Costs 2011/12*, Leeds: Health and Social Care Information Centre.

Heenan, D. (2013) 'Northern Ireland', in C. Ham, D. Heenan, M. Longley and D. Steel (eds), *Integrated Care in Northern Ireland, Scotland and Wales: Lessons for England*, London: King's Fund, pp 2–24.

Jay Report (1979) *Report of the Committee of Inquiry into Mental Handicap Nursing and Care*, London: HMSO.

Jones, R. (2019) Paper presented to Social Work History Network, June 2019.

Laming, Lord (2003) *The Victoria Climbié Inquiry*, Cmnd 5730, London: HMSO.

Levy, A. and Kahan, B. (1991) *The Pindown Experience and the Protection of Children: The Report of the Staffordshire Child Care Inquiry 1990*, Stafford: Staffordshire County Council.

Lieveley, N. and Crosby, G. with Bowman, C. (2011) *The Changing Face of Care Homes*, London: Centre for Policy on Ageing and BUPA.

LGA (Local Government Association) (2019), Press release, 2 July.

NAO (National Audit Office) (2017) *Health and Social Care Integration*, London: National Audit Office.

NAO (2019) *Pressures on Children's Social Care*, London: National Audit Office.

Royal Commission on Long Term Care (1999) *With Respect to Old Age: Long Term Care – Rights and Responsibilities*, Cm 4192-1, London: The Stationery Office.

Seebohm, F. (1968) *Report of the Committee on Local Authority and Allied Personal Social Services*, Cmnd 3703, London: HMSO.

Simpkin, M. (1979) *Trapped within Welfare*, London: Macmillan.

Smith, J. (1971) 'Top jobs in social services', in K. Jones (ed), *The Year Book of Social Policy in Britain 1971*, London: Routledge and Kegan Paul, pp 16–30.

Timmins, N. (2017) *The Five Giants*, 3rd edn, London: William Collins.

Timmins, N. (2019) 'The 1990 NHS and Community Care Act', *Social Work History Network Bulletin*, vol 6, no 1, pp 4–8.

Younghusband, E. (1978) *Social Work in Britain 1950–75, Volume 1*, London: George Allen and Unwin.

3

Regulation and inspection of social work: costly distraction or stimulus to improve?

David N. Jones

How do we know whether social services are meeting the needs of people and using resources effectively? What evidence persuades politicians to support social work and social services? What happens when professionals or services fail to live up to required standards? What is proportionate expenditure on regulation?

People and governments are interested in supporting and controlling those with problems related to health, disability, unemployment, relationship breakdowns and poverty, reflecting moral, religious, political and financial concerns. Governments seek to influence and direct those who provide these services, through management, setting of standards, provision of education and training, monitoring of performance and financial controls. These regulations provide rules and guidance about activity and finance.

This chapter describes regulation of 'social work' and social workers in England, focusing on regulation of services through inspection and of individuals through professional registration. Regulation by legislation, and through qualifications frameworks, are covered in other chapters. Financial controls and audit arrangements are regulation, but are not covered here (MHCLG, 2019). The differing arrangements in Scotland, Wales and Northern Ireland are acknowledged, noting the growing divergence between them.

The chronic institutional instability in recent years since the abolition of the Central Council for Education and Training in Social Work in 2001, caused largely by constant political meddling, must have undermined improvement and contributed to uncertainty and lack of confidence.

Managing performance of social services: the role of inspection

The 1970 Local Authority Social Services Act gave the government power to issue guidance to local councils, and the 1990 NHS and Community Care Act added the power to give directions/instructions. Inspection and performance management have been powerful levers for this purpose.

Inspection can focus on compliance (enforcement) and/or improvement (efficiency) (Rhodes, 1981), which may be seen as 'punitive' or 'supportive' (Davis et al, 2001b). Functions can include: monitoring policy implementation; enforcing accountability; providing evidence about resourcing; providing consultancy and advice; encouraging innovation; and reporting to Parliament.

Social services inspection can be traced from the Elizabethan 'Act for the Releife of the Poore' of 1601 (Slack, 1998), through to the 2012 Welfare Reform Act (Smith 1866, Corbett and Markham, 1867; Younghusband, 1981; Roberts, 1991; Rivett, 2005). A restructured Children's Inspectorate, in response to the 1948 Children Act (developed from the inspectorate created in 1850 to inspect industrial and reformatory schools) was located in the Home Office (Heywood, 1979).

The Seebohm reforms (1968) created a Social Work Service – not an inspectorate – intended to promote better professional practices through 'persuasion and encouragement' (Department of Health and Social Security et al, 1971; Day and Klein, 1990). This transformed into the Social Services Inspectorate (SSI) in 1985, still within the Department of Health, with a mission to: inspect practice; advise on policy and support its implementation; and secure effective management of government business (Social Services Inspectorate, 1985; Gilroy, 2004, p 2). This mix of roles had benefits, but contrasted with independent inspectorates at arm's length from government.

In the absence of a strong, independent, professional social work body, the SSI Chief Inspector became the authoritative voice of social work, defining good practice and providing professional leadership. However, SSI was seen by politicians as too closely identified with the service it was intended to 'police' ('provider capture') (Rouse and Smith, 1999, p 238), lacking a reputation as a fearless enforcer. Inspectors were seen, perhaps unfairly, as out of touch with new developments. SSI was criticised for not preventing service failures like child abuse tragedies and care abuses (Humphrey, 2002, p 465), hindered by a lack of objective measures of 'effectiveness'.

Three related trends transformed thinking in the 1990s. First, politicians embraced global enthusiasm for 'new public management' (including performance management), ostensibly designed to ensure transparency and accountability of public services to citizens. The Treasury demanded performance measures, and some councils experimented with systems such as European Foundation for Quality Management (Kelly and Warr, 1992; Darvill, 1998; Pillinger, 2001). SSI developed a standards-based 'methodology', specifying what it expected to find in inspections (for example, James et al, 1992; Cope, 2001).

Second, government implemented mandatory competitive tendering of services, challenging local council monopolies, those especially of residential and home-based care. Most services ended up being provided outside local government. This transformed the regulatory environment.

Third, the growth of 'consumerism' and concern for 'rights', including service user campaigns, fuelled concerns that public services were insufficiently responsive to individual preferences (Jordan, 1975). Politicians and the public demanded honesty about service quality and problems.

The New Labour government in 1997 transformed how government shaped public services. Inspection was a key instrument (Blythe, 2001; Davis et al, 2001a), supporting implementation of national standards and targets. *Modernising Social Services: Promoting Independence, Improving Protection, Raising Standards* (Department of Health, 1998) proposed improvements in user protection, a revised system of regulation, a new emphasis on training and workforce standards and additional resources for social care.

The Performance Assessment Framework (PAF) (Social Services Inspectorate, 1999; Smith, 2000) defined 80 national performance indicators (PIs) for evaluating and comparing services. Some argue that PIs distort practice by focusing on what can be measured rather than what is important (Philpot, 2001; Seddon, 2003; Gillen, 2004): 'the whole ... effort is directed ... towards passing inspection' (Perryman, 2006, p 148). Some argued that social work and social care are not amenable to quantitative measures (for example, Philpot, 2001; Munro, 2004; Leadbetter, 2006). The Comprehensive Performance Assessment (Department for Communities and Local Government, 2006) later created an overarching local government performance framework, involving all the service inspectorates. Whether targets and indicators provide a realistic snapshot of service quality remains contested (Munro, 2004; Seddon, 2005; McLean et al, 2007). League tables were not popular with local government, but providing evidence of social services achievements ensured political and professional recognition of the essential contribution of social services (see also Martin, 2004).

Alongside these SSI developments, a proposal for a Joint Review Team (JRT) was announced (Department of Health, 1992), originally intended to monitor the substantial funding to local councils for community care reforms. The JRT methodology embraced both performance management and service user perspectives, drawing on quantitative and qualitative evidence (Joint Reviews, 1998, 2000, 2001; Humphrey, 2002, 2003a, 2003b) in a 'unique and experimental methodology' (Humphrey, 2002, p 463) 'more consistent and comprehensive than other social research ... (but also) more problematic' (Humphrey 2003b, p 178). Reviews evaluated social services departments as part of a system including the whole council and other agencies, and posed four key questions: is performance managed effectively, is there best value, are individuals well served and how effective is planning for community needs?

The blunt conclusions in review reports became high risk for councillors and senior managers, so preparation and implementation absorbed considerable resources. Council self-assessments were evaluated through observations and interviews with service users, staff, other agencies, managers and politicians, to reveal the leadership's capacity to understand and direct the organisation. Councils judged to be failing were subjected to a rigorous improvement regime, frequently involving replacement of the Director and sometimes of the lead councillor. Joint Reviews made and broke reputations. All but two councils in England and Wales were reviewed over seven years (1997–2004) (Gilroy, 2004, p 22). The learning from Joint Reviews helped to shape Joint Area Reviews (Ofsted, 2005), the Commission for Social Care Inspection (2005) and Corporate Performance Assessment (Department for Communities and Local Government, 2006).

Other regulatory innovations included: (i) Best Value, designed to replace compulsory competitive tendering with a more rigorous and more user-focused process of internal challenge monitored by the Best Value Inspectorate (Martin et al, 1998; Audit Commission, 2000), drawing on learning from the Joint Review Team (Department of the Environment, Transport and the Regions, 1998; Audit Commission, 1999); (ii) the development of independent inspection units (Davies, 2000, p 301; Waine, 2004); and (iii) increased emphasis on user rights, including new complaints procedures (Malin et al, 2002, p 57).

While SSI and Joint Reviews highlighted improvements in service management, discontent with performance management continued. For many practitioners, the relationship between laborious, computerised data collection and delivering quality services for service users was unbalanced (Smith, 2000), begging the question: 'was the expenditure on preparation, inspection and response worthwhile and proportionate?'

Alongside the public judgements about performance, statutory Special Measures arrangements created wide-ranging powers in relation to 'failing' services (Department of Health Social Services Inspectorate, 2001; National Institute for Social Work, 2001), including transfer of responsibility for managing services to a neighbouring council or independent body. Additional inspection and direct intervention in 'failing' councils and schools did appear to have some positive effects (Barnes, 2003; Barnes and Gurney, 2004; Matthews and Sammons, 2004, 2005; Perryman, 2005): 'the threat of re-inspection for the weakest' has been suggested as the best motivator for improvement (Matthews and Sammons, 2004). Performance Action Teams were used in several councils, bringing additional resources to fund changes necessary to create speedy improvement. Most of the 'failing' councils worked their way out of Special Measures, and the number going into that status dropped (Barnes, 2003; Barnes and Gurney, 2004). In contrast, well-performing services can also deteriorate quickly. The reasons have not been researched, although they are often associated with changes in local political or professional leadership.

As Joint Reviews and other inspectorates delivered more outspoken judgements, publicising the evidence of good and poor services, the impact on staff morale and the ability to improve became more problematic; concerns emerged about the long-term impact on councils judged to be 'failing' and their workforces. Management and organisation undeniably attracted more attention, but practice skills were, arguably, ignored.

By the end of the decade SSI was seen as the most user-focused inspectorate, disseminating good practice, facilitating service improvement and more transparent in its way of working (Local Government Association, 2001, p 3), although the least focused on resource management. Around half of councils considered that SSI and Ofsted inspectors were well equipped for the job, more than any other inspectorate – a significant transformation from the 1980s.

By 2004 central government recognised that the performance regime was having a negative impact on morale and recruitment; there was also concern about the growing cost of inspection (Martin, 2004). A Cabinet Office seminar concluded: 'we need to be better at making performance systems and rewards things that are valued by and motivate public sector workers (Office of Public Services Reform, 2004). Emphasis shifted to empowering local leaders to manage performance systems, while government defined and monitored the infrastructure.

In contrast to the national inspection of local authorities, the regulation of private and voluntary sector services had been undertaken by local councils for decades. However, concerns about 'governance', as a result of growing direct competition between local government and independent sector providers, resulted first in creation of arm's-length independent inspection units within local government and then in the National Care Standards Commission (NCSC) (Waine, 2004; Gummerson, 2006, p 2). All sectors were then subjected to the same regulatory requirements.

In the week that the NCSC launched in 2004, government announced that they would later that year merge it with the SSI and Joint Review Team to form the Commission for Social Care Inspection, creating a national inspectorate for the whole personal social services, for the first time independent of a government department. This did not resolve the instability. As these changes were being implemented, proposals were announced (Office of Public Services Reform, 2003; Audit Commission, 2004; Department of Health, 2004; Commission for Social Care Inspection, 2005) to reduce the volume of inspections and the number of inspectorates (Hampton, 2004, p 2; Cabinet Office, 2006). Children's services inspectors transferred to an enlarged 'new Ofsted' in 2007. Adult social care services inspections merged with the Healthcare Commission from April 2009 to form a single body responsible for regulating both adult social care and health, the Care Quality Commission. For the first time for around 170 years, there was no inspectorate solely for social work and social services. The reliability and credibility of inspection methodologies and their impact in real life is still contentious, but there is no sign that inspection will diminish.

Regulation of social workers: a successful campaign with a sting in the tail?

The first statutory regulation of UK social workers was enacted by the 2000 Care Standards Act; separate regulatory bodies were established in the four countries of the UK. The regulatory body for England, the GSCC, came into being in 2001. Responsibility for regulating social work qualifications transferred to the GSCC and equivalent regulatory bodies in Scotland, Wales and Northern Ireland.

These changes followed a long campaign by BASW and others (Association of Social Workers, 1955; Bamford, 2015). Regulatory bodies provide a foundation of principles and values informing the public about what it should expect and holding practitioners to account – especially important for social work operating in areas of contested values (Shardlow, 1989; Payne, 1996, 1999; Thompson, 2006; Banks et al, 2008; Banks and Nøhr, 2011; Payne, 2012; Parker and Doel, 2013; Reamer, 2013; Truell and Jones, 2015; Professional Standards Authority for Health and Social Care, 2016). A regulatory body also puts social work on an equal footing with related professional groups.

The 1976 BASW AGM approved 'in principle proposals for a scheme of accreditation', providing the basis for the campaign for a regulatory body. A Joint Steering Group included the Association of Directors of Social Services (ADSS), the Association of Directors of Social Work (ADSW), BASW, the Conference of Chief Probation Officers and the Residential Care Association (RCA), with observers from the Department of Health and Social Security (DHSS), CCETSW and the Society of Social Work Students (Joint Steering Group, 1980). Analysis of the arguments noted that social work was alone among the health and welfare professions in not having statutory regulation of training and practice, but concluded that the costs and effort involved in creating a regulator were disproportionate (Malherbe, 1980). The Committee on the Roles and Tasks of Social Workers (Barclay Committee, 1982) was encouraged by BASW to support the case for a regulatory body and concluded that, while there was insufficient support, further consideration was merited. BASW launched a campaign that built support.

Significant resistance came from local government bodies, supported by the main white-collar trade union NALGO (the National and Local Government Officers' Association) (Reed, 1987), arguing that, as employers of most social workers, they already regulated employment. The National Council of Voluntary Organisations was also opposed. There was also resistance from within the profession, arguing that a regulator was elitist and antipathetic to social work values and partnership with service users. The debate shifted as the diversity of providers increased. Local authorities could no longer claim that they regulated the profession through employment, and their need to have mechanisms to monitor standards in the agencies being commissioned was highlighted. Examples of poor decisions by local councillors dealing with cases of unacceptable practice strengthened the case.

The Joseph Rowntree Trust invited key leaders to a consultation held at the Athenaeum Club in London in 1987. Sir William Utting, then Chief Inspector of Social Services, was an active participant. The discussion identified renewed interest in the concept and the Joseph Rowntree Fund financed a project, hosted by the National Institute for Social Work (NISW), to explore the idea (Brand, 1999). NISW convened a small group with similar membership to the former Joint Steering Group (see above), which soon agreed to expand.

The formation of the General Social Services Council Action Group within NISW (chaired by Sir Peter Barclay), with BASW as a founding member, marked the start of a campaign that culminated in the 2000 Care Standards Act (General Social Services Council Action Group, 1993). The Action Group was UK wide and included local government bodies, directors' associations (ADSW and ADSS), professional bodies (BASW and the Social Care Association) and the Trades Union Congress, with observers from CCETSW and the DHSS. Sir William Utting is recorded as representing the NISW Board.

Professor Roy Parker was commissioned to research the case for a regulator, concluding in favour of regulation (Parker, 1990). The Action Group endorsed Parker's recommendation of a statutory regulator for the whole social care sector, of which social work would be a small element. Once all the key stakeholders were aligned, it became easier to lobby the political parties. BASW supported this inclusive approach but some were concerned that including the larger body of social care workers would dominate the work of the regulator and detract from the focus on social work – a debate which continues in different forms in each of the four countries of the UK.

The case for professional regulation was strengthened by European Economic Community directives on mutual recognition of qualifications. The First Directive on Mutual Recognition of Diplomas related to higher diplomas and required member states to recognise qualifications awarded in other countries, provided that the period of study was three years or more and that the occupation was 'regulated' (European Economic Community, 1989). The Second Directive related to other occupations and required a minimum of six months of study as well as formal regulation of the occupation (European Economic Community, 1992). It was seen as likely that UK social work would satisfy the requirements of the First Directive if the length of training were extended to three years, which happened, and the occupation were regulated, which occurred. Mobility of the workforce and the ability to recruit from overseas were important, but probably more significant was the consequence that these Directives established comparators not only between countries but also between professional groups (Jones and Pierce, 1990; Jones, 1999; Lyons and Lawrence, 2006; Lyons and Littlechild, 2006).

The Conservative government procrastinated, but eventually published a response in 1996 (Department of Health, 1996). However, New Labour included the creation of a social care regulator in its 1997 general election manifesto and, once elected, quickly acted on this (Pitkeathley, 2000). The role of the regulators, as set out in *Modernising Social Services* (Department of Health, 1998), was to be responsible for the regulation of social workers and qualifications.

The Office for Public Management consulted on a code of conduct and recommended that there should also be a code of practice for agencies, since social work practice was so linked with the capacity of the agency within which it was delivered (Jones and Corrigan, 2000a, 2000b; Office for Public Management, 2000).

The government decided to implement registration of qualified social workers in England and protection of title in the first instance, leaving a decision about the more numerous social care workforce until later (Department of Health, 1998). The devolved administrations adopted different approaches to this issue, which has created continuing tension and operational challenges.

Regulation of social work in England since 2001

The GSCC opened the register in 2001 (Jerrom, 2001; Jones, 2001) and developed the new degree in Social Work. Service users were concerned whether there would be sufficient resources to implement the new codes in the context of tightening eligibility criteria (Gilbert, 2001). Social workers willingly, if slowly, registered (Brindle, 2004).

The UK regulators initiated a consultation about protection of the title of social worker (GSCC, 2003). The four regulators endorsed UK-wide codes of practice for social care workers and employers (Office for Public Management, 2000; GSCC, 2002). The social worker code underpinned social work practice and disciplinary processes, and so had real force, but the code for employers did not have statutory force and had weaker impact. England later abandoned the code for employers, although it has been retained by the other nations. The first disciplinary hearings into allegations against registered social workers in England were in 2006 (GSCC, 2006; Brindle, 2007).

The GSCC faced growing criticism that disciplinary hearings focused on personal misbehaviour rather than practice quality (Lombard, 2010; McLaughlin, 2010). Long delays in conduct proceedings developed. A critical report by the Council for Healthcare Regulatory Excellence

(2009) identified weaknesses in management and procedures for hearing complaints, and made adverse comparisons with health service regulators. A new Chair and Chief Executive restored its leading role among stakeholders (*Professional Social Work*, 2009). A report comparing models of regulating social work education was never published (Saks, 2009).

The Coalition government announced in 2010, without prior warning, that the GSCC functions would be transferred to the Health Professions Council, to be renamed the Health and Care Professions Council (HCPC). This seemed to be primarily a cost-saving decision, without regard to the development of the social work qualifications framework and practice standards. Social work in England therefore became regulated under a multi-disciplinary structure, while it remained separate in the other nations. The GSCC (2012) published a report summarising a decade of achievements, and a report by the Chief Executive reflected on leadership in closing an organisation (Thompson, 2012).

The HCPC regulates 15 health professions. Social work was the largest professional group and significantly changed the balance of its work. A registered social worker was appointed to the governing board. The HCPC decided not to continue involvement in some areas of work undertaken by the GSCC, such as an active role alongside other stakeholders in service development. HCPC staff and committees took time to adjust to the ethos, politics and language of social work.

The Professional Standards Authority oversees regulatory bodies in health and social care; its highly critical review of the approach to health and social work regulation argued that registrants are 'frightened into compliance' and introduced 'right-touch regulation' as a new approach (Professional Standards Authority, 2015).

This chapter is primarily concerned with regulation. However, regulation is influenced by developments elsewhere (see other chapters), such as the reports on social work education (Croisdale-Appleby, 2014; Narey, 2014), the Social Work Task Force (2009), the Professional Capabilities Framework (PCF) (BASW, 2019) and The College of Social Work (TCSW) (Philpot, 2011).

Throughout this period the Department for Education (DfE) wanted to improve social work with children and families (see, for example, National Audit Office, 2016), as reports of child abuse tragedies continued. This concern appears to have contributed to the 2015 decision to re-create a specific social work regulator in England. The hurried process of forming Social Work England (SWE) stimulated parliamentary battles about its status and structure, probably because the legislation was imposed rather than introduced with customary cross-party and professional consensus (Department for Education and Department of Health, 2018).

The appointments of Lord Patel (a former social worker) as Chair and Colum Conway (a social worker and former Chief Executive of the Northern Ireland regulator) as Chief Executive were widely welcomed. However, the failure to appoint any additional social workers to the Board, which has the final say on qualification requirements and practice standards, provoked professional anger. SWE embarked on an inclusive consultation about practice standards and qualifications (Social Work England, 2019). It remains to be seen what impact the unbalanced membership of the Board will have on professional identity and support for the regulator (Haynes, 2019). SWE assumed responsibility for regulation on 2 December 2019.

It is self-evident that this history of organisational disruption would have significant impact on social work practice and management and on the perception of social workers: three very different regulators in less than 20 years. It is perhaps too soon to evaluate the consequences of that disruption, but it is clear that the advent of regulation did not result in improved professional self-confidence, nor in improved public perceptions, which its advocates had envisaged.

Regulation of social work in Scotland, Wales and Northern Ireland since 2001

The process of regulation in the three smaller nations of the UK has been less disrupted by organisational upheavals. Their arrangements have been characterised by more constructive partnership working between stakeholders and a shared political and professional vision.

Conclusion

Regulation is designed to sustain public confidence, protect ministers, deal with poor practice and ensure value for money. Has regulation enhanced confidence, and was expenditure proportionate? Regulation has focused on outcomes for service users, has shaped good practice and has held local political and professional leaders to account, but it has not guaranteed high-quality services. Politicians, regulators and professionals have not faced up to defining the objective cost of quality services and regulation, including both direct costs and costs of compliance. Regulators have not consistently demonstrated a grasp of reality, identified 'failures' in good time or facilitated improvements;

recent research suggests that methodologies have failed to take account of resource inequalities and that judgements are therefore distorted (Bywaters and Webb, 2018). Effectiveness is difficult to evaluate in diverse and complex social services, but some form of regulation of public services seems to be inevitable for public and political reassurance. How this is most effectively delivered remains a constant challenge.

Acknowledgements

This chapter has drawn heavily on *Regulation of Social Work and Social Workers in the UK* (Jones, 2018). A more detailed discussion of the history of social services inspection and the JRT can be found in Jones (2009).

References

Association of Social Workers (1955) *A Report on Registration and the Social Worker*, Slough: Association of Social Workers.

Audit Commission (1999) *Best Value and the Audit Commission in England*, London: Audit Commission.

Audit Commission (2000) *Seeing is Believing: How the Audit Commission will Carry Out Best Value Inspections in England*, London: Audit Commission, www.audit-commission.gov.uk/reports/NATIONAL-REPORT.asp?CategoryID=&ProdID=08ABFD4C-883E-40d7-B9EA-BCE4D89CD566.

Audit Commission (2004) *A Modern Approach to Inspecting Services: A Consultation on how the Audit Commission will Inspect Local Public Services from 1 April 2005*, London: Audit Commission, www.bestvalueinspections.gov.uk/Products/NATIONAL-REPORT/073E289D-8848–47A6–8D0E-D081253BB8FF/AModernApproachToInspectingServices.pdf.

Bamford, T. (2015) *A Contemporary History of Social Work: Learning from the Past*, Bristol: Policy Press.

Banks, S. and Nøhr, K. (eds) (2011) *Practising Social Work Ethics around the World*, London: Routledge.

Banks, S., Hugman, R., Healy, L., Bozalek, V. and Orme, J. (2008) 'Global ethics for social work: problems and possibilities – papers from the Ethics and Social Welfare Symposium, Durban, July 2008', *Ethics and Social Welfare*, vol 2, pp 276–90.

Barclay Committee (1982) *Social Workers: Their Role and Tasks*, London: Bedford Square Press for the National Institute for Social Work.

Barnes, J. (2003) 'Turning around "failing" organisations: literature review', Department of Health (unpublished), London. jebarnes@supanet.com.

Barnes, J. and Gurney, G. (2004) *Off PAT? Supporting Improvement in Social Care Services: Reviewing the Lessons from the Work of Performance Action Teams with Councils with Social Services Responsibilities*, London: Department of Health.

BASW (2019) *Professional Capabilities Framework (PCF)* [Online]. Available at: https://www.basw.co.uk/professional-development/professional-capabilities-framework-pcf/the-pcf (accessed 29 September 2019).

Blythe, E. (2001) 'The impact of the first term of the new Labour Government on social work in Britain: the interface between education policy and social work', *British Journal of Social Work*, vol 31, pp 563–77.

Brand, D. (1999) *Accountable Care: Developing the General Social Care Council*, York: Joseph Rowntree Foundation.

Brindle, D. (2004) 'Filling in the gaps', *Guardian* Society, 28 July.

Brindle, D. (2007) 'Questionable punishment', *Guardian*, 1 August.

Bywaters, P. and Webb, C. (2018) 'There is clear evidence that links deprivation, expenditure and quality in children's services', *Community Care*, 7 February, https://www.communitycare.co.uk/2018/02/07/clear-evidence-links-deprivation-expenditure-quality-childrens-services/ (accessed 8 November 2019).

Cabinet Office (2006) *Public Service Inspection*, London: Cabinet Office.

Commission for Social Care Inspection (2005) *The State of Social Care in England 2004–5*, London: Commission for Social Care Inspection.

Cope, C. (2001) *Quality on the Way: Inspection of Service Quality Improvements in Social Care*, London: Department of Health,.

Corbett, U. and Markham, W.O. (1867) *Metropolitan Workhouses*, London: Poor Law Board, https://wellcomecollection.org/works/yxkgwren/items?canvas=1&sierraId=b24914915&langCode=eng (accessed 23 September 2019).

Council for Healthcare Regulatory Excellence (2009) *Report and Recommendations to the Secretary of State for Health on the Conduct Function of the General Social Care Council*, www.professionalstandards.org.uk/docs/default-source/publications/special-review-report/general-social-care-council-review-2009.pdf (accessed 7 April 2017).

Croisdale-Appleby, D. (2014) *Re-visioning Social Work Education: An Independent Review*, London: Department of Health, https://www.gov.uk/government/uploads/system/uploads/attachment_data/file/285788/DCA_Accessible.pdf (accessed 1 September 2017).

Darvill, G. (1998) *Organisation, People and Standards*, London: NISW, ADSS, CCETSW.

Davies, C. (2000) *Frameworks for Regulation and Accountability: Threat or Opportunity*, London: Sage Publishing.

Davis, H., Downe, J. and Martin, S. (2001a) *External Inspection of Local Government: Driving Improvement or Drowning in Detail?*, York: YPS.

Davis, H., Downe, J. and Martin, S. (2001b) *The Impact of External Inspection on Local Government*, York: Joseph Rowntree Foundation, www.jrf.org.uk/knowledge/findings/government/921.asp.

Day, P. and Klein, R. (1990) *Inspecting the Inspectorates*, York: Joseph Rowntree Memorial Trust.

Department for Communities and Local Government (2006) *Comprehensive Performance Assessment: An Introduction*, London: DCLG, www.communities.gov.uk/index.asp?id=1133963 (accessed 11 July 2006).

Department for Education and Department of Health (2018) *Social Work England: Consultation on Secondary Legislative Framework*, London: Department for Education, https://consult.education.gov.uk/social-work-england-implementation-team/social-work-england-consultation-on-secondary-legi/supporting_documents/Social%20Work%20EnglandConsultation.pdf (accessed 1 March 2018).

Department of Health (1992) *Inspecting Social Services: A Consultation Document*, London: Department of Health, www.bopcris.ac.uk/cgi-bin/displayrec.pl?searchtext=Inspection&record=/bopall/ref23719.html.

Department of Health (1996) *Obligations of Care: A Consultation Paper on the Setting of Conduct and Practice Standards for Social Services Staff*, London: Department of Health for the UK Health Departments.

Department of Health (1998) *Modernising Social Services: Promoting Independence, Improving Protection, Raising Standards*, London: HMSO, www.dh.gov.uk/PublicationsAndStatistics/Publications/PublicationsPolicyAndGuidance/PublicationsPolicyAndGuidanceArticle/fs/en?CONTENT_ID=4009575&chk=bztPtC.

Department of Health (2004) 'Reid confirms planned merger of Healthcare Commission and Commission for Social Care Inspection', London: Department of Health, www.dh.gov.uk/PublicationsAndStatistics/PressReleases/PressReleasesNotices/fs/en?CONTENT_ID=4106502&chk=kqM72Z.

Department of Health and Social Security, Welsh Office and National Health Service Advisory Service (1971) *National Health Service Hospital Advisory Service: Annual Report for 1969–70*, London: HMSO, www.bopcris.ac.uk/bop1965/ref1907.html.

Department of Health Social Services Inspectorate (2001) 'New "star performance ratings" for social services', London: Department of Health, www.dh.gov.uk/PublicationsAndStatistics/PressReleases/ PressReleasesNotices/fs/en?CONTENT_ID=4014202&chk= KRbnht (accessed 19 September 2006).

Department of the Environment, Transport and the Regions (1998) *Modernising Local Government: Improving Local Services through Best Value*, London: HMSO.

European Economic Community (1989) *A General System for the Recognition of Higher Education Diplomas*, Brussels: European Economic Community.

European Economic Community (1992) *General System for the Recognition of Diplomas: The Second Directive*, Brussels: European Economic Community.

General Social Services Council Action Group (1993) *Final Report*, London: National Institute for Social Work.

Gilbert, H. (2001) 'Clients deliver their verdict on codes of conduct and practice', London: Community Care.

Gillen, S. (2004) 'Child placement upheaval as councils override care plans to bolster ratings', London: Community Care.

Gilroy, D. (2004) *The Social Services Inspectorate: A History – Origins, Impact and Legacy*, London: Department of Health, https://webarchive.nationalarchives.gov.uk/+/www.dh.gov.uk/ assetRoot/04/07/75/95/04077595.pdf.

GSCC (2002) *Codes of Practice for Social Care Workers and Employers*, London: GSCC, www.gscc.org.uk/codes (accessed 3 September 2006).

GSCC (2003) 'Start of consultation on protection of title', London: General Social Care Council, www.gscc.org.uk/news_story. asp?newsID=84.

GSCC (2006) 'First social worker conduct hearing scheduled', London: General Social Care Council, www.gscc.org.uk/News+and+events/ Media+releases/First+social+worker+conduct+hearing+scheduled. htm (accessed 18 April 2006).

GSCC (2012) *Regulating Social Workers (2001–12)*, http://webarchive. nationalarchives.gov.uk/20120703122123/http://www.gscc.org.uk/ cmsFiles/Publications/LR_Regulating_social_workers_2001–12.pdf (accessed 26 February 2017).

Gummerson, M. (2006) 'Regulation of public services: a literature survey', Portsmouth: University of Portsmouth, www.port.ac.uk/ research/rasc/researchworktodate/filetodownload,21971,en.pdf (accessed 7 May 2018).

Hampton, P. (2004) *Reducing Administrative Burdens: Effective Inspection and Enforcement*, London: Her Majesty's Stationery Office.

Haynes, L. (2019) 'Lack of registered social workers on Social Work England board criticised', *Community Care*, 18 April.

Heywood, J. (1979) *Children in Care: The Development of the Service for the Deprived Child* (3rd edn), London: Routledge and Kegan Paul.

Humphrey, J.C. (2002) 'Joint Reviews: retracing the trajectory, decoding the terms', *British Journal of Social Work*, vol 32, pp 463–76.

Humphrey, J.C. (2003a) 'Joint Reviews: judgement day and beyond', *British Journal of Social Work*, vol 33, pp 727–38.

Humphrey, J.C. (2003b) 'Joint Reviews: the methodology in action', *British Journal of Social Work*, vol 33, pp 177–90.

James, A., Brooks, T. and Towell, D. (1992) *Committed to Quality: Quality Assurance in Social Services Departments*, London: Department of Health.

Jerrom, C. (2001) 'Pitkeathley to head up care council,' London: Community Care.

Joint Reviews (1998) *Reviewing Social Services – Guiding You Through*, London: Audit Commission.

Joint Reviews (2000) *Promising Prospects: Joint Reviews Team Fourth Annual Report 1999/2000*, London: Audit Commission.

Joint Reviews (2001) *Reviewing Social Services: Guiding You Through*, London: Audit Commission.

Joint Steering Group (1980) *Accreditation in Social Work: A Second and Final Report*, Birmingham: British Association of Social Workers.

Jones, D.N. (1999) 'Regulating social work: key questions', *Practice*, vol 11, pp 55–63.

Jones, D.N. (2001) 'A new era for social work regulation in the United Kingdom', *Representing Children*, vol 14, pp 81–92.

Jones, D.N. (2009) 'An insider study of Joint Reviews of local authority social services.', PhD thesis, Warwick University.

Jones, D.N. (2018) *Regulation of Social Work and Social Workers in the United Kingdom*, Birmingham: British Association of Social Workers, http://cdn.basw.co.uk/upload/basw_95742–5.pdf (accessed 22 February 2018).

Jones, D.N. and Corrigan, P. (2000a) *Regulating Social Work: A Case Study in Change from the United Kingdom*, Montreal, Canada: International Federation of Social Workers and International Association of Schools of Social Work World Symposium.

Jones, D.N. and Corrigan, P. (2000b) 'Under Review', *Professional Social Work*, October, pp 14–15.

Jones, D.N. and Pierce, R. (1990) *The European Community Directive on Professional Qualifications: The Knowledge, Skills and Values of Social Work in a European Context*, Brussels: International Federation of Social Workers European Region and European Economic Community.

Jordan, B. (1975) *Clients are Fellow Citizens*, Edinburgh: British Association of Social Workers Annual Conference (out of print).

Kelly, D. and Warr, B. (eds) (1992) *Quality Counts: Achieving Quality in Social Care Services*, London, Whiting & Birch.

Leadbetter, M. (2006) 'Media distortions create "crisis of democracy"', *Professional Social Work*, June, p 14.

Local Government Association (2001) *An Inspector Calls: A Survey of Local Authorities on the Impact of Inspection*, London: LGA Publications, www.lga.gov.uk/Documents/Publication/inspections.pdf.

Lombard, D. (2010) 'The past and future of the GSCC conduct system', *Community Care*, www.communitycare.co.uk/2010/01/15/the-past-and-future-of-the-gscc-conduct-system/ (accessed 7 April 2017).

Lyons, K. and Lawrence, S. (2006) *Social Work in Europe: Educating for Change*, Birmingham: BASW Press.

Lyons, K. and Littlechild, B. (eds) (2006) *International Labour Mobility in Social Work*, Birmingham: BASW.

Malherbe, M. (1980) *Accreditation in Social Work: Principles and Issues in Context: A Contribution to the Debate*, London: CCETSW.

Malin, N., Wilmot, S. and Manthorpe, J. (2002) *Key Concepts and Debates in Health and Social Policy*, Maidenhead: Open University Press.

Martin, S. (2004) 'The changing face of public service inspection', *Public Money and Management*, vol 24, pp 3–5.

Martin, S., Hartley, J., Bostock, J., Hands, D. and Sutcliffe, J. (1998) *Best Value: Current Developments and Future Challenges*, London: Local Government Association.

Matthews, P. and Sammons, P. (2004) *Improvement through Inspection: An Evaluation of the Impact of Ofsted's Work*, London: The Office of Standards in Education (Ofsted).

Matthews, P. and Sammons, P. (2005) 'Survival of the weakest: the differential improvement of schools causing concern in England', *London Review of Education*, vol 3, pp 159–76.

McLaughlin, K. (2010) 'The social worker versus the General Social Care Council: an analysis of care standards tribunal hearings and decisions', *British Journal of Social Work*, vol 40, pp 311–27.

McLean, I., Haubrich, D. and Gutiérrez-Romero, R. (2007) 'The perils and pitfalls of performance measurement: the CPA regime for local authorities in England', *Public Money and Management*, vol 27, pp 111–18.

MHCLG (2019) *Independent Review into the Arrangements in place to Support the Transparency and Quality of Local Authority Financial Reporting and External Audit in England*, London: Ministry of Housing Communities and Local Government, https://assets.publishing.service.gov.uk/government/uploads/system/uploads/attachment_data/file/815781/Independent_Review_ToR.pdf (accessed 20 September 2019).

Munro, E. (2004) 'The impact of audit on social work practice', *British Journal of Social Work*, vol 34, pp 1075–95.

Narey, M. (2014) *Making the Education of Social Workers Consistently Effective: Report of Sir Martin Narey's Independent Review of the Education of Children's Social Workers*, London: Department for Education, www.gov.uk/government/publications (accessed 21 May 2014).

National Audit Office (2016) *Children in Need of Help or Protection*, London: National Audit Office, https://www.nao.org.uk/report/children-in-need-of-help-or-protection/ (accessed 22 October 2016).

National Institute for Social Work (2001) *Special Measures Interventions: Working in Local Authorities to Improve Performance in Social Services*, London: NISW. www.nisw.org.uk.

Office for Public Management (2000) 'Draft code of conduct for staff and code of practice for agencies for the General Social Care Council', London: OPM.

Office of Public Services Reform (2003) *Inspecting for Improvement: Developing a Customer Focused Approach*, London: Office of Public Services Reform, www.everychildmatters.gov.uk/_files/410FC0E01AAC0BE1116952A03F88E950.pdf.

Office of Public Services Reform (2004) *Professionals and Performance Management. Public Services Reform Seminars 2004–05, 15 June 2004*, London: Cabinet Office.

Ofsted (2005) *Every Child Matters: Joint Area Reviews of Children's Services*, London: Ofsted, www.ofsted.gov.uk/publications/index.cfm?fuseaction=pubs.displayfile&id=3963&type=pdf.

Parker, J. and Doel, M. (eds) (2013) *Professional Social Work*, London: Sage Publishing.

Parker, R. (1990) *Safeguarding Standards*, London: National Institute for Social Work.

Payne, M. (1996) *What is Professional Social Work?*, Birmingham: Venture Press.

Payne, M. (1999) 'The moral bases of social work', *European Journal of Social Work*, vol 2, pp 247–58.

Payne, M. (2012) 'What's so special about social work and social justice?', *Guardian Professional*, 10 July, https://www.theguardian.com/social-care-network/2012/jul/10/social-work-social-justice?CMP=twt_gu.

Perryman, J. (2005) 'School leadership and management after special measures: discipline without the gaze?', *School Leadership and Management*, vol 25, pp 281–97.

Perryman, J. (2006) 'Panoptic performativity and school inspection regimes: disciplinary mechanisms and life under special measures', *Journal of Education Policy*, vol 21, pp 147–61.

Philpot, T. (2001) 'What a performance', *Community Care*, 18 October, pp 34–5.

Philpot, T. (2011) 'High tensions over establishment of social work college', *Guardian*, 8 December.

Pillinger, J. (2001) *Quality in Social Public Services*, Dublin: European Foundation for the Improvement of Living and Working Conditions.

Pitkeathley, J. (2000) 'General Social Care Council', *Professional Social Work*, vol 1, pp 6.

Professional Social Work (2009) 'GSCC hopes for a Rosier regulatory future', *Professional Social Work*, April, pp 20–1.

Professional Standards Authority for Health and Social Care (2015) *Rethinking Regulation*, London: Professional Standards Authority for Health and Social Care, https://www.professionalstandards.org.uk/docs/default-source/publications/thought-paper/rethinking-regulation-2015.pdf?sfvrsn=edf77f20_14 (accessed 31 January 2018).

Professional Standards Authority for Health and Social Care (2016) 'Professional identities and regulation: a literature review', London: Professional Standards Authority for Health and Social Care, www.professionalstandards.org.uk/docs/default-source/publications/professional-identities-and-regulation---a-literature-review.pdf?sfvrsn=0 (accessed 8 January 2017).

Reamer, F. (2013) *Social Work Values and Ethics*, New York: Columbia University Press.

Reed, D. (1987) 'Why we say "no"', *Community Care*, 17 September, pp 20–1.

Rhodes, G. (1981) *Inspectorates in British Government: Law Enforcement and Standards of Efficiency*, London: George Allen and Unwin.

Rivett, G. (2005) *Poor Law Infirmaries*, www.nhshistory.net/poor_law_infirmaries.htm (accessed 9 April 2014).

Roberts, A. (1991) *England's Poor Law Commissioners and the Trade in Pauper Lunacy 1834–1847*, www.mdx.ac.uk/www/study/Mott.htm#AfterMott (accessed 23 November 2004).

Rouse, J. and Smith, G. (1999) 'Accountability', in M. Powell (ed), *New Labour, New Welfare State?*, Bristol: Policy Press.

Saks, M. (2009) 'Discussion document: the regulation of social work education', London: General Social Care Council (unpublished).

Seddon, J. (2003) *Written Submission to Public Administration Select Committee's Inquiry into Public Sector Performance Targets*, Buckingham: Vanguard Education.

Seddon, J. (2005) *Adult Social Care: A Systems Analysis and a Better Way Forward*, Buckingham: Vanguard Education.

Seebohm, F. (1968) *Report of the Committee on Local Authority and Allied Personal Social Services*, London: HMSO.

Shardlow, S. (ed) (1989) *The Values of Change in Social Work*, London: Routledge.

Slack, P. (1998) *From Reformation to Improvement: Public Welfare in Early Modern England*, Oxford: Oxford University Press.

Smith, E. (1866) *Report to the Poor Law Board on the Metropolitan Workhouse Infirmaries etc*, London: House of Commons.

Smith, G. (2000) 'Is PAF reaching the troops? A follow-up to the performance survey of councillors and managers', *Management Issues in Social Care*, vol 7, pp 37–41.

Social Services Inspectorate (1985) *The Social Services Inspectorate of the Department of Health and Social Security: Mission Statement*, London: Department of Health and Social Security.

Social Services Inspectorate (1999) *Social Services Performance in 1998/99: The Personal Social Services Performance Assessment Framework*, London: Department of Health.

Social Work England (2019) *Reshaping Standards, Enabling Change: Consultation Response*, Sheffield, Social Work England, https://socialworkengland.org.uk/wp-content/uploads/2019/09/CONSULTATION-REPORT_FINAL.pdf (accessed 19 September 2019).

Social Work Task Force (2009) *Building a Safe, Confident Future: The Final Report of the Social Work Task Force*, London: Department for Children, Schools and Families, http://webarchive.nationalarchives.gov.uk/20130403221302/https://www.education.gov.uk/publications/eOrderingDownload/01114–2009DOM-EN.pdf (accessed 8 January 2018).

Thompson, N. (2006) 'Professionalism: help or hindrance?', *Professional Social Work*, March, p 7.

Thompson, P. (2012) 'Leadership for organisational success – a case study from closing an organisation', London: General Social Care Council (unpublished).

Truell, R. and Jones, D.N. (2015) 'Global agenda for social work and social development', in J.D. Wright (editor-in-chief), *International Encyclopedia of the Social and Behavioral Sciences* (2nd edn), Oxford: Elsevier.

Waine, B. (2004) *Regulation and Inspection of Adult Social Care Services – Baseline Study*, Department of Health, London, www.masc.bham.ac.uk/baseline/base1.htm.

Younghusband, E. (1981) *The Newest Profession: A Short History of Social Work*, London: Community Care/IPC Business Press.

4

Continuity and change in the knowledge base for social work

June Thoburn

Introduction

Given the potentially ambitious scope of the title, this is essentially a personal perspective. It draws on my experiences as: a student on a postgraduate child care officer course in 1962; a child and family and then a generalist 'patch' social worker; a social work lecturer and researcher; a board member of the General Social Care Council (GSCC); and in the voluntary sector. References to key texts are woven into a commentary on the changing views between the 1950s and the late 2010s about necessary knowledge for social workers in the early stages of their career. Detailed knowledge needed for more specialist and supervisory roles is beyond the scope of this chapter.

In academic curriculum terms, social work, like public and social policy, law and education, is an applied social science discipline that, over time, has developed its own knowledge base, adding in insights from economics, social history, ethics, sociology, medicine and health sciences, psychology, criminology, demography and management. In broad terms, the areas of knowledge come under the overlapping areas of:

- social science disciplines (the socio-political/legal context);
- understanding human development and relationships (the internal/relational world);
- theories, approaches and methods for social work practice.

These have to be brought together in response to the social worker's need for an understanding of relationships (within families and communities, with adults and children in need of services and with professionals). In one of the first UK articles addressing this question the founding editor of the *British Journal of Social Work*, Olive Stevenson (1971, pp 225–37), invited the reader 'to think in terms of "frames of reference" for understanding and helping people in difficulty. Such frames of reference overlap, complement each other and, at times, conflict.'

At the start of the period explored in this volume, knowledge for practice came mainly from the first two areas, but over time the research base and published literature on the third has greatly expanded. This chapter summarises the early social sciences-dominated phase up to the 1960s before exploring these three 'frames of reference' after 1970, when, with the expansion of schools of social work, the balance shifted. Some courses continued to 'buy in' 'service teaching' from the faculties of sociology, social policy, psychology, medicine and law, while other teams of social work lecturers provided the social science teaching from within their own number. Discrete courses on 'sociology' or 'psychology' typically became 'social work and society' or 'human growth and development'.

The respective contributions of research reports, refereed journal articles, the professional press, practice wisdom and experts by experience are considered. The chapter ends with reference to current debates, played out in mainstream and social media as well as in professional and policy debates, on who is in the driving seat in determining the knowledge base for social work.

The social science foundations

The social science knowledge base up to the 1970s

During this period when social work training in the UK expanded (see Chapter 1) the social science curriculum developed considerably, especially in the areas of social policy and sociology. It brought in knowledge of community and class (Wilmott and Young, 1957) and explored the roots of social problems and the rationale for public and social services (Titmuss, 1968). These were essential readings for an understanding of where social work fitted within the post-war welfare state.

The debates between 'universalism' and 'targeted' responses to social problems, and social work's response to them, especially poverty, were rehearsed in both professional and more general publications, including the influential *New Society*, first published in 1962. In 1959 Barbara Wootton, a highly respected professor of economics, used a chapter on social work (Wootton et al, 1959) to provide what Stevenson (2013, p 77) subsequently described as a 'trenchant critique of social work'. She summarises Wootton's argument that 'social work had taken a wrong turning away from the alleviation of material and social problems towards a preoccupation with the inner worlds of clients, borrowing (pretentiously she argues) from psychoanalytic theory' (Stevenson, 2013, p 77). Stevenson (1963) used an early issue of *New Society* to refute this assertion. In 'The Understanding Caseworker' she outlined for a non-social work readership how social caseworkers concern themselves with outer as well as inner worlds.

During the 1960s and 1970s Sir Keith Joseph, who as Secretary of State for Social Services was accountable for social work policy in the Heath government, held a view contrary to those of both Wootton and Stevenson. In a 1973 speech to Directors of Social Services, reflecting on the 'cycle of deprivation' and the 'underclass' theories propounded at the time by US economist Charles Murray, he saw the social work role as focusing on individual problems and 'problem families' (Joseph, 1973).

This debate in the public arena was an example of an early 'polemic' about the nature of social work. Around the same time pamphlets published by the Child Poverty Action Group (CPAG; set up in 1965 and to which many social workers and students belonged) reported on the facts and 'the feel' of poverty. Data and interview-based research publications drawing on sociological and social policy theories became available, notably Peter Townsend's (1962) powerful indictment of the care of the elderly, *The Last Refuge*. This period saw the early empirical research studies specifically focusing on social work and related social services. In the field of child care, data-based analyses by social policy PhD graduates joined social work reading lists (Parker, 1966; Packman, 1969).

Understanding the law and relevant legislation had to be an important part of the curriculum (I still have the 1933 Children and Young Persons Act and 1948 Children Act and fostering regulations provided to me by the Home Office before I started my child care officer training). Section 1 of the 1963 Children and Young Persons Act, empowering social workers to provide 'preventive' services in the family home, owed much to the advocacy of the growing band of policy-aware social workers and academics.

This period saw the start of data- and interview-based research specifically on social work conducted by social policy and social work academics. As well as the 1963 Children and Young Persons Act, the (1968) Seebohm Committee recommendations were informed by empirical research on those who provided and those who were the clients of the existing services. Importantly, just before the new social services departments were set up, 1970 saw the publication of research by Mayer and Timms that introduced social workers to research based on what their clients had to say about them.

Social science knowledge for social work after 1970

The social sciences remained essential components of courses preparing social workers to practise across the needs and age groups, but adapted to the (changing) roles and tasks of UK social work practitioners. Social policy academics, especially, continued to play a leading role in the development of the social work knowledge base and research agenda. Peter Townsend followed up his research on elder care with studies of all areas of poverty and deprivation, leading to his 1979 tour de force, *Poverty in the United Kingdom*. He and Roy Parker (both members of Titmuss's LSE social policy team; see Titmuss, 1968) had key roles in the Bristol University social work programme. Dennis Marsden (1969) brought new knowledge from research based on interviews with single-parent families. Bob Holman combined social work academic leadership with research and advocacy for improved services for families experiencing material deprivation. A 1976 CPAG pamphlet, *Inequality in Child Care*, broadened out in 1978 into *Poverty, Explanations of Social Deprivation* (Holman, 1978). More modest in size but having an impact on the child care officers and their tutors of the time was the detailed qualitative research by Herbert and Wilson (1978) on parenting in poor environments.

The linkages between poverty, inequality and politics were taken up by social work lecturers within the growing number of social work courses. Social work academics and practitioners helped to develop British Association of Social Workers (BASW) policies on social work responses to poverty, and social policy knowledge was used by social work leaders and practitioners to lobby for change, as with the implementation of the 1977 Housing (Homeless Persons) Act. At this point the contribution of the media to the knowledge base can be brought in. The powerful 1966 BBC TV programme *Cathy Come Home* and the early episodes of the Granada documentary *Seven Up!* (1964) made their contributions to the curriculum and to motivations for social workers to engage with policy issues. More debatable was the impact on social work knowledge of official and media reporting on child deaths and chronic abuse, in which social workers were involved as inquiry chairs or members, but also as practitioners whose work came under scrutiny (Butler and Drakeford, 2011).

Despite the growing role played by government advisory or regulatory bodies (referred to in other chapters), programmes varied in the emphasis they placed on the social sciences. However, the curriculum guidance and accreditation process for schools of social work led gradually, and increasingly after the GSCC began to accredit qualifying social work education, to a narrowing of the knowledge base.

The curriculum for generic social workers further narrowed when the Home Office concluded that probation officers were not social workers and should have a separate criminal justice-focused training. Criminology as a contributory discipline faded from many social work departments.

The emphasis was increasingly on the knowledge base for front-line social work practice, but still incorporating essential knowledge from the contributory disciplines and basic knowledge necessary to work across age and needs groups. In recognition that, as recommended by the Seebohm Committee, social workers should initially be 'generalists', the concept of 'transferability' and adaptation of knowledge from one client group and setting to another came into prominence. It was recognised that in two years (and three, when the honours degree became a requirement for registration in 2001) it would not be possible for students to study all areas of the curriculum and experience placements in all the main settings. They were therefore required to demonstrate how relevant cross-disciplinary learning for practice in one setting could be transferred and supplemented for practice in a different setting. Theses and dissertations were points where knowledge for practice from the contributory disciplines could be assessed.

Knowledge from social administration about the interlocking systems required to meet welfare needs tended to be integrated across the curriculum. While the importance of inter-professional practice was recognised, in qualifying programmes the emphasis tended to be on learning *about* other professions and agencies, often integrated within the 'social work and society' knowledge stream. Learning '*how to*' work with other professionals and agencies, including across statutory and voluntary sectors, during qualifying training depended on the placements experienced. Taught modules on mental health practice and child protection, and more recently adult protection, became increasingly important, bringing in practitioners from paediatrics or psychiatry. However, it was recognised that post-qualifying training was essential for acquiring the necessary knowledge for practice in specialist areas such as fostering and adoption, palliative care, forensic social work and working with hearing-impaired clients. This trend was further expanded when mental health legislation in 1983 introduced the role of the Approved Social Worker (subsequently the Approved Mental Health Professional), for which completion of an approved post-qualifying course was required.

As the UK became home to more diverse populations the curriculum incorporated knowledge from sociology, cultural studies and demography about the diverse ethnic groups now needing social work services, and about practice that was not discriminatory, whether in terms of ethnicity, gender, immigration status, age or sexual orientation (CCETSW, 1991). Also advocated by Central Council for Education and Training in Social Work (CCETSW), and subsequently required by GSCC, the views of people who use services, reported by increasingly vocal service user-led and voluntary sector groups, permeated the curriculum (see Chapter 8).

Understanding human development and relationships

Two British figures from psychology and psychiatry whose work had a profound influence on social workers' understanding of the 'inner worlds' of their clients were psychiatrists John Bowlby and Donald Winnicott. Bowlby's (1951) theories of attachment, separation and loss were essential reading on social work courses of the day. Donald Winnicott (see Stevenson, 2013) was an influential teacher on the London School of Economics and Political Science (LSE) mental health and child care courses, whose theories around 'good enough parenting' were incorporated into the teaching of human growth and development. Both were reinforced in many programmes by the research-based films of James and Joyce Robertson (1971) on young children in brief separation.

From the 1940s onwards publications by the US ecologist Urie Bronfenbrenner (see Bronfenbrenner, 1992) had a growing impact on practice with communities, groups and individuals in the US and UK. His ecological systems theories informed social work in communities and participatory practice models. Together with systems theory, developed in the 1950s by von Bertalanffy, ecological theories also informed specific methods such as systemic family therapy. The work on social learning theory by behavioural psychologists in the US, especially as developed into theories of cognitive behaviour therapy, were prominent in the curricula of some schools of social work (Sheldon, 2011).

In the area of adult mental health and family relationships, the early knowledge base drew on the work of psychiatrists and included R.D. Laing's 'anti-psychiatry' texts, including *The Divided Self* (1960). From the US, psychologist Carl Rogers' theories of *person-centred counselling* and Eric Berne's theories of *transactional analysis* (as popularised in *Games People Play*, 1964) found their way into and are still to be found in aspects of modern social work theory. Of importance within the mental health social work curriculum were the writings of Maxwell Jones on therapeutic communities. Developed during the Second World War, they became sources for those working in psychiatric hospitals and for the prison-based probation officers (Jones, 1968).

These writers continue to have an impact on the social work knowledge base, but their influence was increasingly mediated through a greater focus on social work practice, notably by child psychiatrist and leading researcher Michael Rutter (1971), who reinterpreted Bowlby's attachment theories for the changing family.

Theories, approaches and methods for direct social work practice

Social work approaches and methods before 1970

The scholars at the LSE, led by Richard Titmuss, rubbed shoulders with teachers and students on two highly influential social work training programmes, for psychiatric social workers led by Kay McDougall and for child care officers led by Clare Britton/Winnicott (see Stevenson, 2013). The emphasis for these two programmes was on psycho-social casework, much influenced by key texts from the US exploring 'the casework relationship' (Biestek, 1957; Perlman, 1957). These were influential in UK schools of social work for many years in that they acknowledged these roots but differentiated social work from its psychodynamic early influences. Eileen Younghusband's generic social work training course (also at the LSE) placed a greater emphasis on context and, influenced by US social work academic Charlotte Towle's (1962) *Common Human Needs*, advocated a model of social work practice that better fitted within a welfare state and rights-based context (Younghusband, 1964). Florence Hollis's (1964) development of theories of social work as a 'psycho-social' process continued as a basic text for many years.

Influenced by US writers, but with essentially British roots in the war-time pacifist movement, the Family Service Units (FSUs) developed a model of working with families living in especially disadvantaged circumstances. FSUs, along with the Tavistock Clinic's psychiatric social workers, were important in the development of the knowledge base for practice in that they provided practice placements for many of this early generation of social work students, many of whom moved into social work lecturing roles. One of the few UK social work texts available to me in 1963 was Fred Philp and Noel Timms' (1963) *The Problem of the Problem Family*, which, despite its unpromising title, was a detailed practice text based on working intensively with a small group of families. Because of the expansion of the Home Office child care and probation courses the emphasis tended to be on social work within statutory services, with books and articles specifically on aspects of these services beginning to be required reading.

Towards the end of this period of development the Seebohm Report (essential reading then and now) broadly came down on the side of Younghusband. Social workers were to be values-based, community-aware, creative helpers for people going through difficult times, rather than therapists, although they also needed to have skills to work with people in distress and experiencing relationship difficulties. In 1969, as part of the debate leading to the Seebohm Report, Adrian Sinfield, a member of the influential LSE social policy faculty, published a Fabian Society tract, *Which Way for Social Work?*, arguing for a curriculum and approach based on understandings of poverty and disadvantage, and for theories of community work and advocacy to be part of the social work curriculum. The originators of and contributors to the CaseCon collective (Bailey and Brake, 1975) were advocates of a more radical model of practice (Corrigan and Leonard, 1978), taught especially at the University of Warwick Department of Social Work.

There remained considerable scope for social work departments to decide on the respective weight to be placed on different approaches to practice. Some included community work as a social work method, until this was separated out from the social work role by CCETSW curriculum guidance, which increasingly required a focus on casework with individuals and families. Other subject areas that tended to fall out of the knowledge-for-practice curriculum on most (but not all) qualifying social work programmes included advocacy, neighbourhood social work and anti-poverty approaches. Group work and group care diminished in importance after the commonly adopted practice for a short placement in a residential care setting was no longer required by CCETSW.

Theories, approaches and methods for practice after 1970

The 1970s saw the publication of texts written by social work academics who had moved into this role after gaining experience as social workers or probation officers. Some of these explored the overarching roles and tasks of social workers within different settings, classic examples being Martin Davies' (1994) *The Essential Social Worker* and Malcolm Payne's publications starting in 1982 with *Social Work in Teams* (an early work in BASW's Practical Social Work series of publications, covering all needs and age groups) and through to his 2014 *Modern Social Work Theory*. Another example of an influential text combining theories and roles is David Howe's (1987) *An Introduction to Social Work Theory*, grouping social workers, broadly, as either 'seekers after meaning' or 'fixers'.

It is not unusual to find social work students and practitioners, social work employers and civil servants erroneously splitting 'academic' learning from 'practice learning' (as acquired on practice placements). Or for students and practitioners to say that they don't make much use of 'theory' in their practice, as if there were a single 'social work theory'. This is a misunderstanding of the extent to which knowledge across all parts of the curriculum is acquired on placement, and of the sequences on social work approaches and methods across the age and needs groups that are central to the 'academic' curriculum. Having concentrated in the above sections on 'theories for understanding', in this section I refer to theories (in the plural) for direct practice. I further break 'theories' down into the approaches, specific methods and tools or techniques for practice that have found their way into the social work knowledge base.

The ideas of the early writers referred to above influenced the new generation of UK-based writers on social work practice within statutory (mainly local government) settings providing services across the age and needs groups. The 'start where the client is' maxim of earlier writers on casework, alongside some ideas from behavioural texts, was carried through into 'task centred social work' (Doel and Marsh, 1992) and is recognisable in 'strengths-based' practice and solution-focused therapy as introduced and adapted more recently from the US. Although the worker–client relationship was intrinsic to these developments of the casework knowledge base it was implicit rather than explicit. In contrast to the earlier period, there were very few texts with 'relationship' in the title between the 1970s and the 2000s, since when relationship-based practice has had a resurgence (Ruch et al, 2010). Relationship-based psycho-social casework and its essential component, empathy (Howe, 2012), may have gone underground, but they remained central to most social work programmes throughout this period.

The transatlantic influence continued, from early texts on casework through to the introduction of newly developed (by psychologists as well as social work educators) 'interventions', notably behavioural social work, which had an impact especially on mental health and probation practice (Sheldon, 2011) and adaptations of systems theory, especially through the introduction of family therapy as a social work method. The adoption by some local authorities of specific interventions developed in the US or Australia – sometimes referred to as 'manualised' programmes because authorities purchase manuals and training to ensure 'programme fidelity' – is a more recent development.

Ecological and systems theories (combined with learning from social administration about the different agencies providing social services who needed to work together) found their way into the UK practice curriculum. These fitted well with post-Seebohm practice, and especially with patch-based social work (Hadley and McGrath, 1980), as did another US import, the unitary methods approach, which argued for combining casework, group work and neighbourhood approaches according to the requirements of each situation. Bob Holman's special contribution, based on his experiences first in Bath and then Easterhouse in Scotland (see Holman, 2000), was to the development and practice of community social work, which emphasised the involvement of those who made use of the services. The BASW series of publications both on generalist practice and on work with specific needs and age groups, and UK-based journals, especially *British Journal of Social Work* and the professional magazines *Social Work Today*, *Community Care* and *Professional Social Work*, have all played a part in disseminating particular approaches and methods for social work practice.

Some of those who have contributed to the knowledge base combined theories and approaches to practice and specific methods for working with individuals or families. An example is Systemic Family Therapy (practised by a range of professionals, especially in the field of adult and child mental health, as well as by some social workers), which combines systems theory with a specific model of working with families. Similarly, behavioural theories adapted from psychology may inform a specific approach to practice (as with cognitive behavioural social work; see Sheldon, 2011) or may inform a broader approach to understanding those who need services and form a backcloth to the use of a fuller range of methods for helping.

In the area of adult social services changing roles are documented, for example by the work of Joan Orme and Bryan Glastonbury (Glastonbury and Orme, 1993) on care management (see Chapter 2). However, the theoretical approaches to and methods for practice referred to above have relevance across adult and child and family social work. After initial training, as workers move into specialist practice, those working in specialist mental health, addictions and disability fields or palliative care need to be familiar with the relevant knowledge from psychology, medicine and pharmacy that is essential for collaborative practice.

The debates around approaches, as well as appropriate methods to be included in the social work practitioner's 'tool box', have carried through from the 1970s to today. With respect to approaches, the cause of 'broadly' neighbourhood-based social work is outlined in Featherstone et al (2014). The call for poverty-informed practice is re-emerging, due to the impact of austerity on adults and children who need services. In 2018 Hadley and Hatch restated the values and contribution of 'patch-based' social work.

Social work knowledge has also been influenced by educational theorists — especially relevant to those who become team leaders, supervisors, or practice educators — and by changing management theories. Bamford's (1982) book was one of the earlier texts written by a local authority senior manager with a social work background. Social policy continues to be a central area of knowledge as exemplified by the commentaries and critiques of Jones (2019) on outsourcing.

Research knowledge for and by social workers

It is not unrelated to the strong tradition of UK research on social work issues and practice since the 1960s that most professors and lecturers in schools of social work had social work practice experience before moving into teaching and research. Data on clients of child care officers and probation officers was collected by the Home Office in the 1950s and incorporated into research publications. From then on first a trickle and now a good flow of social workers moved into social work education after or while completing and publishing research-based doctorates.

From the mid-1960s onwards social work practitioners, managers and academics collaborated to develop a particular model of 'mixed methods research' heavily influenced by the Dartington Social Research Unit. This was often funded by government agencies, but also by research arms of charitable trusts such as Rowntree, Nuffield and Mind. Typically, officially collected data was combined with data from case records and interviews with social workers and clients. The focus might be on outcomes (variously defined) for adults or children, but more often was on the services provided and the views of those who either did or did not receive a service.

An early influence on the importance of researchers reporting to social workers on what their clients thought of them was Mayer and Timms (1970, *The Client Speaks*). An example of this mixed-methods approach that had a place in social work education at the time was the Stevenson and Parsloe (1978) evaluation of the new social services departments. Rowe and Lambert (1974, *Children Who Wait*) influenced both the 1975 Children Act and the 1989 Children Act. Jane Rowe played a leading role in pulling together the first of 11 Department of Health (DH) funded *Messages from Research*, which were overviews of government-funded research reporting on all aspects of child and family social work. These had impacts on policy as well as practice, introducing, for example, the concept of 'permanence' and showcasing the importance of knowledge needed to balance family support with child protection.

Some researchers have explored discrete areas of need, as, for example, the social worker/gerontology collaborations of Phillips et al (2000), while others have evaluated particular social work approaches or methods. This latter trend continues with the setting up of the What Works Centre, as does the ongoing debate about appropriate methods for researching social services and social work practice and the balance between experimental design and qualitative methods.

The legal knowledge base

Possibly more than in many other jurisdictions, because most social work is practised as part of publicly provided social or mental health services, sequences on law for social workers figure prominently. Indeed, this is one of the few areas of the curriculum that is usually tested by a formal exam. In adult services there has been a need to take on board changes in community care and mental health legislation that provide the mandate for local authority and health service practitioners. Legal issues around domestic violence, addictions and immigration are also relevant to practice across the age and needs groups.

Child and family social work legislation will be referred to in another chapter. It is important to note that a large number of social workers are employed via the Children and Family Court Advisory and Support Service to provide social work advice to the family courts. A small number of qualified social workers also work within local authority Youth Offending Teams.

Across the age and needs groups, it has been essential for the legal implications of a succession of reports following child and vulnerable-adult deaths, serious injury or sexual abuse and exploitation to be incorporated into knowledge for practice.

Conclusions

The respective places of social science disciplines, systems knowledge and the more technical aspects of practice were rehearsed in 2014 when the DH and Department for Education (DfE) commissioned separate reports on social work education. These reached different conclusions on whether social work education should be broadly based to equip graduates to practise at a beginning level across age and needs groups and settings (Croisdale-Appleby, 2014) or should equip them for practice in specialist child and family teams (Narey, 2014). Then in its early stages, the Frontline apprenticeship model of fast-track training for local authority child and family social work has subsequently greatly expanded, and been joined by Think Ahead, based on similar lines but with a mental health specialism (see Thoburn, 2017). The other fast-track child and family specialist programme (Step Up) continues, but is more closely linked with the 'mainstream' universities and curricula.

Questions around the knowledge base for social work education and training posed and debated in the print and social media and within the profession by these and other developments include: is there space in the social work curriculum for relationship-based social work; task-centred/strengths-based approaches; community-/advocacy-/partnerships-based approaches? Can manualised programmes and (usually narrowly defined) 'evidence-based practice' fit alongside 'practice wisdom' and the voices of experts by experience within the agreed knowledge base?

And, finally, what are the respective places of government ministers, the regulator, the inspectorates, social workers and their managers and professional associations, social work educators/researchers in schools of social work, voluntary sector and commercial sectors; the media; and those who need social work services in determining what should be the knowledge base both for generalist social work and for specialist areas of practice?

The years covered in this overview have seen cumulative changes between the respective influences of these. A movement can be seen from predominance of the universities and experienced professionals in service-leader roles and through professional associations, through an increased role for social work researchers, to a much expanded role for government and government 'arm's-length' bodies. The two Chief Social Workers have become, to different extents, more the spokespersons for the government of the day and less (as was originally intended) the professional social workers explaining and speaking up for social work within government. The link with research-based knowledge generated in schools of social work has been further considerably weakened by the government-funded Innovations programmes and the What Works Centre (prioritising some areas of knowledge, research methods and models of practice over others; see Jones, 2019; Tunstill, 2019). Although it was not intended to be an arbiter of social work knowledge, the fact that Social Work England, the new regulator of social work education as well as practice, appears to have set its face against having any registered social workers or social work academics on its board may further weaken what I would argue is the necessary partnership of all the above in shaping the social work knowledge curriculum.

In summary, and despite these recent changes, most social work programmes still follow the Croisdale-Appleby (2014) rather than the Narey (2014) recommendations and continue to ensure a balanced curriculum integrating knowledge about the explanations, extent and nature of social, psychological and relationship difficulties and the services needed to address these with the values, knowledge and skills for direct practice. This is closely allied with the Professional Capabilities Framework (PCF), developed by the Social Work Reform Board but taken forward by BASW, rather than the narrower, government-initiated DfE and DH Knowledge and Skills Statements endorsed by the two Chief Social Workers.

I want to end with a Twitter comment addressed to a university researcher colleague that points to the growing importance of social media in enabling practitioners and experts-by-experience to enter this debate about the knowledge base for social work and thus 'what is social work':

> Can I just say; one piece of your research was used in our yr2 research module on the social work degree. We had to analyse it, but reading it is how I came to follow you and your work. ('Joseph Cormack', Twitter, 30 August 2019)

References

Bailey, R. and Brake, M. (1975) (eds) *Radical Social Work*, London: Edward Arnold.

Bamford, T. (1982) *Managing Social Work*, London: Tavistock.

BBC (British Broadcasting Company) (1966) *Cathy Come Home*.

Berne, E. (1964) *Games People Play*, New York: Grove Press.

Biestek, F. (1957) *The Casework Relationship*, New York: Loyola University Press.

Bowlby, J. (1951) *Maternal Care and Mental Health,* Geneva: WHO.

Bronfenbrenner, U. (1992) 'Ecological systems theory', in U. Bronfenbrenner (ed), *Making Human Beings Human: Bioecological Perspectives on Human Development*, Thousand Oaks, CA: Sage, pp 106–73.

Butler, I. and Drakeford, M. (2011) *Social Work on Trial: The Colwell Inquiry*, Bristol: Policy Press.

CCETSW (1991) *One Small Step Towards Racial Justice: The Teaching of Antiracism in Diploma in Social Work Programmes*, London: CCETSW.

Corrigan, P. and Leonard, P. (1978) *Social Work Practice under Capitalism*, London: Macmillan.

Croisdale-Appleby, D. (2014) *Re-visioning Social Work Education*, London: DH.

Davies, M. (1994) *The Essential Social Worker*, London: Routledge.

Doel, M. and Marsh, P. (1992) *Task Centred Social Work*, London: Routledge.

Featherstone, B., White, S. and Morris, K. (2014) *Re-imagining Child Protection*, Bristol: Policy Press.

Glastonbury, B. and Orme, J. (1993) *Care Management: Tasks and Workloads*, Birmingham: BASW.

Hadley, R. and McGrath, M. (1980) *When Social Services are Local*, London: Allen and Unwin.

Herbert, H. and Wilson, G. (1978) *Parents and Children in the Inner City*, London: Routledge, Kegan, Paul.

Hollis, F. (1964) *Casework: A Psychosocial Therapy*, New York: Random House.

Holman, R. (1976) *Inequality in Child Care*, London: CPAG.

Holman, R. (1978) *Poverty: Explanations of Social Deprivation*, London: Martin Robertson.

Holman, B. (2000) *Kids at the Door Revisited*, London: Russell House.

Howe, D. (1987) *An Introduction to Social Work Theory*, Basingstoke: Palgrave Macmillan.

Howe, D. (2012) *Empathy, What It Is and Why It Matters*, Basingstoke: Palgrave Macmillan.

Jones, M. (1968) *Social Psychiatry in Practice. The Idea of a Therapeutic Community*, Harmondsworth: Penguin.

Jones, R. (2019) *In Whose Interest? The Privatisation of Child Protection and Social Work*, Bristol: Policy Press.

Joseph, K. (1973) 'The cycle of deprivation', *Community Schools Gazette*, vol 67, no 2, pp 61–72.

Laing, R.D. (1960) *The Divided Self*, London: Tavistock.

Marsden, D. (1969) *Mothers Alone*, London: Allen Lane.

Mayer, J. and Timms, N. (1970) *The Client Speaks*, London: Routledge, Kegan, Paul.

Narey, M. (2014) *Making the Education of Social Workers Consistently Effective*, London: DfE.

Packman, J. (1969) *Child Care Needs and Numbers*, London: Allen and Unwin.

Parker, R. (1966) *Decision in Child Care*, London: Allen and Unwin.

Payne, M. (1982) *Social Work in Teams*, London: Macmillan.

Payne, M. (2014) *Modern Social Work Theory* (4th edn), Oxford: Oxford University Press.

Perlman, H. (1957) *Social Casework: A Problem-solving Process*, Chicago: University of Chicago Press.

Phillips. J., Bernard, M., Phillipson, C. and Ogg, J. (2000) 'Social support in later life: a study of three areas', *British Journal of Social Work*, vol 30, no 6, pp 837–53.

Philp, F. and Timms, N. (1963) *The Problem of the Problem Family*, London: FSU.

Robertson, J. and Robertson, J. (1971) 'Young children in brief separation', *Psychoanalytic Study of the Child*, vol 26, pp 264–315.

Rowe, J. and Lambert, L. (1974) *Children Who Wait*, London: BAAF.

Ruch, G., Turney, D. and Ward, A. (2010) *Relationship-based Social Work: Getting to the Heart of Practice*, London: Jessica Kingsley.

Rutter, M. (1971) *Maternal Deprivation Reassessed*, Harmondsworth: Penguin.

Sheldon, B. (2011) *Cognitive-Behavioural Therapy*, London: Routledge.

Sinfield, A. (1969) *Which Way for Social Work?*, London: Fabian Society.

Stevenson, O. (1963) 'The understanding caseworker', *New Society*, 1 August, pp 84–96.

Stevenson, O. (1971) 'Knowledge for social work', *British Journal of Social Work*, vol 1, no 2, pp 225–37.

Stevenson, O. (2013) *Reflections on a Life in Social Work*, Buckingham: Hinton House.

Stevenson, O. and Parsloe, P. (1978) *Social Services Teams*, London: DH.

Thoburn, J. (2017) 'In defence of a university social work education', *Journal of Children's Services*, vol 12, no 2, pp 37–106.

Titmuss, R. (1968) *Commitment to Welfare*, London: Allen and Unwin.

Towle, C. (1962) *Common Human Needs*, Washington DC: National Association of Social Workers.

Townsend, P. (1962) *The Last Refuge*, London: Routledge and Kegan Paul.

Townsend, P. (1979) *Poverty in the United Kingdom*, Harmondsworth: Penguin.

Tunstill, J. (2019) 'Pruned, policed and privatised: the knowledge base for children and families social work in England and Wales in 2019', *Social Work and Social Sciences Review*, vol 20, no 2, pp 57–76.

Wilmott, M. and Young, M. (1957) *Family and Kinship in East London*, London: Routledge and Kegan Paul.

Wootton, B., Seal, V. and Chambers, R. (1959) *Social Science and Social Pathology*, London: Allen & Unwin.

Younghusband, E. (1964) *Social Work and Social Change*, London: Allen and Unwin.

5

Social work education: learning from the past?

Hilary Tompsett

Introduction

Social work education and training provides a gateway to an extraordinary profession that can change lives. This chapter identifies seven questions that have shaped educational approaches since 1970 in the light of changing contexts and considers key challenges affecting social work education now, before suggesting some future directions, priorities and risks. While this chapter addresses the whole of the UK, developments in England are discussed more fully, with comparisons made wherever possible across the four nations.

Background and changing contexts

Views on how to prepare social work students and trainees appropriately have been subject to contention, change (Bamford, 2015) and political, regulatory and higher education influences. Societal expectations of social workers and public perceptions of the profession expressed in the media have also shifted over time, influenced by crises or tragedies, such as the death of Peter Connelly ('Baby P') reported in 2008, and consequent reports, recommendations and legal changes.

Changing governmental policy positions regarding the profession have influenced education decisions, such as the 1995 separation of probation from social work training for England and Wales, and organisational systems, such as employment arrangements for health service social workers; increased outsourcing of services to the private, voluntary and independent sectors; and divided responsibility for social work between different government departments – currently the Department for Education (DfE) and the Department of Health and Social Care. Preparing social workers for different role descriptions and multiple employers has required considerable adaptation by education providers. Devolution across the UK since 1998 has resulted in further, separate, and not uniform, development (Smith, 2008) and increased divergence in social work practice and education, particularly in England.

Significant regulatory changes have occurred since the 1970 establishment of the Central Council for Education and Training in Social Work (CCETSW) as the UK-wide regulator (see Chapter 3). From 2001, Care Councils in England (General Social Care Council, GSCC), Scotland (Scottish Social Services Council, SSSC), Northern Ireland (Northern Ireland Social Care Council, NISCC) and Wales (Care Council for Wales, CCW, later Social Care Wales, SCW) established separate qualification frameworks. After GSCC's closure in 2012, England's regulatory arrangements underwent further change, transferring first to the Health and Care Professions Council (HCPC) and then in December 2019 to Social Work England (SWE). CCETSW's awards, the Certificate of Qualification in Social Work (CQSW), and the Certificate in Social Service (CSS) for social care, established in 1971 and 1977 respectively, were replaced in 1989 by the single Diploma of Social Work (DipSW). The current UK-wide degree-level minimum qualification, introduced 24 years later in 2003, is now subject to considerable variation of routes. Postgraduate routes have constituted a smaller proportion of qualifying courses, although this is rapidly changing in England − 7% in 2003, 42% in 2012 (GSCC, 2012b, p 14).

The higher education environment changed with the introduction in 1998 of tuition fees across the UK, the lifting of controls on student numbers in 2015 (although not in Northern Ireland; see Hillman, 2014; Murphy, 2019), and a widening participation agenda for access to higher education institutions (HEIs). The creation of a market-place for student applications, increased pressure on research activity and excellence, and hard financial considerations contributed to social work course closures in England (for example, Oxford and LSE, in the 1980s, and more recently Exeter, Reading and Southampton) – a trend not reflected in other nations of the UK. GSCC reported 22 courses closed between 2001 and 2012, although not in 22 HEIs (GSCC, 2012b, p 11). New courses have emerged in post-1992 universities or through government-sponsored fast-track routes or apprenticeships.

Key questions shaping educational approaches

What are the nature of the profession and the discipline of social work?

Is it a profession at all? After long-standing debates on whether social work is a semi-profession, becoming a registered profession with protected title and required registration (achieved in 2005) should have established for the first time a new status that recognises specific skills, territory, knowledge base and guarded entry into the profession (Payne, 2006; Rogowski, 2010). The introduction of the degree minimum should also have given social work, as a professional discipline, comparable status with other degree-level professions, such as psychology, teaching and (from 2009) nursing. How social work is viewed as an academic and practice-related discipline by governments and educational establishments affects the importance and value attributed to having a strong research base within a university to support teaching (Chapter 4).

What are we preparing social workers for? One professional role or many?

The generic qualifications of CQSW and CSS reflected preparation for one profession, capable of responding to entire families' problems. The 1988 Griffiths Report, implemented through the 1990 NHS and Community Care Act, signalled the move towards commissioning rather than providing care services, requiring education to prepare students for possible case or care manager roles. With the introduction of this and the 1989 Children Act, services reverted to specialist teams and roles with children and families, adults, and those experiencing mental health problems. DipSW's introduction in 1989 still signified education for an integrated profession, with specialisation after initial qualification, as, for example, Approved Social Worker status under the 1983 Mental Health Act for mental health social workers. GSCC's Post Qualifying Framework in 1995 established named awards across all specialisms, and by the end of the 1990s probation training was completely separate.

Throughout this period, 'practice readiness' or 'preparedness' was regarded as the goal of social work education, but it is the 'fit between social work education and agency expectations' (Marsh and Triseliotis, 1996, p 2) that affects whether students emerging from courses are welcomed by employers. Anxiety experienced by many social workers after qualification, identified by Marsh and Triseliotis in relation to undertaking new roles, resource constraints, bureaucracy levels and access to support and supervision, was still evident in later research (Bates et al, 2010), suggesting that newly qualified social workers felt only partially prepared for work roles. Such anxiety is common in other new professionals (Moriarty et al, 2011).

England's Social Work Reform Board (SWRB, 2010), established after the Social Work Task Force Report (SWTF, 2009), used 'readiness for direct practice' as a threshold definition (TCSW, 2012) for when students should go out on placement (later associated with eligibility for bursary funding, Gov-UK, 2019a). The SWRB emphasised that workers should be 'safe to practise' on entry to work, and recommended the introduction in 2012 of an Assessed and Supported Year in Employment after qualification, mirroring the Assessed Year in Employment in Northern Ireland since 2007.

Who will make good social workers?

Views on this differ: whether they need to represent the communities they serve and the interests of those they are working with and/ or whether people with particular characteristics, profile or prior academic achievement will make better social workers and have better success rates (MacAlister, 2012).

CCETSW's DipSW requirements (CCETSW, 1991, p 30) restricted qualification to students reaching a minimum of 22 years of age. Removal of the age bar in 2003 brought 'a significant expansion in the number of individuals under the age of 20 enrolling to the degree' (GSCC, 2012b, p 27). Despite this, the median age of students has not really changed, from 32 years in 1998 (Eborall and Garmeson, 2001, p 77) to 32.5 years in 2012 (GSCC, 2012a, p 20). The DH's Degree Rules (DH, 2002) stipulated that HEIs should have strategies to ensure recruitment of students broadly representative of the wider population. By 2012 there was greater diversity among degree students than in average university student populations – 16% of students describing themselves as Black/Black British (GSCC, 2012b, p 24). However, 'in terms of age-groups, the lowest pass rate was experienced by those under 20 at enrolment' (GSCC, 2012b, p 27), and 'of all ethnic groups, [it] was … black students (74%) [who] also had the joint highest withdrawal rate (19%)' (GSCC, 2012b, p 35).

In 2009 the SWTF expressed concerns about the calibre of students recruited to the degree. The workforce increasingly needed to be research informed and to be able to deal with complex and difficult cases in inter-professional contexts as workloads shifted away from preventive to high-risk protective service needs. The SWRB criticised both the intake and the robustness of recruitment methods in England, including levels of spoken and written English. While they valued experience and maturity (additional to, not instead of, academic ability), candidates' learning from their life/work experience was also important, and it was noted in some research that students with extensive social care experience have had lower progression rates than their peers (Holmstrom and Taylor, 2008). The degree evaluation confirmed that postgraduates had higher pass rates than undergraduates (81% to 66%) (McNay, 2008, p 7). The desire to attract high academic achievers influenced the development of fast-track routes in 2013.

Discussion on who will make good social workers is frequently overtaken by questions as to how we can recruit sufficient applicants to fill social work vacancies and keep those we have trained already.

How many social work recruits do we need?

Since the 1976 Birch Working Party Report on workforce planning and training for the social services (DHSS, 1976), ongoing concerns across the UK about the numbers of social workers needed have been complicated by fluctuations in student recruitment. Separate from predictable delays in entry to the workforce – for example, with the change from the two-year DipSW to the three-year degree in 2003 (DH, 2000) – there have been large falls in applications; for example, between 1995 and 1998 DipSW applicant numbers fell from 11,526 to 6,600 (around 55%). This was explained by the lack of financial support for students (in the context of new higher education (HE) fees), but also by the poor image of social work, the variety of different qualifications and levels and the lack of consensus among employers about which jobs required DipSW qualifications (Eborall and Garmeson, 2001). The introduction of the degree raised actual student numbers – from 2,759 to 6,364 per year by 2010 (GSCC, 2012b, pp 18/19) – but in 2016/17, for example, of 4,220 students qualified, only 74% were in a social work job six months later (Turner, 2019).

The average career of a social worker, estimated as 7.7 years, compares poorly with 25 for doctors, 15 for nurses and 28 for pharmacists (Curtis et al, 2010). Estimating workforce numbers is complex, but an over-focus on recruitment rather than retention risks wasting recruitment costs and reducing practitioner experience and continuity in the workplace. Continuing changing roles and tasks, work pressures, reductions in resources and posts and larger caseloads are still affecting retention (Baginsky, 2013).

Who is best to make decisions about social work education?

Defining threshold knowledge, skills and values for the profession has been made more complex in England by different perspectives as to how and by whom this should be done: by employers, professional bodies (as in the US), HEIs/education providers (as in Canada), regulators or even politicians (as in the UK). Different descriptions of education/assessment methods in terms of outcomes, competences or capabilities (Moriarty et al, 2011, 2015) have led to perceived confusion and lack of clarity, particularly as HE providers must comply with university/Council for National Academic Awards requirements and, from 2000, The Quality Assurance Agency's Benchmark Statement – resulting in a multitude of requirements.

Government-led initiatives on workforce needs and appropriate roles and tasks have shaped decisions about student numbers, bursaries, routes to the profession and length of time needed to qualify. Despite the SWRB's programme of improvement for the whole social work system, which commanded sector-wide stakeholder support and the universal introduction of education changes in HEIs from 2013, the government commissioned two new separate reviews of social work education (Narey, 2014; Croisdale-Appleby, 2014).

When HCPC took over social work regulation in England they dispensed with National Occupational Standards (Skills for Care, 2014), used elsewhere in the UK, and did not adopt the SWRB's Professional Capabilities Framework (PCF). Instead, existing Standards of Proficiency for HCPC's 15 other professions were revised after consultation with social work organisations and published alongside a detailed guide comparing these with the PCF (HCPC, 2012). The multiple requirements were criticised in both of the England reviews: Narey, commissioned by DfE, favoured the PCF, while Croisdale-Appleby, commissioned by DH, recommended a single, integrated set of standards. Then England's two Chief Social Workers, appointed in 2014 as the SWRB was disbanded, generated two Knowledge and Skills (post-qualifying) Statements (Gov-UK, 2019b, 2019c), adding to the different frameworks. Reviews in Scotland (SSSC, 2016), Wales (SCW, 2018) and Northern Ireland (NISCC, 2015) reflect greater stakeholder collaboration and agreement on future frameworks, and Northern Ireland's Framework, unlike England's, adopted Croisdale-Appleby's recommendation to prepare social workers for skills as a 'practitioner, professional and social scientist'.

Expansion of courses accompanied growth in student numbers on the degree courses: by 2012, 307 courses were approved at 83 HEIs. Recruitment to HEIs in England is institutionally no longer capped, but the DH cap on bursary places, introduced in 2010 (currently 1,500 postgraduate and 2,500 undergraduate places; Gov-UK, 2019a) is now affecting enrolment to traditional courses in England. The bursary was initially significant in attracting more diverse applications

(McNay, 2008, p 8), but in terms of numbers, data for 2016/17 shows that postgraduate enrolments rose by 13% while undergraduate numbers fell 12% to 2,640 (Skills for Care, 2018, in Turner, 2019). Government support for expanding fast-track routes is also affecting recruitment, but not in a planned way.

Sponsored routes, mainly for people already working in local authorities, were introduced from 2012 via Step Up to Social Work programmes in employer/HEI partnerships. In 2013, Frontline programmes were developed to attract high-calibre entrants to children's social work, offer leadership/management potential opportunities and address shortages; these were modelled on Teach First, a scheme to attract graduates into teaching, and followed in 2016 by Think Ahead for mental health trainees, and apprenticeship models from 2017. While conventional courses take two to three years and apprenticeships typically take 36 months, Step Up programmes, originally 18 months long, now take 14 months and Frontline and Think Ahead qualifications are achievable within one year (through intensive summer schools and work placements under employment arrangements). Such models are not without criticism: for preparing students for specific roles rather than a profession and offering limited practice experience, theory, underpinning research and time for reflection and critical evaluation (Croisdale-Appleby, 2014). It is also not clear whether these routes will have currency or equivalence internationally, or even across the UK (McNicoll, 2017).

A Parliamentary Select Committee report (HMSO, 2009) challenged why social work needs so many HEIs to train approximately 5,000 students a year, when 30 medical courses train 9,000 medical students annually. GSCC responded that social work students are frequently more mature, local and have more financial and family constraints than traditional medical students, but are also more likely to join the local workforce. Funding can be seen to impact on recruitment and retention, but this is only part of motivation.

The level of cross-sector cooperation affects decisions and outcomes. The changes introduced in 2014 by the Northern Ireland regulator (NISCC) to control the qualification (degree-level only) and number of qualifying places were negotiated and agreed with HEIs. Care Councils outside England have been more influential in shaping wider educational developments – for example, in Scotland, prescribing specific compulsory post-qualification training. Regulators, such as General Medical Council, HCPC and the General Optical Council, work closely with the professional colleges; the role of BASW is critical for the future, especially in upholding the PCF in England (BASW,

2019), which was welcomed by social workers for their professional identity.

What's important in social work education?

Curriculum and programme content

The knowledge base for social work has aspects of both continuity and change (see Chapter 4). Many elements of curriculum content have remained constant in programme descriptions, such as human growth and development, methods, law and ethics, although emphasis and language have adapted to match policy, legal and service contexts and priorities. Elements removed or diminished since the 1970s, such as welfare benefits after the introduction of rights officers, have not lessened the importance of addressing inequality (Walker, 2002). Community and group work, taught as core skills post-Seebohm (1968) to address social problems beyond individuals, were superseded in the 1980s–1990s by teaching on case/care management to meet the need for budgetary, commissioning and supervision skills. Course design has had to reflect the rising importance of inter-professionalism (Barr, 2002) and international perspectives. Early programmes adopted North American social work models, while later ones emphasised the global nature of the profession by, for example, international placements or reference to the international definition of social work (IFSW, 2014).

Social work methods teaching in the 1970s reflected predominantly individual casework approaches, alongside short-term casework models and crisis intervention. Radical perspectives challenged these models, arguing that 'psychoanalytically dominated caseworker(s)' see 'social problems as the products of [clients'] internal worlds', while 'the real cause of social problems is economic and political oppression' (Parsloe, 1975). A Curriculum Guide constructed for TCSW (now hosted by BASW) describes an extensive range of methods and intervention theories for the 21st century, reflecting greater emphasis on empowerment models:

> Systems theory; ecological perspective/person-in-environment; psychosocial; psychodynamic/psychoanalytic; attachment theory; attachment-based interventions; social constructivism; feminist theory and practice; critical social work; radical social work; groupwork theory and practice; anti-discriminatory and anti-oppressive theory and practice; power and empowerment; the strengths perspective;

behavioural theory; cognitive theory; cognitive behavioural therapy; assessment …; advocacy; community work/ development; person-centred approach; relationship-based social work; narrative practice/therapy; life story work and life review; art and/or play therapy; mediation approaches; family therapy/systemic practice; task-centred social work; motivational interviewing; solution-focused practice; crisis theory and intervention. (Teater, 2012)

Underpinning of professional ethics and focus on service users

Teaching of ethics and values has remained core to social work education, helping to shape professionalism and enabling students to work with respect for individuals, families and communities (Biestek, 1957; Banks, 2006). Since social work became a registered profession in 2005, professional Codes of Conduct and Ethics (BASW's from 1971/72, and country regulators') have formalised these. The recent refocusing on 'the relationship at the heart/centre of social work practice' (Wilson et al, 2008) resonates with what frequently motivates students into social work, alongside principles of social justice.

From early years, hearing the 'client's' voice was important (Mayer and Timms, 1970). Empowerment and co-production in social work practice and meaningful involvement of service users and carers in education (Beresford et al, 1994) have now been applied across recruitment, course design, evaluation and delivery, and skills practice, feedback and assessment (see Chapter 8). Although CCETSW required partnership with employers, all social work regulators now embed service user and carer involvement in their education standards (DH, 2002; SSSC, 2003; NISCC, 2015; HCPC, 2017; SCW, 2018; and SWE, 2019a). It was noteworthy that HCPC agreed to make service user involvement a requirement for all the other 15 professions they regulate, after taking over social work regulation in England in 2012 (HCPC Education Committee, Minutes, 6 June 2013, item 9).

Education for anti-discriminatory practice

The rising emphasis in social work programmes from the 1970s–1980s on teaching for anti-discriminatory practice was evident in regulatory requirements (CCETSW, 1991) and educational research (for example, Clifford and Burke, 2005). It was to ensure that students were prepared 'for ethnically sensitive practice', to 'challenge and confront institutional and other forms of racism' and 'combat … discrimination based on age gender, sexual orientation, class, disability, culture, religion, language (including sign language) or nationality' (CCETSW, 1991, p 11).

Subsequent governments criticised this emphasis as overly 'politically correct'. Tim Yeo, a Junior Health Minister, as reported in *Social Work Today* in 1992, advocated a 'common sense approach to transracial adoptive placements', reinforced by Virginia Bottomley, the Health Minister, calling on CCETSW to adopt a more balanced approach, with 'no place in the training of social workers for politically correct notions, for the domination of ideology and textbook theories over practical skills for children. Social workers have a difficult job to do and their decisions should not be informed by fashionable theories, but by sensible, time-honoured principles and values' (Walker, 2002). CCETSW's 1991 statements/policies on anti-racism, equal opportunities and the Welsh language were revised in 1995. More recent challenges (Michael Gove, Secretary of State for Education, in 2011) have echoed similar governmental views on trans-racial adoptions.

Preparation for practice and placements

From the earliest programmes, students had to 'meet a satisfactory standard in fieldwork' (Cree, 2018) and develop skills for practice, particularly communication skills (Trevithick, 2012). Video-recording technology, introduced in the 2000s with Practice Learning suites ('Skills Labs'), and service user and carer involvement radically altered teaching, feedback and assessment methods (Moss et al, 2007; Tompsett et al, 2017). Students on placement (Parker, 2006) identified that they felt insufficiently prepared in emotional resilience for coping with violent service user responses, possibly reflecting workplace pressures. Preparing social workers for new and changing professional situations and roles brought a sharper focus to the teaching of critical thinking and reflection skills (Fook et al, 2000; Munro, 2011).

Accredited practice teachers (recognised by the Practice Teachers Award, 1989–2011), to support and assess students on placement (CCETSW, 1991, pp 26–7), have now evolved into Practice Educators, still regarded as vital, despite the pressure, due to shortages, to use placements with differently qualified professionals supervising. As the vice-chancellor of a university with a medical school commented verbally at a Universities UK seminar on Social Work Education in May 2009, 'Social Workers can be supervised by a non-Social Worker? Medics would never agree to that'. Standards in England now require oversight by a named Practice Educator who is a registered social worker (SWE, 2019b, p 11).

The time allocated to practice placements (initially as much as 50%) reflects their importance and has been consistent in UK-wide course design and regulatory guidance, although actual requirements have changed and varied over time, particularly since devolution. Placements now generally require 200 days in practice, with, in England, mandatory attendance, 30 designated skills days, a final placement of 100 days and the inclusion of a statutory setting (SWE, 2019b).

Who should pay? And what does it cost?

In recent years, since 2012, hybrid arrangements (part employer-/ part government-funded) with Step Up, Frontline, Think Ahead and Apprenticeship models are increasingly preferred by government departments in England, but these still constitute a small proportion of qualifying routes, accounting for only 29% of all students in 2015/16 (Turner, 2019). A DfE-commissioned report in 2010 on the unit costs of different models of qualifying education concluded that, when comparing the cost to the government, traditional routes are significantly cheaper, with the lowest cost overall being for undergraduate routes; postgraduate routes cost over half as much again, with Step Up costing just under half as much and Frontline a little over three times more. When costed in terms of the economy, the costs of Step Up are lowest and those of undergraduate routes highest – the difference being accounted for by 'opportunity costs', that is because traditional routes do not offer employment opportunities (Cutmore and Rodger, 2016, p 47).

Despite the funding for placements, shortages have increased over the years and have contributed to student dissatisfaction, regulatory quality concerns and criticisms of student unpreparedness for roles in which there were fewer placements (McNay, 2008; GSCC, 2012b, p 30). It is clear, however, that students are bearing much of the cost themselves.

Challenges impacting on social work education now

Do employers and HEIs agree on what makes a good social worker?

There are still debates about what level of performance we are educating social workers for. Do they need to be specialist in one area at qualification, 'hitting the ground running' in their first employment, and qualifying in the fastest time possible? Or are we educating professionals to join a profession at the competent 'advanced beginner' level (Dreyfus, 2004; Fook et al, 2000, adapted in Akhtar, 2013, p 68), while gaining specialist experience post-qualification with mentoring and supervision? Diminishing on-the-job training budgets in local authorities and ongoing retention issues have encouraged short-term solutions and quicker, work-based qualifying routes to specialist jobs with a reduced curriculum and education. This will have a long-term effect on the profession and professionals and there is no strong evidence yet that these routes improve retention.

Will/do we learn from evaluation?

Commissioned reviews have taken place of DipSW (Lyons and Manion, 2004), the degree (McNay, 2008), Frontline (Maxwell et al, 2016), Step Up and Think Ahead (Smith et al, 2018, 2019), alongside research to evaluate and learn from the literature (Moriarty et al, 2015). While evaluations balance some positive student feedback from fast-track programmes and identify issues and potential improvements, decisions are frequently made before evaluations are completed – for example, to support further cohorts of Step Up and Frontline (Turner, 2014). Research suggests that we should be doing much more to support retention (Baginsky, 2013).

The ongoing divide between government departments

The ongoing divide between government departments continues to challenge an integrated profession in England. Potential further independence moves within other nations of the UK, after Brexit, threaten further divergence in the light of financial and political priorities. Lack of a sector-wide social work forum (compare SWRB) is particularly noticeable in England, despite the establishment of BASW's Standing Conference in association with the Joint University Council Social Work Education Committee (JUC-SWEC) (the UK-wide membership organisation of universities offering social work education) and the Association of Professors of Social Work.

Are we international enough?

In terms of educating UK social workers to be members of a global profession, are we international enough, or are we primarily focused on solving the employment shortages in our own country? There is an important role for UK-based organisations to raise their eyes to the horizon and support international research, for example, BASW and JUC-SWEC working in association with the IFSW.

Where to next?

Social work still has a problem with its public image, and has focused too much in past years on recruitment to solve workforce shortages. There needs to be greater attention to retention, reducing high caseloads, addressing austerity and cutbacks and enabling quality relationship work to be practised under good supervision. The professional title, identity and register, and raising the minimum education to degree level should bring greater parity with other professions, but social work still lacks a strong post-qualifying framework of specialist qualifications.

While government and HEIs are apparently promoting postgraduate routes to social work education, matched by bursary trends in England, retention of undergraduate programmes and maintenance of bursaries are important. Multiple models of entry/education have a place in supporting diversity of students and of the workforce, but clearer evidence is needed to assess the impact on retention rates and workforce shortages and to compare costs. It is also essential that evidence-based generic models of initial qualification are offered within strong, research-based HEIs to safeguard research and evidence to support professional practice. The numbers of HEIs offering social work education may reduce in future (compare Northern Ireland, with only two HEIs), but properly supported partnerships between employers and HEIs so as to provide sufficient quality placements and supervision will remain key.

The impacts of Brexit, and political upheaval following the outcome of this on the economy, public sector and higher education, are as yet unknown and raise potential future uncertainty. Many are anxious about risk to the existence of the profession in such a rapidly changing world. While poverty and inequality are still prevalent and increasing, the need for social work remains (Jones, 2012) but outsourcing or reallocation of tasks to less or differently qualified roles and professionals may lead to reductions in numbers of social workers, the hardening of professional differences geared to specific job roles and consequent educational shrinkage to minimum requirements.

The social work profession, and social work education, have always been dynamic and evolving, adapting to new circumstances and needs as we learn by looking back on the many changes that have taken place since 1970. The strength of the research and education sector lies in ensuring that social work's fundamental core values underpin all their work. Collaboration between HEIs, employers, regulatory bodies, professional organisations and governments of whatever hue has characterised the best transitions of the past so as to keep academic and practice learning relevant to current contexts. Despite the uncertainties ahead, this brings hope for the future of the profession, professionals and students, and for outcomes for people who need the services of social workers.

References

Akhtar, F. (2013) *Mastering Social Work Values and Ethics*, London: Jessica Kingsley.

Baginsky, M. (2013) 'Retaining experienced social workers in children's services: the challenge facing Local Authorities in England', London: King's College, www.kcl.ac.uk/scwru/pubs/2013/reports/baginsky13retaining.pdf.

Bamford, T. (2015) *A Contemporary History of Social Work: Learning from the Past*, London: Policy Press.

Banks, S. (2006) *Ethics and Values in Social Work*, Basingstoke: Palgrave Macmillan.

Barr, H. (2002) *Interprofessional Education: Today, Yesterday and Tomorrow*, London: LTSN for Health Sciences and Practice.

BASW (2019) 'Professional Capabilities Framework', www.basw.co.uk/professional-development/professional-capabilities-framework-pcf.

Bates, N., Immins, T., Parker, J., Keen, S., Rutter, L., Brown, K. and Zsigo, Z. (2010) 'Baptism of fire: the first year in the life of a newly qualified social worker', *Social Work Education*, vol 29, no 2, pp 152–170.

Beresford, P. with Page, L. and Stevens, A. (1994) 'Changing the culture: involving service users in social work education', CCETSW Paper 32.2, London: Central Council for Education and Training in Social Work.

Biestek, F. (1957) *The Casework Relationship*, Chicago: Loyola University Press.

CCETSW (1991) *DipSW: Rules and Requirements for the Diploma in Social Work, Paper 30*, London: Central Council for Education and Training in Social Work.

Clifford, D. and Burke, B. (2005) 'Developing anti-oppressive ethics in the new curriculum', *Social Work Education*, vol 24, no 6, pp 677–92.

Cree, V. (2018) 'Celebrating 100 years of social work at Edinburgh University', www.socialwork.ed.ac.uk/centenary/learning/academic_learning.

Croisdale-Appleby, D. (2014) *Re-visioning Social Work Education, An Independent Review*, www.gov.uk/government/publications/social-work-education-review.

Curtis, L., Moriarty, J. and Netten, A. (2010) 'The expected working life of a social worker', *British Journal of Social Work*, vol 40, pp 1628–43.

Cutmore, M. and Rodger, J. (2016) *Comparing the Costs of Social Work Qualification Routes*, London: DfE, assets.publishing.service.gov.uk/government/uploads/system/uploads/attachment_data/file/510361/DFE-RR517-Social-work-qualification-routes-comparing_the_costs.pdf.

DH (2000) *A Quality Strategy for Social Care, Consultation Document*, London: Department of Health.

DH (2002) *Requirements for Social Work Training*, London: Department of Health, www.scie.org.uk/publications/guides/guide04/files/requirements-for-social-work-training.pdf?res=true.

DHSS (1976) *Birch Working Party Report*, London: Department of Health and Social Security.

Dreyfus, S.E. (2004) 'The five-stage model of adult skill acquisition', *Bulletin of Science, Technology & Society*, vol 24, no 3, 177–81, bst.sagepub.com/content/24/3/177.

Eborall, C. and Garmeson, K. (2001) 'Desk research on recruitment and retention in social care and social work', prepared for COI Communications for the Department of Health, London: Department of Health.

Fook, J., Ryan, M. and Hawkins, L. (2000) *Professional Expertise: Practice, Theory and Education for Working in Uncertainty*, London: Whiting and Birch.

Gov-UK (2019a) 'Social work education in the 2019 academic year: information for HEIs and students', assets.publishing.service.gov.uk/government/uploads/system/uploads/attachment_data/file/813511/Social_Work_Bursary_2019_Information_pack.pdf.

Gov-UK (2019b) 'Knowledge and skills for child and family social work', www.gov.uk/government/publications/knowledge-and-skills-statements-for-child-and-family-social-work.

Gov-UK (2019c) 'Adult social work post-qualifying standards: knowledge and skills statements', www.gov.uk/government/publications/adult-social-work-post-qualifying-standards-knowledge-and-skills-statement.

GSCC (2012a) *Regulating Social Work Education 2001–12 Learning Report*, London: General Social Care Council, www.nationalarchives.gov.uk.

GSCC (2012b) *Regulating Social Workers 2001–12 Learning Report*, London: General Social Care Council, www.nationalarchives.gov.uk.

HCPC (2012) 'Standards of proficiency for social workers in England', London: Health and Care Professions Council, www.hcpcuk.org/assets/documents/ 10003B08Standardsofproficiency-SocialworkersinEngland.pdf.

HCPC (2017) 'Standards of education and training', London: Health and Care Professions Council, www.hcpc-uk.org/globalassets/resources/standards/standards-of-education-and-training.pdf.

Hillman, N. (2014) 'A guide to the removal of student number controls', Oxford: Higher Education Policy Institute, www.hepi.ac.uk/wp-content/uploads/2014/09/Clean-copy-of-SNC-paper.pdf.

HMSO (2009) *House of Commons Select Committee Proceedings: Children and Families Social Work*, London: Her Majesty's Stationery Office.

Holmstrom, C. and Taylor, I. (2008) 'Researching admissions: what can we learn about selection of applicants from findings about students in difficulty on a social work programme?' *Social Work Education*, vol 27, no 8, pp 819–36.

IFSW (2014) 'Global definition of social work', Melbourne: International Federation of Social Workers, ifsw.org/policies/definition-of-social-work/.

Jones, R. (2012) 'The best of times, the worst of times: social work and its moment', *British Journal of Social Work*, vol 44, pp 485–502.

Lyons, K. and Manion, K. (2004) 'Goodbye DipSW: trends in student satisfaction and employment outcomes: Some implications for the new award', *Social Work Education*, vol 23, pp 133–48.

MacAlister, J. (2012) *Frontline: Improving the Children's Social Work Profession*, London: IPPR, www.ippr.org/files/images/media/files/publication/2013/03/frontline-childrens-social-work_Oct2012_9705.pdf?noredirect=1.

Marsh, P. and Triseliotis, J. (1996) *Ready to Practice? Social Workers and Probation Officers: Their Training and First Year in Work*, Aldershot: Avebury.

Maxwell, N., Scourfield, J., Le Zhang, M., de Villiers, T., Pithouse, A. and Tayyaba, S. (2016) *Independent Evaluation of the Frontline Pilot: Research Report*, www.gov.uk/government/publications.

Mayer, J.E. and Timms, N. (1970) *The Client Speaks*, New York: Atherton Press.

McNay, M. (ed) (2008) 'Evaluation of the new social work degree qualification in England', London: King's College, www.kcl.ac.uk/ scwru/pubs/2008/evaluationteammcnay2008evaluation-execsumm. pdf.

McNicoll, A. (2017) 'Frontline graduates face restrictions on practicing outside of England', London: Community Care, www. communitycare.co.uk/2017/04/03/frontline-graduates-face-restrictions-practising-outside-england/.

Moriarty, J., Baginsky, M. and Manthorpe, J. (2015) 'Literature review of roles and issues within the social work profession in England', www.socialwelfare.bl.uk/subject-areas/services-activity/social-work-care- services/socialcareworkforceresearchunit/ 174392moriarty-et-al-2015-PSA.pdf.

Moriarty, J., Manthorpe, J., Stevens, M. and Hussein, S. (2011) 'Making the transition: comparing research on newly qualified social workers', *British Journal of Social Work*, vol 41, no 7, 1340–56.

Moss, B., Dunkerly, M., Price, B., Sullivan, W., Reynolds, M. and Yates, B. (2007) 'Skills laboratories and the new social work degree: one small step towards best practice? Service users' and carers' perspectives', *Social Work Education*, vol 26, pp 708–22.

Munro, E. (2011) *The Munro Review of Child Protection: A Child-centred System*, www.gov.uk/government/publications/ munro-review-of-child-protection-final-report-a-child-centred-system.

Murphy, B. (2019) 'The cap that doesn't fit: student numbers in Northern Ireland' (guest blog), Oxford: Higher Education Policy Institute, www.hepi.ac.uk/2019/02/18/the-cap-that-doesnt-fit-student-numbers-in-northern-ireland/.

Narey, M. (2014) *Making the Education of Social Workers Consistently Effective*, www.gov.uk/government/publications/making-the-education-of-social-workers-consistently-effective.

NISCC (Northern Ireland Social Care Council) (2015) *Northern Ireland Framework Specification for the Degree in Social Work*, niscc. info/storage/resources/20151020_niframeworkspecificationfv_publishedsept2014_amendedoct2015_jh.pdf.

Parker, J. (2006) 'Developing perceptions of competence during practice learning', *British Journal of Social Work*, vol 36, pp 1017–36.

Parsloe, P. (1975) 'Book review of Brake, R. and Bailey, M. (eds), *Radical Social Work*, New York: Pantheon Books', *British Journal of Social Work*, watermark.silverchair.com/6–2-283.pdf.

Payne, M. (2006) *What is Professional Social Work?*, Bristol: The Policy Press.

Rogowski, S. (2010) *Social Work: The Rise and Fall of a Profession*, Bristol: Policy Press.

SCW (2018) *Framework for the Degree in Social Work in Wales*, Cardiff: Social Care Wales, socialcare.wales/learning-and-development/regulation-of-social-work-education-and-training#section-30395-anchor.

Seebohm Report (1968) *Report of the Interdepartmental Committee on Local Authority and Allied Personal Social Services*, http://filestore.nationalarchives.gov.uk/pdfs/small/cab-129-138-c-88.pdf.

Skills for Care (2014) *National Occupational Standards*, www.ukstandards.org.uk/NOS.

Skills for Care (2018) *Social Work Education 2018 Skills for Care Analysis of Higher Education Statistics Agency (HESA) Data*, www.skillsforcare.org.uk/workforceintelligence.

Smith, C. (2008) *Devolution in the UK: Powers and Structures in Scotland, Wales and Northern Ireland (Briefing Paper, No 1)*, Edinburgh: The University of Edinburgh/NSPCC Centre for UK-wide Learning in Child Protection.

Smith, R., Russell, C., Stepanova, E., Venn, L., Carpenter, J. and Patsios, D. (2018) *Evaluation of Step Up to Social Work, Cohorts 1 and 2: 3-years and 5-years on*, Durham/Bristol: Durham and Bristol Universities, London: Department for Education, assets.publishing.service.gov.uk/government/uploads/system/uploads/attachment_data/file/707085/Step_Up_to_Social_Work_evaluation-3_and_5_years_on.pdf.

Smith, R., Russell, C., Stepanova, E., Venn, L., Carpenter, J. and Patsios, D. (2019) *Independent Evaluation of the Think Ahead Programme*, Durham/Bristol: Durham and Bristol Universities, thinkahead.org/news-item/independent-evaluation-of-the-think-ahead-programme-draws-positive-conclusions/.

SSSC (2003) *Framework for Social Work Education in Scotland*, Edinburgh: Scottish Social Services Council, www.sssc.uk.com/knowledgebase/article/KA-02074/en-us.

SSSC (2016) *Review of Social Work Education Statement on progress 2015–2016*, Edinburgh: Scottish Social Services Council.

SWE (Social Work England) (2019a) *Consultation on Standards*. Available from socialworkengland.org.uk/education-and-training-standards/.

SWE (2019b) *Practice Placement Guidance*, socialworkengland.org.uk/wp-content/uploads/2019/07/Practice_Placements_Guidance_FINAL.pdf.

SWRB (Social Work Reform Board) (2010) *Building a safe and confident future: Full detailed proposals from the Social Work Reform Board*, www. gov.uk/government/collections/social-work-reform-board.

SWTF (Social Work Task Force) (2009) *Building a safe and confident future*, London: Department for Children, Schools and Families, webarchive.nationalarchives.gov.uk/20130403221302/https:// www.education.gov.uk/publications/eOrderingDownload/01114– 2009DOM-EN.pdf.

TCSW (The College of Social Work) (2012) *Readiness for Direct Practice*. Available from https://www.basw.co.uk/professional-development/ professional-capabilities-framework-pcf/the-pcf/readiness.

Teater, B. (2012) *Curriculum Guide: Social Work Intervention Methods, produced for the College of Social Work*, www.basw.co.uk/system/files/ resources/basw_104913–2_0.pdf.

Tompsett, H., Henderson, K., Mathew Byrne, J., Gaskell Mew, E. and Tompsett, C. (2017) 'Self-efficacy and outcomes: validating a measure comparing social work students' perceived and assessed ability in core pre-placement skills', *British Journal of Social Work online*, www. bjswonline.com/doi/full/10.1093/bjsw/bcx001.

Trevithick, P. (2012) *Social Work Skills and Knowledge: A Practice Handbook*, Buckingham: Open University Press.

Turner, A. (2014) 'Government to support fourth cohort of Step Up to Social work trainees', *Community Care*, 11 June, www.communitycare. co.uk/2014/06/11/government-support-fourth-cohort-step-social- work-trainees/.

Turner, A. (2019) 'Postgraduate social work enrolments rise as undergraduate numbers fall and fast-track expansion continues', *Community Care*, 23 January, www.communitycare.co.uk/2019/01/23/ postgraduate-social-work-enrolments-rise-undergraduate-numbers- fall-fast-track-expansion-continues/.

Walker, H. (2002) *A Genealogy of Equality: The Curriculum for Social Work Education and Training*, London: Woburn.

Wilson, K., Ruch., G., Lymbery, M. and Cooper, A. (2008) *Valuepack: Social Work: An Introduction to Contemporary Practice*, London: Longman.

6

Practising social work

Guy Shennan

Introduction: a practitioner's account

Given the nature of social work, with all its messiness, it might be fitting to begin a chapter on changes in social work practice since 1970 with something of a paradox. The logician Irving Copi presented the philosophical problem of identity (in the sense of sameness) across time via the following two statements about change, each of which appears to be true, but inconsistent with the other.

1. If a changing thing really changes, there can't literally be one and the same thing before and after the change.
2. However, if there isn't literally one and the same thing before and after the change, then nothing has really undergone any change. (cited in Gallois, 2016)

So, for talk about changes in social work practice to make sense there might need to be something unchanging about it too, some essence that enables 'social work' in 2020 to be recognised as such by a time traveller familiar with 'social work' in 1970. Given the changes that have taken place, I suspect that such recognition might not always immediately be forthcoming. One of the implications of these comments is that change and identity, or sameness, are bound up with and dependent upon each other. In this chapter, therefore, as well as describing some of the changes to it, I will also be interested in some of the attempts in the period under consideration to define social work, to endow it with some timeless characteristics. Paradoxically again, perhaps, such definitions and conceptions have themselves been subject to change over time.

The most simple definition of social work practice might be what it is that social workers do, although this would be circular. Moreover, one of my main contentions will be that what social workers do is often now not so much social work as a professional activity but, rather, that they are operationalising policy determined outside of the profession, for example by government. The professional practice of social work has been described as 'knowledge, skills, and values in action' (Trevithick, 2012, p 45), which suggests that tracing changes in social work practice requires us to pay attention to shifts in its underpinning knowledge and value bases. Such shifts connect with ideas about whose knowledges are perceived to be important. Some changes to social work practice have arisen from a greater attention to service users' knowledges (I do not mean to suggest that this attention has been anywhere near sufficient), which are experientially based (Beresford, 2000). Other experiential knowledge that has not been sufficiently drawn upon perhaps is that of social work practitioners themselves (Gordon, 2018), in a period that has seen a rise in managerialism (Stevenson, 2005) and, some have argued, an insufficient valuing of social workers who remain in practice (Minty, 1995). In this context I should declare that the author of this chapter has always remained a practitioner. In the 50 years since 1970, both feminism (Evans, 1995) and constructivism (Parton and O'Byrne, 2000) have challenged traditional notions of dispassionate knowledge, which can be communicated in some neutral fashion independently of who is doing the communicating (Humphries, 1988). Of the many different accounts of changes in social work practice that could be constructed, among the influences that have led to the one presented here are my experiences, values and preferences. So let me declare some of these, in the interests of transparency, and also so as to signal some topics that I shall consider during the chapter.

I qualified as a social worker in 1989, considering myself fortunate to have trained at the University of Sheffield, given the emphasis there on practice models such as task-centred practice (Doel and Marsh, 1992) and its role in the development of 'client studies' (Sainsbury, 1975; Fisher, 1983). With pre-course experience in mental health, I envisaged specialising in this area, but wanted a generic social work post first. When I arrived in one, I discovered that it was generic more or less in name only, and that I was in effect a specialist social worker with children and families. This role was formalised after the 'big bang' of the implementation of the 1989 Children Act and the 1990 NHS and Community Care Act (Dickens, 2011) and the creation in our social services department of separate children's and adults' teams.

I moved from a patch-based children and families team to a duty team, looking for spaces to work therapeutically – to help people –

which was not easy, given the increasing focus on child protection. During this time I trained in solution-focused practice, which I began using in my social work in the duty team (Hogg and Wheeler, 2004), later specialising in the approach with a voluntary organisation, the Family Service Unit (Shennan, 2003). Since my last local authority position, in 2004, I have continued to specialise in solution-focused practice, first employed in a private clinic and training centre (Shennan, 2019) and now independently, as a practitioner, consultant and trainer. Although working outside the mainstream of social work during this time, I have remained a registered social worker and a member of the British Association of Social Workers (BASW), which I chaired from 2014 to 2018. Another relevant aspect of my personal experience, given the devolution of the past 20 years or so, is that it has mainly been in England, which will inevitably lead to a bias in this chapter towards developments there.

These are some of the experiences that affect my view of developments in social work practice since the unification of the profession in 1970. I was in short trousers when Seebohm reported and BASW was formed, and still when Maria Colwell was killed, and a few months short of voting age when Mrs Thatcher was first elected in 1979 and the age that we now call neoliberal began.

All these events had a huge impact on the development of social work during the period under review, which I am about to sketch in general terms. We should, though, be careful about thinking of this as a purely linear progression. Rather than having arrived at certain changes by a particular point in time, we can think of social work as always 'in the middle' of travelling, during which 'core debates and dilemmas come round again and again' (Dickens, 2011, p 23). These debates often focus on tensions that have been around modern social work since its late 19th-century beginnings, some of which will be evident in what follows.

Changing conceptions of social work

These include tensions between care and control, maintenance and change, policing and helping. In the third of these pairs of (apparent) opposites, the balance 40 years ago was very much towards the latter for one leading social work thinker. Bill Jordan has offered a number of characterisations of social work, including in this opening sentence of a book published in 1979: 'It sounds simpleminded to talk of social work as "helping people"; yet it is difficult to find a better way of describing what social workers try to do' (Jordan, 1979, p 1).

The conception of social work set out shortly afterwards in the Barclay Report (1982) was based on investigations of what social workers actually did, appraised alongside views of what they are needed to do. To the relief of social workers, I am sure, this Working Party, set up at the request of the Secretary of State for Social Services and chaired by Peter Barclay, concluded that social workers *are* needed, to carry out two activities, which they termed 'counselling' and 'social care planning'. Their choice of words was potentially confusing, especially in the case of counselling, which they used as an alternative to 'social casework'. It will help in understanding their choice if we note that at this time the three 'methods' that social workers were commonly said to use were casework, group work and community work. Casework, originally simply denoting the work done with particular 'cases', had come to mean something more, suggesting the purposeful use of the worker–client relationship to facilitate change, or accommodation to what could not be changed (Roberts and Nee, 1970). Its association with psychodynamic approaches to social work in particular, which were falling from favour from the 1970s onwards (Payne and Reith-Hall, 2019, p 16), made casework an unfashionable term, and this contributed to Barclay's choice. Each of these words used to encapsulate a major part of social work activity – casework, counselling, even helping – might sound odd to contemporary social work ears. They might be translated today as 'direct work' – in contrast, for example, to 'care management', or to signal how little time social workers now typically spend, directly, with service users (BASW, 2018a).

Barclay also challenged the notion that casework, group work and community work were distinct methods, as had Leonard (1975) in his exploration of a paradigm for radical social work, seeing them, rather, as signifying who the social worker was working with in each case and arguing that counselling and social care planning could each be used with individuals, groups and communities. The Working Party's overall vision was encapsulated in a chapter called 'Towards community social work', although, despite this future-oriented title, they acknowledged that they were really just repeating Seebohm's recommendations. Community social work and its patch-based variation were popular during the 1980s (Hadley et al, 1987) and, I believe, still feature in the aspirations of many practitioners today – including in the case of this author – but they have largely fallen victim to the child protection orientation that I am shortly to describe.

Continuing his attempts to characterise social work, Jordan (1987) suggested that two activities that played a powerful role in its self-image – counselling (in its usual meaning, rather than that assigned by Barclay) and advocacy – did not actually feature prominently in everyday practice. What social workers did on a day-to-day basis he called 'informal negotiation', which was concerned with fairness in 'the final distribution of welfare that takes place in society' (Jordan, 1987, p 136). In contrast to the expert approaches of the old professions – such as medicine, law and teaching, practised in the professional territories of hospitals, courts and schools – social workers were willing 'to forsake the formality of their roles, and to "mix" it with ordinary people in their "natural" settings, using the informality of their methods as a means of negotiating solutions to problems rather than imposing them' (Jordan, 1987, p 140). This was an appealing picture of social work to a student entering the profession at that time – and I believe that it has much to offer still in terms of a vision of what social work can be – but it was soon to be at odds with what was happening on the ground, and perhaps already was by the time it was published. I had still to learn that the contents of books and journals did not always match actual social work activity. This was hidden from me as a student social worker on placement, as the contexts in which I worked and the caseloads I was given enabled me to develop skills in helping approaches such as task-centred social work.

As I have mentioned, on qualifying I wanted to continue to develop my experience by working as a generic social worker. It may be that I was just too late, as the re-emergence of specialisation had recently been reported (Challis and Ferlie, 1988), or that I had misunderstood the idea of genericism, in which case I was probably not alone. There has always been potential for confusion about what or who was being described as 'generic' (Minty, 1995; Stevenson, 2005), in part because a department could be providing a generic service in which individual workers specialised. The latter usually refers to areas of work defined by service user group, but then different specialist workers could be using generic social work values, knowledge and skills. To convey the latter meaning, the word 'holistic' has frequently come to replace 'generic' – for example, in the case of a holistic model of social work assessment (Lloyd and Taylor, 1995). Recent concerns about a fragmentation of social work (Boahen and Wiles, 2019) have led to a holistic notion of practice being promoted as an essential aspect of a unified profession, for example by the Professional Capabilities Framework (PCF). An important feature of the PCF is that it was created and is owned by the social work profession (BASW, 2018b), and it has been used to underpin a holistic, or generic, skill set for social work practice (Davies and Jones, 2016).

From professional to procedural knowledge

In my first post as a qualified worker I was expecting to have a generic caseload, but the reality was quite different, as it contained at any time at the most one token non-child care 'case'. Within this restriction of my caseload there was a further narrowing still. Up to the late 1980s social work had had a preventive tradition, which in the children and families field focused on preventing children having to come into care (Stepney, 2014), but I found myself in the early stages of a process by which 'social work has been reduced to a very narrow concern with child protection' (Parton, 2014, p 2042). This reduction was accompanied by significant shifts in the type of knowledge on which practice was based. A series of high-profile child death inquiries, together with government-led and media-supported critiques of public sector professionals, particularly marked in the case of social work, had contributed to a loss of confidence in social workers and an associated decrease in professional autonomy. Social work practice was becoming increasingly proceduralised, with the importance of child protection procedures being underlined at all times. When I met the Deputy Area Officer during my induction, the main message that he left this keen but anxious newly qualified worker with was that if I followed procedures I would be fine. Some time later, on one of my duty days, we received a referral indicating some concern about a child. The Area Officer appeared at the duty desk and a prolonged discussion with the duty manager ensued, focused entirely on whether or not the referral should be dealt with under child protection procedures. At this distance I do not recall the discussion's outcome regarding what was done for the child, but I do know that it influenced my understanding of the type of knowledge that was expected to inform my practice.

A distinction has been drawn between occupational and organisational professionalism (Fenton, 2016), with the former basing practice on knowledge and values developed by the occupation, or profession, while in the latter, practice is led by agency 'knowledge' – procedures, targets and performance indicators, budgetary imperatives and so on. In his article on prevention Stepney (2014) frequently uses the phrase 'policy to practice'; another way of viewing this occupational and organisational distinction is to contrast theory-based practice with policy-based practice. Social work theory comes very much from the profession (Payne and Reith-Hall, 2019), yet much of what social workers now do is governed by policy, legislation and statutory guidance. The impact of a particular practice can also vary depending on whether it has originated from within the profession or from outside policy, as we shall see later in the case of strengths-based practice.

One area of social work practice where we can see clearly how organisational has tended to supplant occupational professionalism is that of assessment. In child protection, guides, checklists and manuals have proliferated, and I recall one of my lecturers saying that the 'Orange Book' (Department of Health, 1988) should be on every social worker's desk. What I do not recall is input on how to use this manual and its lists of questions to support a professional analysis, it tending instead to elicit large amounts of information that could be relayed to managers to then use in their decision making. A bureaucratic approach to assessment spread from child protection more widely across children and families social work, from the Looked After Children Assessment and Action Records (Knight and Caveney, 1998), to the Assessment Framework (Department of Health, 2000) and today's 'Child in Need' assessments and plans. Information technology enabled an intensification of this central prescription and performance management via the widely criticised Integrated Children's System (White et al, 2010). This level of prescription, including strict time scales for the completion of assessments, was criticised by Munro in her 2011 review of child protection, which put forward a series of recommendations aimed at reducing bureaucracy and revitalising professional practice, although the extent to which these have been implemented is unclear in the dual context of austerity and a huge increase in care proceedings.

A similar narrowing of the social work role can be seen in social work practice with adults, which is 'increasingly restricted to the act of assessment' (Lymbery, 2005, p 43). Following the 1990 NHS and Community Care Act, whose market-oriented demands saw emerge a 'procedural, deprofessionalised model of social work practice' (Whittington, 2016, p 1944), social workers turned into care managers, organising packages of care to meet assessed need. In England the assessment of adults' needs and eligibility for care and support is now governed by the 2014 Care Act, and it has been argued that policies on eligibility criteria create a standardised and resource-led view of need, rather than one based on the unique lived experience of each individual (Slasberg and Beresford, 2017). As ever, practice cannot escape the context in which it takes place, and under austerity the practice of assessment is impacted upon more than ever by the question of how much need can be afforded. Eligibility policies answer this 'by creating a circular definition of "need", whereby a "need" is only a need if there is the resource to meet it' (Slasberg and Beresford, 2017, p 1263).

Contrasting definitions

Another of social work's tensions concerns the extent to which statutory powers are used, compared to working with people on a voluntary basis. The characterisations of social work above, with helping and informal negotiation at their centre, came from a time when there was 'relatively little overt statutory work' (Barclay, 1982, p 13) and statutory action was 'a last resort' (Jordan, 1987, p 136). Since the early 1990s the accelerating dominance of child protection has led to a significant increase in the number of children in public care, and the last decade since 2010 in particular has seen large rises in care proceedings (Thomas, 2018). The 2014 Care Act has also put the safeguarding of adults on a statutory footing for the first time and in the last decade since 2010 there has been a sharp rise in compulsory detentions in England under the 1983 Mental Health Act (Care Quality Commission, 2018). As with the rise in care proceedings, there will be numerous reasons for this, but, as social workers still constitute the large majority of Approved Mental Health Professionals, this rise in compulsory detentions does contribute, alongside these other protection and safeguarding practices and increased use of statutory powers, to a particular picture of contemporary social work.

This picture was reflected in the 'Public Description of Social Work' included in the final report of the Social Work Task Force (2009), set up following the death of Peter Connelly in 2008, which began: 'Social work helps adults and children to be safe so they can cope and take control of their lives again.' The foregrounding of safety reflects the shift in social work's focus over the years that I have outlined. The report continues: 'Social workers make life better for people in crisis who are struggling to cope, feel alone and cannot sort out their problems unaided', and while I appreciate that the intention was to write in 'plain English' to aid public understanding, what I think is missing here is the 'social' aspect of social work. The markedly different 'Global Definition of Social Work' was agreed five years later by the International Federation of Social Workers (IFSW) and the International Association of Schools of Social Work (IASSW):

> Social work is a practice-based profession and an academic discipline that promotes social change and development, social cohesion, and the empowerment and liberation of people. Principles of social justice, human rights, collective responsibility and respect for diversities are central to social work. Underpinned by theories of social work, social

sciences, humanities and indigenous knowledge, social work engages people and structures to address life challenges and enhance wellbeing. (IFSW, 2014)

While it would be wise not to confuse the aspirations underlying such a definition 'with what the vast majority of state-directed social workers actually do in their practice' (Jones and Lavalette, 2013, p 150), this offers a bolder vision of social work practice that can act as a counterpoint to the narrowing we have seen in the UK since the late 1970s. One of the reasons for this is that it is based on the theories, knowledges and practices of social work as a profession, rather than on the imperatives of the organisations in which social workers are employed. I shall turn now to some profession-led practice developments, which I believe to have been among the most important of the past 50 years. Up to around 1970, social work practice was in the main influenced, if not dominated, by psychoanalytic theory (Stevenson, 2005), and I believe that, in some respects in each case, the approaches I am about to consider can all be seen as reactions to this. The reduction of this influence and the development of other approaches arose from various empirical, theoretical and ideological shifts, leading to the growth of short-term and collaborative approaches, radical social work and strengths-based perspectives.

'Retaining a commitment to good practice'

Research began to cast doubt on the effectiveness of long-term social work, including an influential study that compared outcomes of extended casework and planned short-term work (Reid and Shyne, 1969). The researchers, unexpectedly, found that families who had just eight sessions made more progress than those who received a more open-ended service. The consideration of the features of the short-term work that contributed to its greater success led to the development of the task-centred approach (Reid and Epstein, 1972). Central to this was an agreement reached by the worker and client, incorporating the target problems, goals and a time limit for the work.

Task-centred practice has to an extent remained influential (Cauvain, 2019), one reason for which may lie in its distinctiveness in being developed within the social work profession. Other models of practice that share some of its features, notably a goal focus and brevity, have originated outside – for example, behavioural social work (Hudson and Macdonald, 1986) and some systemic and family therapy approaches (Burnham, 1986). Systemic practices have experienced a resurgence of interest since around 2010, following the promotion of the 'Hackney model' (Goodman and Trowler, 2012).

Another feature of task-centred practice is the collaborative nature of the worker–service user relationship that it both requires and engenders. Again, moves in this more egalitarian direction reached far wider than just this one approach. The 1970s arrived in the midst of an age of radical political activity, which inevitably affected social work. Radical social workers believed that social work was always liable to be just attaching sticking plasters to the individual casualties of societal inequalities, and that more fundamental change was needed. This included change in the relationships between social workers and the people with whom they worked, from authoritarian towards dialogical styles, as 'radical change can only come from consciousness developed as a result of exchange rather than imposition' (Leonard, 1975, p 59). One critique at that time noted that feminist ideas were added rather than integrated into radical social work, and advocated using the feminist concept of 'pre-figurative politics', with its emphasis on creating different forms of social relations, exemplified by Women's Aid Refuges (Hudson, 1985). As the relationships within these services were not based on a view of women as victims, but drew rather on 'the collective power of women' (Hudson, 1985, p 648), this may also be seen as anticipating the strengths perspective that was to develop in social work some years later.

Radical social work suffered a similar fate to community social work in the 1980s and 1990s, but then resurfaced with remarkable vigour and in new forms in the 2000s. As social work had shifted, so too did the nature of radical practice, and what was now radical included 'retaining a commitment to good practice' (Ferguson and Woodward, 2009, p 153). This saw good practice as resisting the dehumanising tendency of proceduralisation, which included forming relationships with service users and carers based on social work values. As in its previous incarnation, radical practice should also include collective activity and political campaigning, and it is a moot point whether such action can be part of social work practice or is engaged in outside – for example, with trade unions. Unfortunately, we do not have the space to debate this here.

Collaborative practices, and the use of explicit agreements between worker and client, were also supported by a body of research that consisted of what were initially called 'client studies', one of the first being reported in the classic *The Client Speaks* (Mayer and Timms, 1970). This showed social workers and their clients often at cross-purposes, with a typical comment coming from a client apparently frustrated that while the social worker was wanting to talk about her relationship with her mother, she wanted help with the gas bill. Shared understandings also required significant shifts in recording practices, and sharing records with clients became part of moves towards a more transparent social work (Doel and Lawson, 1986). Similarly, and it is almost hard to credit now that these were not always standard practices, service users began to be invited to meetings that concerned them, such as case conferences. In the child protection field this was part of a wider attempt to work in 'partnership with families' (Platt and Shemmings, 1996), following research showing the importance of constructive relationships for good outcomes for children (Department of Health, 1995). That such partnership working has been hard to sustain is evident from concerns continuing to be voiced about authoritarian styles of child protection practice (Featherstone et al, 2014), and renewed calls for working collaboratively with parents (Mellon, 2017). These renewed calls go further, though, by proposing engagement with new forms of parent self-organisation and peer advocacy, drawing on pioneering work, for example in New York (Tobis, 2013). This chimes with a critique of the client studies tradition, which, while acknowledging that such studies do ensure that service users' knowledge is included in social work theorising, at least to a degree, points out that this knowledge is interpreted and mediated by social work academics and practitioners (Beresford, 2000). Service users can be the authors, and not only the subjects, of research and practice developments, as is suggested by the term 'co-production'.

Co-production is sometimes used as a synonym for the sort of collaborative practices described above, but its meaning can stretch further, for example when used in combination with the policy of personalisation in adult social care (Hunter and Ritchie, 2007). This aims to increase choice and control for adult users over the social care services they receive, which suggests a good fit with the values underpinning social work practice. This, however, has been compromised by inadequate resourcing (Lymbery, 2012). An example of the potential of co-production to enter the child protection arena has been provided by an enquiry that put families who had experienced child protection in touch with front-line social workers in order to influence service design and delivery (Surviving Safeguarding, 2019).

Those seeking a more co-productive model of child protection have detected possibilities in 'strengths-based casework' (Featherstone et al, 2018, p 122), and the shift from a deficit-based towards a strengths perspective has been described as 'an important development of the 21st century' (Payne and Reith-Hall, 2019, p 15). We need to distinguish here between overarching perspectives and methodologies that can put these into practice. Since the publication of the first article to mention a strengths perspective for social work practice (Weick et al, 1989), one critique of this has concerned the 'lack of a specific set of techniques or skills to implement the fundamental idea' (Blundo et al, 2019, p 220). Common to the social care legislation that has been passed in each nation of the UK in recent years is an expectation that social work practice will be strengths-based. There is a concern that this is an example of policy-based, or statute-led, practice, which does not necessarily give social workers the means to work in this way.

Some specific methods have been situated under this umbrella term, with Payne and Reith-Hall (2019) suggesting solution-focused practice, motivational interviewing, narrative social work and mindfulness, while the chapter on strengths-based approaches in a well-known book on assessment in social work adds the 'Resilience model' (Milner et al, 2015). Having trained in solution-focused practice in 1995, I immediately found that I could use it in my work in a children and families duty team, and to good effect. This included both using aspects of the approach in an unplanned way, opportunities for which frequently presented themselves, and also using the whole model in a more structured fashion. We were able to do the latter by separating the referrals that we received into two groups, one being third-party reports of concern and the other requests for help from family members. The solution-focused approach, in common with other helping models of social work, is most straightforwardly applied following a request for help. As social work has been led from helping to policing, with managers claiming that the former is not its 'core business', and people needing help ceasing to request it for fear of the latter, such approaches have been hard to sustain. What has happened in some cases is that they become adapted for use in the more controlling side of social work, sometimes accompanied by claims that they will have a humanising effect on this, as for example with the Signs of Safety model for child protection practice (Turnell and Edwards, 1999), which is influenced by the solution-focused approach. When whole departments then implement such an approach, dangers arise of its bureaucratisation (Baginsky et al, 2017) and a slide from theory- to policy-based practice.

Conclusion

So, is there some underlying essence of social work that has remained constant in the face of all these changes of the 50 years since 1970? It is hard to say that there is. What I believe has remained constant is the commitment of so many social workers to practising in a way that fits with the values of their profession – a commitment that is embodied in their professional association (whether or not they are members) that has now been constant for 50 years; and values that have an explicit statement in the profession's Code of Ethics, which was first written 45 years ago (BASW, 2014). This commitment often needs to be accompanied by a moral courage (Fenton, 2016), given the level of difficulty involved in practising in an ethical way in the face of the forces of managerialism and proceduralisation that I have outlined. It should not be this difficult, though. Whether or not collective activity and campaigning can be a part of social work practice itself, they are very much needed in order to achieve changes in its context so that accounts of the next 50 years can tell a different story: a story of social work practices led by social workers ourselves, in full and equal partnership with the people we serve.

References

Baginsky, M., Moriarty, J., Manthorpe, J., Beecham, J. and Hickman. B. (2017) *Evaluation of Signs of Safety in 10 Pilots*, London: Department for Education.

Barclay, P. (chair) (1982) *Social Workers: Their Role and Tasks*, London: Bedford Square Press.

BASW (2014) 'Code of Ethics', https://www.basw.co.uk/about-basw/code-ethics.

BASW (2018a) *80–20 Campaign: How Much 'Direct' Time do Social Workers Spend with Children and Families?*, https://www.basw.co.uk/resources/80–20-campaign-final-report-2018.

BASW (2018b) *Professional Capabilities Framework*, https://www.basw.co.uk/professional-development/professional-capabilities-framework-pdf.

Beresford, P. (2000) 'Service users' knowledges and social work theory: conflict or collaboration?', *British Journal of Social Work*, vol 30, pp 489–503.

Blundo, R., Bolton, K. and Lehmann, P. (2019) 'Strengths perspective: critical analysis of the influence on social work', in M. Payne and E. Reith-Hall (eds), *The Routledge Handbook of Social Work Theory*, Abingdon: Routledge, pp 216–23.

Boahen, G. and Wiles, F. (2019) *Professionalism and Self-management*, London: Open University Press.

Burnham, J. (1986) *Family Therapy: First Steps Towards a Systemic Approach*, London: Tavistock.

Care Quality Commission (2018) *Mental Health Act: The Rise in the Use of the MHA to Detain People in England*, London: Care Quality Commission, https://www.cqc.org.uk/sites/default/files/20180123_mhadetentions_report.pdf.

Cauvain, S. (2019) 'Task-centred practice', in M. Payne and E. Reith-Hall (eds), *The Routledge Handbook of Social Work Theory*, Abingdon: Routledge, pp 205–15.

Challis, D. and Ferlie, M. (1988) 'The myth of generic practice: specialisation in social work', *Journal of Social Policy*, vol 17, pp 1–22.

Davies, K. and Jones, R. (eds) (2016) *Skills for Social Work Practice*, London: Palgrave Macmillan.

Department of Health (1988) *Protecting Children: A Guide for Social Workers Undertaking a Comprehensive Assessment*, London: HMSO.

Department of Health (1995) *Child Protection: Messages from Research*, London: HMSO.

Department of Health (2000) *Framework for the Assessment of Children in Need and their Families*, London: The Stationery Office.

Dickens, J. (2011) 'Social work in England at a watershed – as always: from the Seebohm Report to the Social Work Task Force', *British Journal of Social Work*, vol 41, pp 22–39.

Doel, M. and Lawson, B. (1986) 'Open records: the client's right to partnership', *British Journal of Social Work*, vol 16, pp 407–30.

Doel, M. and Marsh, P. (1992) *Task-centred Social Work*, London: Ashgate.

Evans, J. (1995) *Feminist Theory Today: An Introduction to Second-wave Feminism*, London: Sage.

Featherstone, B., White, S. and Morris, K. (2014) *Re-imagining Child Protection: Towards Humane Social Work with Children and Families*, Bristol: Policy Press.

Featherstone, B., Gupta, A., Morris, K. and White, S. (2018) *Protecting Children: A Social Model*, Bristol: Policy Press.

Fenton, J. (2016) 'Organisational professionalism and moral courage: contradictory concepts in social work?', *Critical and Radical Social Work*, vol 4, pp 199–216.

Ferguson, I. and Woodward, R. (2009) *Radical Social Work in Practice: Making a Difference*, Bristol: Policy Press.

Fisher, M. (ed) (1983) *Speaking of Clients*, Sheffield: University of Sheffield Joint Unit for Social Services Research.

Gallois, A. (2016) 'Identity over time', in E.N. Zalta (ed), *The Stanford Encyclopedia of Philosophy*, https://plato.stanford.edu/archives/win2016/entries/identity-time/.

Goodman, S. and Trowler, I. (eds) (2012) *Social Work Reclaimed: Innovative Frameworks for Child and Family Social Work Practice*, London: Jessica Kingsley.

Gordon, J. (2018) 'The voice of the social worker: a narrative literature review', *British Journal of Social Work*, vol 48, pp 1333–50.

Hadley, R., Cooper, M., Dale, P. and Stacy, G. (1987) *A Community Social Worker's Handbook*, London: Tavistock.

Hogg, V. and Wheeler, J. (2004) 'Miracles R Them: solution-focused practice in a Social Services duty team', *Practice*, vol 16, pp 299–314.

Hudson, A. (1985) 'Feminism and social work: resistance or dialogue?' *British Journal of Social Work*, vol 15, pp 635–55.

Hudson, B. and Macdonald, G. (1986) *Behavioural Social Work: An Introduction*, London: Macmillan.

Humphries, B. (1988) 'Adult learning in social work education: towards liberation or domestication?', *Critical Social Policy*, vol 23, pp 4–21.

Hunter, S. and Ritchie, P. (eds) (2007) *Co-production and Personalisation in Social Care: Changing Relationships in the Provision of Social Care*, London: Jessica Kingsley.

IFSW (2014) 'Global Definition of Social Work', ifsw.org/what-is-social-work/global-definition-of-social-work/.

Jones, C. and Lavalette, M. (2013) 'The two souls of social work: exploring the roots of "popular social work"', *Critical and Radical Social Work*, vol 1, pp 147–65.

Jordan, B. (1979) *Helping in Social Work*, London: Routledge and Kegan Paul.

Jordan, B. (1987) 'Counselling, advocacy and negotiation', *British Journal of Social Work*, vol 17, pp 135–46.

Knight, T. and Caveney, S. (1998) 'Assessment and action records: will they promote good parenting?', *British Journal of Social Work*, vol 28, pp 29–43.

Leonard, P. (1975) 'Towards a paradigm for radical practice', in R. Bailey and M. Brake (eds), *Radical Social Work*, London: Edward Arnold, pp 46–61.

Lloyd, M. and Taylor, C. (1995) 'From Hollis to the Orange Book: developing a holistic model of social work assessment', *British Journal of Social Work*, vol 25, pp 691–710.

Lymbery, M. (2005) *Social Work with Older People: Context, Policy and Practice*, London: Sage.

Lymbery, M. (2012) 'Social work and personalisation', *British Journal of Social Work*, vol 42, pp 783–92.

Mayer, J. and Timms, N. (1970) *The Client Speaks: Working Class Impressions of Casework*, London: Routledge and Kegan Paul.

Mellon, M. (2017) *Child Protection: Listening To and Learning From Parents*, Glasgow: Iriss, https://www.iriss.org.uk/resources/insights/child-protection-listening-and-learning-parents.

Milner, J., Myers, S. and O'Byrne, P. (2015) *Assessment in Social Work* (4th edn), London: Red Globe Press.

Minty, B. (1995) 'Social work's five deadly sins', *Social Work and Social Sciences Review*, vol 6, pp 48–63.

Munro, E. (2011) *The Munro Review of Child Protection: Final Report: A Child-centred System*, London: The Stationery Office.

Parton, N. (2014) 'Social work, child protection and politics: some critical and constructive reflections', *British Journal of Social Work*, vol 44, pp 2042–56.

Parton, N. and O'Byrne, P. (2000) *Constructive Social Work*, Basingstoke: Palgrave Macmillan.

Payne, M. and Reith-Hall, E. (2019) *The Routledge Handbook of Social Work Theory*, Abingdon: Routledge.

Platt, D. and Shemmings, D. (eds) (1996) *Making Enquiries into Alleged Child Abuse and Neglect: Partnership with Families*, Chichester: Wiley.

Reid, W. and Epstein, L. (1972) *Task-centred Casework*, New York: Columbia University Press.

Reid, W. and Shyne, A. (1969) *Brief and Extended Casework*, New York: Columbia University Press.

Roberts, R. and Nee, R. (1970) *Theories of Social Casework*, Chicago: University of Chicago Press.

Sainsbury, E. (1975) *Social Work with Families: Perceptions of Social Casework among Clients of a Family Service Unit*, London: Routledge and Kegan Paul.

Shennan, G. (2003) 'The Early Response Project: a voluntary sector contribution to CAMHS', *Child and Adolescent Mental Health in Primary Care*, vol 1, no 2, pp 46–50.

Shennan, G. (2019) *Solution-focused Practice: Effective Communication to Facilitate Change* (2nd edn), London: Red Globe Press.

Slasberg, C. and Beresford, P. (2017) 'The need to bring an end to the era of eligibility policies for a person-centred, financially sustainable future', *Disability & Society*, vol 32, pp 1263–8.

Social Work Task Force (2009) *Building a Safe, Confident Future: The Final Report of the Social Work Task Force*, https://webarchive.nationalarchives.gov.uk/20130403221302/https://www.education.gov.uk/publications/ eOrderingDownload/01114–2009DOM-EN.pdf.

Stepney, P. (2014) 'Prevention in social work: the final frontier?', *Critical and Radical Social Work*, vol 2, pp 305–20.

Stevenson, O. (2005) 'Genericism and specialization: the story since 1970', *British Journal of Social Work*, vol 35, pp 569–86.

Surviving Safeguarding (2019) 'How a family-led child protection enquiry built trust between social workers and families', *Community Care*, https://www.communitycare.co.uk/2019/04/12/family-led-child-protection-enquiry-built-trust-social-workers-families/.

Thomas, C. (2018) *Care Crisis Review*, London: Family Rights Group https://www.frg.org.uk/images/Care_Crisis/Care-Crisis-Review-Factors-report-FINAL.pdf.

Tobis, D. (2013) *From Pariahs to Partners: How Parents and their Allies Changed New York City's Child Welfare System*, New York: Oxford University Press.

Trevithick, P. (2012) *Social Work Skills and Knowledge: A Practice Handbook* (3rd edn), Maidenhead: Open University Press.

Turnell, A. and Edwards, S. (1999) *Signs of Safety: A Solution and Safety Oriented Approach to Child Protection Casework*, New York: Norton.

Weick, A., Rapp, C., Sullivan, W. and Kisthardt, W. (1989) 'A strengths perspective for social work practice', *Social Work*, vol 34, pp 350–89.

White, S., Wastell, D., Broadhurst, K. and Hall, C. (2010) 'When policy o'erleaps itself: the 'tragic tale' of the Integrated Children's System', *Critical Social Policy*, vol 30, pp 405–29.

Whittington, C. (2016) 'The promised liberation of adult social work under England's 2014 Care Act: genuine prospect or false prospectus?', *British Journal of Social Work*, vol 46, pp 1942–61.

7

Looking back, looking forward: two personal views

Part I: Looking back
Malcolm Jordan

Social work's a business now
Except of course it's not
There's no 'win-win' for shareholders
We work with the have nots
Those left behind by GDP
No second homes in France
It's Sanctions and the Food bank now
Loan sharks at the door
Social work's a business now
No need to help the poor. (Unwin, 2017)

Back in 1970 social work was practised in a variety of specialised settings. These included medical and psychiatric hospitals, child guidance clinics, probation, and local authority children's, health and welfare departments. Only a minority of social workers in the local authority services were qualified.

Social workers also worked in a variety of voluntary organisations, mostly dealing with the care of children, elderly people or individuals with disabilities. In addition, there were highly specialised agencies concerned with distressed families of which Family Service Units and the Family Welfare Association were prime examples. Work was usually in small groups that included senior workers and team leaders. In the many welfare departments controlled by Medical Officers of Health, social workers could be overwhelmed by the authority of the medical model.

If you worked in any of these environments you carried a number of 'cases' and were responsible for all aspects of that work: the amount of time you spent with each, how often you visited (aware of the costs of travel and so on), the specific methods you used and when to close a 'case'. You were of course able to seek advice and support from peers or in supervision to examine the issues you might be facing with any specific situation. In some large organisations there would be team leaders and a principal who could be called upon for extra resources, or for advice on particularly complex cases. What bound all this together was the concept of professionalism, promoted and enforced where necessary by professional associations. Social workers sought leadership, a sort of taken-for-granted function combining responsibility and a degree of charisma.

In the 1960s we were a committed, hard-working and dispersed group of workers with little public recognition or authority – a weakly defined profession with porous boundaries, often set within more powerful organisations.

To some extent this changed in 1968 with the publication of the Seebohm Report (1968). Before considering the implications of that, we need to try to clarify two key terms that continue to be a feature for social work today: professionalism and leadership. You will notice that the word 'manager' has not yet been used. In an extensive three-year study in the late 1960s of social workers in a southern county, examining their backgrounds, experience and expectations of the effects of the Seebohm changes, in all the answers to thousands of questions the word 'manager' was mentioned only once. Administration was important, but had no managerial authority.

Whether social work is a profession or would want to be one is a long-disputed question. The standard definition of a profession is that it requires expert knowledge, a recognised qualification restricting entry, a code of practice requiring high codes of conduct, integrity and a method of discipline. It was argued, in opposition to claims of professional status, that our knowledge base was weak; that we had no restriction on entry and few methods of dismissal by our peers. The claims of social work have been strengthened by the slow development of our own knowledge base; research and the establishment of the GSCC; and the achievement of protected occupational status in 2005. This leaves the question as to whether we really want to be seen as a profession along with the long-established and elite occupations of law and medicine. From this comes the dislike of the term 'client' or 'patient', which came to be seen as demeaning terms. I have never thought that this applied to social work, and although I have reluctantly adopted the current term of 'service user', I've always thought it less personal and respectful than 'client'. Leadership is a more difficult term to define: it has a much longer history and a highly personal element that is not easy to categorise. My best definition comes from a speech that I heard Sir John Hunt, leader in 1953 of the first successful Everest expedition, give to adult army cadet leaders in March 1955:

> The power to inspire others to discover and give of their best. It demands that the leader operates from within the group, not from above it; setting a fine example, but not stealing initiative: taking his share of the joint task. The spirit of this is 'Let's try this' not 'You do this' ... it's the attitude that the leader's job is only one of the jobs to be done; it's the art of persuading each other member of the group that his is also an essential job and its development his own responsibility; it's the art of blending all these efforts to produce a combined result.

The question of leadership faded from fashion sometime in the group-think of the 1960s and, surprisingly, remained in the shadows throughout the Thatcher years and into the 1990s. But I note that it now seems to be coming back into fashion, possibly as a response to excessively prescriptive management (Fairholm and Fairholm, 2009).

In respect of training and practice the Seebohm proposals were generally welcomed, if somewhat misunderstood. Within a local authority's new social service department, social work was to be based in teams offering a generic service to local communities. Some idea of the radical thinking of the Committee was their statement that:

> At many points in this report we have stressed that we see our proposals not simply in terms of organisation but as embodying a wider conception of social services, directed to the well being of the whole community and not only of social casualties, and seeing the community it serves as the basis of its authority, resources and effectiveness. (Seebohm, 1968, para 474)

One issue that divided opinion was the size, complexity and power of the bureaucratic structure of the average local authority. There was some comfort that the Director would, for the first time, be recognised as a chief officer on an equal basis to the powerful departments of education and finance. A charismatic experienced social worker as leader would work wonders. There was as much reality in this expectation as in the above quote on accountability. The situation was summed up by Sir William Utting, Chief Social Services Inspector for

England and Wales at the Department of Health and Social Security from 1976 to 1991.

> What Local Authorities wanted was a nice, tidy, buttoned down department whose achievements and low cost would be a credit, come the next election. The workforce, on the other hand, swollen by the unqualified and politicised intake of the 1970s wanted the New Jerusalem for their clients and themselves – and now! (Utting, 2002)

A reflection of some of the difficulties of the time can be seen in the experience of a well-qualified new Director who, inviting front-line staff to his office for a welcome chat, found that some would often be late or just fail to show up. One, when asked for an explanation, said 'I don't think you're a vital part of the department. It's people like me, at the sharp end, who really get things done' (*Community Care*, 1998). Such an exchange was a hangover from administration, which was seen as of lesser status, being there to ensure that the resources were available to enable social workers to get on with their job. It also reflected the views promoted by the radical magazine *Case Con*, which attacked the managerialism of the new social services departments in issue after issue of lively commentary, often in cartoon drawings of besuited, massive-salaried Directors on their heading the Seebohm Factories of downtrodden workers forced to suppress needy applicants (Weinstein, 2011).

As the new social services departments settled down a process of inevitable osmosis into the culture, language and system of local government pushed Directors to formalise their position as top-level managers. They were required to spell out the purpose, goals and key policies for their departments, to create a recognisable structure that would effectively execute those policies and control budgets. Then they could communicate with their fellow chief officers. In large authorities, where second-level Divisional Directors had been established, they morphed into managers in most aspects of their role, although some continued to deal with cases. My recollection is that below that level the professional ethics and processes of social work remained relatively untainted.

In 1979 the Conservative government under Margaret Thatcher came to power and adopted the policies of deregulation, privatisation of public assets, reductions in public spending and attacks on trade union power that were aspects of neoliberalism. She spelt out her views:

I think we have gone through a period when too many children and people have been given to understand 'I have a problem, it is the Government's job to cope with it!' or 'I have a problem, I will go and get a grant to cope with it!' 'I am homeless, the Government must house me!' and so they are casting their problems on society and who is society? There is no such thing as society! There are individual men and women and there are families and no government can do anything except through people and people look to themselves first. It is our duty to look after ourselves and then also to help look after our neighbour and life is a reciprocal business and people have got the entitlements too much in mind without the obligations, because there is no such thing as an entitlement unless someone has first met an obligation. (Thatcher, 1987)

Patch teams

The incoming government was concerned that many social workers were left-wing activists. There was uncertainty and disagreement about what social workers were for and what they did. The situation was not helped by a 1980 publication, *Can Social Work Survive?*, that in some ways repeated the historic attack by Barbara Wootton (Wootton, 1959). The book's attack was concentrated on the assumed lack of science in social work. 'When compassion is not held in check by the discipline of science then the result is both misplaced and dangerous' (Brewer and Lait, 1980). The authors' solution, not surprisingly, was that social work should be returned to the NHS. While I and many colleagues saw the book as a self-righteous, ill-disciplined publication, it became a significant factor in the Secretary of State's decision to ask the social reformer Sir Peter Barclay, Chairman of the National Institute for Social Work, to undertake a study of the role and tasks of social workers. This intervention led to the publication in 1982 of a report that had relatively little impact (Barclay, 1982).

The main outcome was to support the community involvement of social workers through the creation of small 'Patch' teams, the purpose of which was getting to know and interact with the residents of an area. It envisaged that the teams would coordinate local agencies to provide the best services. Patch teams were taken up, but rarely delivered the scale of community engagement envisaged.

The next major review into community care followed the dramatic escalation in costs to social security of payments for residential and nursing care as described in Chapter 2. Local authorities moved to divest themselves of homes in order to have the fees met by social security, and no test of need was applied. Sir Roy Griffiths, Chairman of Sainsburys supermarkets, was appointed to carry out the review of the community-based, challengingly interactive world of social care. In 1988 Griffiths concluded by recommending that local authorities should take a leadership role to assess local needs and then manage the provision of services by existing local private or voluntary agencies, which should promote the fashionable idea of choice and innovation (Griffiths, 1988). Clear lines of accountability and responsibility would be required; social services departments would assess individual needs and design flexible packages of care from the available range of services. In short, Care Management successfully entwined social workers into management by requiring that case workers should know the unit costs of each package.

The government's response was to introduce the 1990 NHS and Community Care Act, which, by and large, followed many of the Griffiths recommendations. It placed full responsibility on local authorities to carry out needs assessments and means testing of individuals in need. This was a customer–assessor–purchaser–provider route in a care market setting. While this recognised the social work profession's skill in assessment, the need to tie this into detailed costs led to the computerisation of processes. Recording and financial management threatened the personal worker–client relationship, often placing the social worker in an ambiguous position. It encouraged local authorities to move out of direct provision of residential and day care services, a process for which they were ill prepared and resulting in some very vague care standards.

Unfortunately the deteriorating economic situation led to further cuts in public services under the auspices of new public management. A key part of this was the further tightening of the now established dynamic of the purchaser–provider split. The then Home Secretary, Kenneth Clarke, commented: 'The new accountability that we seek from our public services will not be achieved simply because men of goodwill and reasonableness wish that it be so. The new accountability is the new radicalism.' The radicalism was of course based on the assumption that private provision was better and less expensive than local government care. I have never seen any independent research to justify this claim. Thus developed a minor tsunami of imposed techniques, including league tables, targets, frequent audits and so on. To ensure that everything was as tight as possible a small army of auditors were recruited who could pore over the statistics far from the human situations at the front line. One by-product was the ability of local managers to manipulate the statistics to the advantage of their service whenever possible.

New Labour

In 1997 Labour was returned to power under the leadership of Tony Blair. In the early years of his ten-year premiership he followed many of his predecessors' policies in accepting the role of private companies in health and social care. The three Es of economy, efficiency and effectiveness were used to encourage local authorities to focus on the processes between expenditure and outcome. Were these internal processes the sharpest and most cost-effective means of achieving the desired goal? If not, why not, and did the result coincide with the pre-set goals? For social services departments this consumed a considerable amount of management time and required the provision of a slew of statistics for government. The 1999 Local Government Act aimed to ease reliance on the three Es. It abolished the compulsory competitive tendering model by introducing the concept of Best Value in an attempt to counter the competitive contract system's reliance on the sole cost of a bid. In future, purchasers were to seek partnership with providers, while still using the three Es framework. In pursuing Best Value, authorities had to consult ratepayers, providers and service users. Nine years later, in 2008, we experienced the world financial crash, precipitated by a combination of irresponsible lending by American banks and clever computer programs that few understood. This threatened our domestic budgets and led to a general election in 2010 and a Coalition government. Instead of punishing the banks for their behaviour, the government imposed a severe programme of austerity on public services and the most vulnerable members of society. So far as education and social services were concerned, this was managed by increasing the market mechanisms already in place.

These were the years in local government when management – the main function of chief officers and middle managers – spread down to the front-line staff. The impact required a psychological change in the latter's approach to their work, in which there was a high tension between professional ethics and the skills of a book-keeper. Costs were measured against need, with social work case recording forming a critical point in every assessment. All this was tightly controlled and monitored locally and nationally by the Care Quality Commission. This was managerialism writ large across every public service. Managerialism had supplanted management by denying the humanity of traditional, rationale-based management and inserting a belief that there is a class of individuals who, by their special skills and knowledge, will infiltrate organisations to make them super-efficient. The ideology is firmly anti-professional and believes that measurement in every detail of an organisation leads to the best outcome. These elements are a direct challenge to professionals, who consequently feel deskilled and restricted in their activities. The level of stress increased as the basis of action seemed to be that everyone and everything has its price (Adams et al, 2008).

I work as a volunteer with young offenders. From time to time the Youth Justice Board requires that we be brought up to date with the latest legislation and policies. Before setting up the required full-day meeting to bring us up to scratch, the manager has to submit not an obvious, straightforward professional case, but a Business Plan arguing that the costs of the event, including a basic buffet at lunch time, are justified in terms of Value for Money. The fact that some 20 of us are giving a day of our time for free seems not to count. As this applies to every manager in the county one wonders how many extra staff have been employed to handle all these requests. These techniques and the requirement to justify every act in terms of cost spread distrust and fear of constant surveillance throughout the organisation, and diminish the professional standing of front-line staff coping with the stresses of their daily work.

The prolonged imposition of Conservative austerity measures has led to terrible cuts in resources, inadequate staffing and the pressure of high caseloads forcing departments to impose thresholds at the point of entry to services. Currently you need to be in a severe mental health or child care crisis, or desperately destitute, disabled or homeless, in order to get through the front door. Early intervention is impossible, often meaning higher costs later. There are long waiting lists in order to be assessed for mental health, family distress or support for disabilities. In the event, some service users find themselves in NHS emergency care or in police custody, thus complicating their lives.

Given the difficulty of measuring the outcomes of social work interventions, measurement has turned to prescribed time-scales between referral, assessment and intervention or, for example, the time to prepare a report for court. This ignores the chaotic lives of many service users. Given the pressure of work, staff sickness and the chaotic circumstances that face most interventions, the net result is that staff have to provide justifications explaining why these arbitrary targets have not been met, with consequently more pressure and stress. Social workers spend 80% of their time on office tasks (usually computerised) and only 20% face to face with service users (BASW, 2018). Social workers are becoming technicians, rather than autonomous professionals, increasingly forced to see work through financial statistics, leading to packages of care being seen as commodities.

As resources diminished, local authorities introduced a triage system of assessment for all new referrals in an attempt to limit demand. Given the variability of these policies, in 2003 the government introduced Fair Access to Care, with four levels of need: critical, substantial, moderate and low. Figures issued by the Care Quality Commission showed that those assessed as 'substantial' rose from 53% in 2005/06 to 83% by 2012/13 (Bamford, 2015).

The Personalisation policy, lauded in the early 2000s, was intended to increase the independence of service users with an impairment by allocating them their own budgets, enabling them to make their own choice of care provisions as 'customers' in the social care market-place. Although these principles remain, programmes have suffered under the effects of austerity, thus limiting choice just at a time when elderly service users have more complex needs. More recently, some local authorities seem to have developed an Orwellian use of language as they seek to disguise these cuts as a service improvement (SWAN, 2019). Bristol City Council launched their Better Lives policy, part of which required increased monitoring and scrutiny of how individuals were spending their budgets. Thus, people with a disability were required to keep a detailed daily diary indicating their activities in 15-minute slots. So, if they watched TV or snoozed these periods were added up to support a case that their care could be cut, even for individuals receiving 24-hour care. A system of pre-paid credit cards was introduced, which meant that the authority could more easily monitor spending or reduce the budget to individuals. There was evidence that service users felt threatened if they refused to use such cards. This policy has been challenged by local activist groups, who remain in discussion with the Bristol City Council,

Can social work survive?

What of the future for social care and social work? While there are many challenges ahead, my faith in social work and social workers remains positive. The politicians' favourite pastime of a reorganisation will not be far off. A full review of social care in England was promised by the government in March 2017, confirmed in the Conservative Party election manifesto of 2019 and repeated in the Queen's Speech in

October 2019. This review was to result in a Green Paper, allowing for public consultation. The fact that it has been re-promised and delayed several times is no surprise, given the complexity of the diverse care systems run by local authorities, their historical roots and structures as compared with the NHS and the financial arrangements that both have inherited. As the government have focused almost entirely on Brexit since 2016 critical welfare issues affecting millions of citizens have been swept aside, along with many other domestic policies.

Recent government changes in social work training are clear examples of neoliberalism's opposition to professionalism and an attempt to enhance managerialism. For social work these are Step Up for Social Work, launched in 2009, Frontline four years later and Think Ahead more recently. The first two focus on work with children, or more specifically child protection, and the third on mental health. The titles convey a message of a future that will be made better than anything that social workers have now. Given the blurb that accompanied the launch of Frontline, rapid promotion is assured. Learn how to be a social worker and get inducted to management, all within 14 months!

The government have invested heavily in these initiatives, which cost about three times as much per trainee as the three-year degree courses. This is all the more surprising, given that the entry criterion for the Fast Track courses is a 2:1 honours degree, although some flexibility has more recently been allowed. This is a divisive initiative, threatening to create different levels of work and also inserting narrowly trained specialist workers among those with a wider, more generically trained approach. There has never been any comprehensive, independent evaluation of this new system, including how trainees fare once in employment, and their retention rates. All this is far removed from the free-flowing, creative mixture of high-level education and training practised in the late 1970s, one example of which was my involvement in the course run in Maidstone that sought to develop competent, critically thinking and creative social workers.

A further example of expensively misunderstood anti-professional initiatives is the government's implementation of the National Assessment and Accreditation System (NAAS). This has cost well over £50 million. It aims to produce 'Accredited' child care social workers whose employers consider them ready for testing after a period of practice. Launched in 2017, the first contracts were awarded to the construction company Mott Macdonald and the accountants Deloitte. It was initially intended that 30,000 social workers would complete accreditation by 2020. The scheme requires social workers to attend a regional assessment centre to complete a series of tests including enacted 'real' social work scenes. All this of course takes no account of the austerity environment in which many service users live (Jones, 2018). The principal social work organisations and Unison raised serious objections long before the launch, including the existence of well-established continuous professional development (CPD) systems. The design is unaltered but implementation phases have been delayed and it is now on a voluntary basis. NAAS is now being tried out in five authorities, with only a trickle of workers taking part. In July 2018 the British Association of Social Workers (BASW) and the Social Workers Union (SWU) issued a joint press statement recognising this fact and offering support to social workers who opted into the scheme, while pointedly not supporting the scheme. They further commented that

> NAAS must also not be a distraction from the more fundamental issues facing children's social work across all 152 local authorities in England – such as workforce stability, reasonable workloads, supportive management and supervisory access and ongoing access to CPD. Underpinning everything is the need for sufficient resources to meet rising demand from children and families, particularly those increasingly impoverished through widespread austerity policies. (*Community Care*, 2018)

Unison's view is that NAAS heaps more pressure on social workers and threatens to create a two-tier system. Their survey showed that 99% of respondents were opposed to the scheme and Unison discouraged members from any involvement with NAAS.

What has been the effect on social workers of austerity and managerialism? Following a SWU initiative with Bath Spa University, Dr Jermaine Ravalier conducted research into the working conditions of social workers in cooperation with BASW. Following an exploratory survey in 2017, a more detailed questionnaire was completed by over 3,000 social workers in 2018. The situation had deteriorated within that short period and was very disturbing. Measured against the Health and Safety Executive's Management Standard Indicators, social workers presented with the highest levels of stress and sickness absence of all care sectors across the country. Job satisfaction varied from only 18% to 26%. Some 66% of social workers planned to leave their posts within the next few months and 50% planned to leave the profession altogether. The survey revealed high levels of stress, average working weeks of up to 11 hours above contract and the numbers of staff working when ill (presenteeism). The causes of stress were high workloads, lack of managerial support, too much time spent on repeatedly over-recording the same information and hot-desking. There was also a marked increase in bad behaviour towards social workers (Ravalier and Boichat, 2018).

Following these results BASW and SWU launched a 'Respect Social Workers' campaign and intensively lobbied Parliament, resulting in an excellent 90-minute debate in the House of Lords. They continue to press for a Commons debate and further action. Dr Ravalier planned to publish a 'Social Worker Wellbeing and Working Conditions: Best Practice Toolkit' in autumn 2019. Neil Thompson has recently drawn attention to the circular effect of stress across all levels of the structure. As staff go sick or burn out they are replaced by agency staff, who quickly leave the toxic environment. This creates more stress, further damaging the service to those in need of help (Thompson, 2019).

Given these challenges, attention naturally turned to the work already undertaken on well-being. This has been an issue for many years, a concern that each individual takes responsibility for their own mental and physical wellness, that of their immediate group and society. There have been attempts by the Office for National Statistics to measure well-being, and discussions on how this may modify the measure of GDP, which is solely based on the economy. It is now creeping into government. For example, the 2014 Social Services and Well-being Act passed by the Welsh Assembly requires coordination and partnership by public authorities with a view to improving the well-being of people. It is now widely promoted and is included in BASW's 2018 Professional Capabilities Framework.

I am vastly encouraged by the enthusiasm, determination and commitment of social workers and students whom I meet in conferences held by SWU, BASW and SWAN and on the front line. However hard pressed, they are willing to join colleagues in national or local branches of Associations and Unions. This is social action in practice, which has been a consistent historical element of social work.

In 2017 a group of social workers walked the 100 miles from Birmingham to Liverpool promoting the SWU/BASW campaign against austerity and to promote social justice. Following this, BASW has taken more radical steps, and through the joint SWU/ BASW Anti-Austerity Group. This has included publication of the Campaign Action Pack to help social workers to promote action in their organisations and communities and the *Anti-Poverty Practice Guide* to urge practitioners to put poverty at the centre of their practice and to help them achieve this (BASW, 2019). Let's join together on behalf of those with lived experience of terrible poverty and the oppressive, alienating effects of managerialism.

Part II: Looking forward
Emma Gant

Introduction

This is written from the perspective of a newly qualified social worker who came late to a social work career after raising a family and working in various roles in health and education. I came into social work because I became very aware of my white, middle-class privilege and appalled by the social inequality I was witnessing. My hope was that becoming a social worker would equip me with the knowledge and tools to tackle these injustices and enable me to educate others about the barriers and discrimination so many families face.

My degree course exceeded all my expectations. Not only did it provide all these tools and knowledge, it also gave me the ability to consider every aspect of society and social work from a critical perspective. There were robust modules covering the effects of poverty, the construction of society, elements of power and the history of social work. We also covered group work and social work in the community. All these, and many others, were deconstructed and considered from different perspectives. Assessment of these modules was by submission of an essay requiring evidence of wide reading and critical evaluation of the subject matter. We were also provided with direct practice sessions on practical issues such as communication, disabilities, substance misuse and domestic violence. Many of these sessions were provided by people with personal experience either as service users or as social workers. We were also required to complete two work placements and document our work in great detail. All these experiences led me to believe I had found my passion in life. I joined BASW and attended conferences and meetings in my spare time, fuelling my commitment to my new profession. I was full of excitement at bringing my enthusiasm, energy and expertise to my role as a Newly Qualified Children and Families social worker for a local authority. I was determined to use my Assessed and Supported Year in Employment (ASYE) to good effect: to continue to expand my knowledge and practice skills and to ensure that the local authority supported me in this.

On being offered a Newly Qualified Social Worker (NQSW) role with a local authority on the ASYE programme, workers must complete a training programme and are, effectively, on probation for their first year in employment. The programme involves quarterly critical logs, observations and obtaining feedback from other professionals and children and families they have worked with. A review meeting must take place for each three-month period and the assessor (line manager) must complete a report following the Professional Capabilities Framework detailing the NQSW's performance and further training needs. The programme run by the local authority I worked for was well organised, with learning ensuring that NQSWs were supported in gaining good practice experience and, in theory, protected study time. However, in reality, the coordinators had little power to influence management decisions about allocated study time, and line managers were expected to act as assessors with no time allowances for the considerable paperwork and extra practice time needed, nor any additional remuneration. In my experience the programme was not respected by some of the management, and guidelines were not followed, nor given precedence over practice issues. Given the high caseloads and the pressing needs of families in crisis, one can understand why this happened. However, it meant a loss of opportunities to give NQSWs the support they needed to become well-rounded, experienced social workers.

Factory work

The constraints of working in the UK's current system of statutory children's social care have drawn analogies to working in a factory (Cooper, 2010). The local authority I was working in certainly felt like a factory. When I first started I was confused. I wasn't expecting to be working in a factory; I was expecting to be advocating for young people, supporting parents, protecting children. I had bought a whole bagful of child- and family-friendly materials to enable me to connect with children and families. I rarely had time to use them. The expectation was to 'do' lots of things in very short time-scales. There was no time for making connections and building real relationships. In the 'do' box were visits, assessments, safety plans, family plans and a host of other paperwork and recording. The managers counted the assessments and visits, sending weekly performance management targets with large red sections to those whose recordings were not hitting deadlines. This produced a highly tense atmosphere, I felt anxious about getting all the recording and processing done within the time-scales. I had a real feeling of tension about whom I should be more anxious about – the families or the management.

Have I held all the right meetings, and recorded that? Does holding a meeting make things better for this family? Had nobody read the Munro Report? Had they heard of it? Did they care? Can I talk about the poverty, discrimination and oppression that I am witnessing? How do I challenge the inherent racism that I am witnessing? My dreams of addressing these barriers by using the research and academic learning I carried had to be put on hold while I adjusted to the traumatic new environment I found myself in. Each month at the ASYE meetings I was able to reflect on and process these experiences. It was when these ceased (at around six months) that I began to find the role extremely difficult.

From a NQSW's point of view there is the heady feeling of earning a significant wage after being a student for three or four years, coupled with the kudos of finally achieving the status of a registered professional. That has to be balanced against the realisation that you will not be able properly to put into practice the values and awareness from your course. It seemed that social workers were rushing around, imposing unachievable child protection plans on families experiencing poverty, insecure housing and insecure work.

The problem is that there has been a shift in social work policy from support of families to scrutiny and judgement, and a simultaneous increase in poverty and societal inequalities (Featherstone et al, 2014; Sharland, 2006). Lack of funding reduces the social work relationship to one of preoccupation about the level of provision of service rather than the impact of that service on family relationships.

As an NQSW completing my ASYE I used my critical logs and portfolio to document my deep sense of the dissonance between my aspirations as a social worker and my experience of being expected to follow local authority procedures without question. Indeed, this resulted in a recommendation that I fail my ASYE because what I had written would bring the local authority into disrepute. A manager insisted that I should change my critical log in order for her to recommend a pass, despite there being no concerns about my practice. I refused to do so.

Working conditions

On joining the local authority I experienced the level of disruption and change that was affecting the new safeguarding units that had been formed following a 'restructuring'. At the time there was no unit for me to join formally, and thus I was seconded to one of the units that was at full capacity and needed support to fulfil its safeguarding duties. This entailed undertaking small pieces of direct work with children and families whom I had previously not met. On my first morning I had no formal induction or welcome pack. Fortunately, as I had completed my placement at the same setting I was familiar with it and had a laptop and phone available to me. Once introduced to the Consultant Social Worker I would be working with, I was left to my own devices.

A practitioner whose organisation does not prioritise their physical, emotional and educational needs is less able to meet those of children and families and thus will be ineffective in facilitating meaningful change for them. In a new professional role, and my first paid employment for some years, I understood the need to be independent and to step in to assist the organisation to fulfil its duties, and my own, in safeguarding local children and families. Adams and Sheard (2013) emphasise the importance of NQSWs learning to walk before they run, and developing good habits from the beginning. They also recognise the difficulties of doing this in the current climate of increased workloads and diminishing resources. Unfortunately, in such situations leaders resort to 'bunker mentality'. They refuse to receive information that is counter to what they want to believe, and this results in failing systems (Elgot and Walker, 2019).

Local authority social work managers sometimes ignore the reality of the terrible working condition their social workers experience; impossibly high caseloads, extremely long working hours; and unrealistic expectations to fulfil statutory obligations. Any social worker not meeting these impossible targets can be attacked. But the human question for the future is: can the imperfect social worker manage to do more good than harm in the time and circumstance in which they find themselves (Docx, 2019)? This is discussed in an article about a local authority Child in Care team where senior managers had little understanding of the actual work taking place and of what the significance of the review meetings was for all parties, in particular for the child. The senior managers did not see how their interaction with the Independent Reviewing Officer (a nominally independent experienced social worker charged with holding the local authority to account for its work with children in care) and social worker was critical for the child to be able to fully participate in the meetings. Indeed, some felt that this was not the role of the social worker at all (Diaz and Alyward, 2019).

There is no doubt that there are some very committed people working in most localities, but the overall atmosphere is one of 'rabbits in the headlights'. Social work managers struggle against all odds to meet their statutory requirements; six-weekly social work visits become mere tick-box exercises. Workforce morale is suffering and the emphasis is on 'keeping going', with no time for looking outside the box for innovations (Aynsley-Green, 2019). Numerous families requiring services, due to the direct effects of austerity, bedroom tax and Universal Credit, are confronted with a lack of staff and poor retention due to working conditions. Some local authorities are becoming toxic working environments.

Social workers as feminists

As a woman and mother myself, through my social work education I have become very aware of many types of systemic discrimination throughout British society. This has driven my passion as a committed feminist to question practices that reinforce this discrimination and oppress those who find themselves disempowered. For me as a NQSW this was a daunting prospect. Finding ways to raise this issue with experienced professionals was a constant source of anxiety for me. I experienced many illustrations of this discrimination, and in many of these situations I felt unable to challenge colleagues. I feared the power of experienced workers to influence the outcome of my ASYE.

Colleagues did not seem to share my newly acquired understanding of the world as one where women are continually disempowered by a patriarchal system. My attempts to explore the reasons behind this lack of critical engagement with gender equality led to puzzlement and a lack of understanding.

The experience felt not dissimilar to that of a person in an abusive relationship, where to disagree or to assert one's own needs is met with disregard, or worse. It is easy to see how a person in an abusive relationship may quickly begin to experience mental ill health. This led me to question the numbers of mothers being referred to our service with mental health difficulties who have been abused by partners or, historically, by parents or other relatives. The acceptance of the medical model by our service shocked me. Where there was no explicit disclosure of abuse, there seemed to be no exploration of the mental health aspect of these women's lives other than the reliance on mental health professionals to prescribe medication in order for children to be protected from an underperforming mother.

Humphreys and Thiara (2003) document the direct link between abusive relationships and severe emotional distress and highlight that professionals' inability to recognise and acknowledge the trauma that is being experienced adds to women's lack of agency and image of self-worth.

The missing narrative of women involved in child protection is discussed by McGhee and Waterhouse (2017). They point out the importance of motherhood as a societal symbol and how this needs to be understood if true partnership with these women is to be achieved. By prioritising relationship building with the mothers I have worked with, I have enabled them to achieve change. Feeling contained and understood has given them a new narrative, one that enables them to grow towards new possibilities, rather than expending energy fighting the existing constraints within which their lives are prescribed.

Child in Need

My initial observations of the implementation of the Child in Need process were that it was oppressive and undermining for the mother. Far from working in partnership, I witnessed a Child in Need meeting where both child's and mother's needs were ignored. Later I was able to work this case myself, forming a good relationship with the mother, the health visitor and the family worker, and we were able to progress the case positively and step the case back down to Early Help. This required sustained, quality time spent with the mother. Making use of the good relationships that I had established with other professionals enabled me to identify their input and that the children's existing relationships with these other professionals gave the needed protective factors to enable the family to move on.

The ability to manage risk is an important aspect of good social work practice. Risk-averse social work is overly oppressive and results in high numbers of child protection cases that overload already stretched services (Featherstone et al, 2011). Social inequalities should be addressed in order to ensure it is child need and abuse, not poverty, that is leading to child protection interventions.

Child protection

Working with families at this level of risk requires the collation of clear evidence to substantiate decision making. Senior managers and the system require that social workers should be completely firm in their preferred course of action. While it is clearly necessary for social workers to be clear about the direction they see a case to be going in, it is also essential for hypotheses to be changed in light of new information. When thresholds are high, social workers are put in the position of taking an extreme position about a family, encouraging them to paint a very dark picture in order to secure the help and support they need to mitigate risk for the children.

This adversarial system does not encourage open, critical reflection and discussion, instead producing a 'them and us' ethos where senior managers are the gatekeepers of resources and social workers are the advocates for action. In other situations, where a social worker is seen as being non-reactive to a potentially high-risk scenario, their professional judgement will be disregarded, and management will implement such action as they see fit, despite having little personal knowledge of the case. This lack of reflection and case direction from afar is confusing and extremely daunting for an inexperienced social worker and can lead to Imposter Phenomenon (IP) or Syndrome (Urwin, 2018). This is when a worker begins to doubt their abilities and feels unworthy of their position and that they are able to carry out their work due only to luck, rather than being confident that it is their skills and knowledge that enable them to do so. Urwin's research found that less-experienced social workers are more likely to experience this, and describes how it may be linked to levels of organisation support. IP may affect social workers' practice, causing them to over-prepare or to procrastinate. Neither of these mechanisms is sustainable long term, so it is important for good management to identify workers experiencing IP, support them to recognise their achievements and accept that they are 'good enough'.

The point is that change in any context cannot occur without robust collaborative relationships that enable transparent, open, honest and non-judgemental dialogue about the realities being experienced by all stakeholders. As Singh and Cowden (2009) point out, it is important for social workers to consider how decisions are made about who is allowed to speak, and whether, as witnesses to abuse of power and authority, it is their moral duty to assert this as knowledge, not as a contested value base.

Hostile environment

In 2009, the House of Lords considered the law in the case of *G v Southwark Borough Council* (referred to as the '*Southwark* judgment'). This ruling clearly affirms the responsibility of children's social care to assess young people aged under 18 who present themselves as being homeless or at risk of homelessness. Despite this, the local authority deems these young people to be resourceful, and they are required to continue sofa surfing and lodging with friends and relatives.

The political climate in which we are currently living appears to me to have infiltrated the working ethos of the local authority and affected social work managers. The 'hostile environment' that Theresa May initiated has filtered down, causing a culture of a 'doubt first, help later' approach to anyone who may not have recourse to public funds, or those on the edge of eligibility on account of their age.

This has been very evident in my work with 17-year-olds struggling with the pressures of difficult parental relationships. In addition, pregnant women or women with small children or babies who are experiencing domestic violence are met with stark choices, as the local authority does not appear to consider their children as being 'in need' and refuses to fund alternative accommodation if the housing authority does not accept their application. Topping and McIntyre (2018) document this change in government policy, citing cases where husbands' narrative of situations have been accepted, rather than challenged, and migrant women have faced a choice between deportation or continued abuse. I supported a young Romanian woman who had just had her baby prematurely and was staying with a friend. She had no recourse to public funds and had been unable to work during her pregnancy. Due to government policy, her position was that she was not entitled to housing or benefits. She was thus forced to return to her ex-partner in another area and rely on him for accommodation and income. My single assessment documented that in my professional opinion her human rights had been contravened by the local authority.

Shoesmith (2016) writes with good authority about the media as fuelling such stigmatisation by labelling these families as the 'moral underclass'. 'Othering' is the sociological process of creating distance between those considered normal and groups who appear to threaten society by contaminating it, either physically or psychologically. Ferguson (2011) discusses the relationship of social workers with this process. In addition, Shoesmith (2016) describes how social workers become concerned not to be associated with such groups. There seemed to be no questioning of the reinforcement of these processes by the social workers' acceptance of them.

Featherstone et al (2014) emphasise the importance for social workers of understanding their own emotional responses to demonised groups in order to challenge such discrimination, as opposed to reinforcing it. This was my expectation as part of my ASYE and my regular supervision. Unfortunately, although my manager had empathy for the families we worked with she did not share my view of the political issues that affected them. Our supervision sessions consisted of case discussions and limited emotional support with regard to difficult cases and how these were impacting on me, but no academic exploration of wider issues.

Social work managers have to act as gatekeepers of local authority funds, but they should also advocate for those who have no voice. The failure to do so caused me to question my role as a local authority social worker. My energy should be harnessed in supporting such people, not in fighting the system designed to protect them and their children from harm. The political climate of austerity has dulled some social workers' ability to see past political rhetoric and to stay true to social work values.

On one occasion I housed a 17-year-old girl under section 17, as the local authority refused to accommodate her under section 20 because they did not want to accept the responsibility of supporting her post-18. The district manager, who agreed with my reasoning, was employed by an agency. On arriving in the office the following Monday I learned that his contract had been terminated unexpectedly. There was no managerial information to inform staff of this change. This in itself caused, in me as well as others, an atmosphere of anxiety, as the clear implication was that workers must not challenge management protocol.

This toxic environment caused me to question myself constantly, as I could not avoid the cognitive dissonance. I questioned my decision to enter the social work profession. This resulted in my experiencing high levels of anxiety and a certain level of depression. My strategy, as documented by Urwin (2018), was one of procrastination, and I was very aware that I was working well below my capacity. Following the Health and Care Professions Council guidelines, I acknowledged this and, following a visit to my GP, made the decision to take some time off work in order to recalibrate my mental health. This was not an easy decision to make. Despite the current highlighting of mental health, there is still a great deal stigma attached to it and many social workers who feel the need to step out for a period of time will not admit to their mental health being an issue, but use a physical health need to inform their sickness period. Indeed, employers will document sickness and these records will be passed to future employers, meaning that those who are honest about the rigours of our profession may be discriminated against.

The Conservative government's decision to continue with austerity measures has impacted greatly on the children and families I have been working with. The cap on Housing Benefit has left many families with rent arrears, trapping them in unsuitable accommodation and thus often in a cycle of despair, leading to further problems such as unemployment and mental ill health. In addition, benefit changes, such as sanctions and the changes to the assessment for Personal Independence Payments, have further penalised those least able to create positive change in their lives, and therefore the lives of their children. Working with people who are experiencing such situations on a daily basis has been emotionally challenging and I at times found it difficult to remain optimistic and to be creative in the face of such systemic injustice. The Code of Ethics for Social Work (BASW, 2012) states that social workers, committed to the promotion of social justice, have a duty to challenge unjust policies and practices. We have the knowledge to do so.

Anti-oppressive practice is a social work approach that identifies, names and questions the power imbalances that result from stigma and discrimination (Thompson, 2012). Burke and Harrison (2002) note that reflexivity is one of the main principles for anti-oppressive social work practice, enabling the continual questioning of the causes of social inequalities and changing practice accordingly. Sheedy (2013, p 107) also states the need for social work as a profession to continually question the accepted categorisation of groups and thus challenge structural oppression. Critically reflective social work can produce not just tokenistic gestures but informed knowledge by which to challenge internalised assumptions about particular social groups. This can bring about improved outcomes in everyday practice at the personal level, as well as culturally through challenging organisational procedures, and structurally through social workers' involvement in policy planning and political engagement through non-governmental organisations such as SWAN and the Social Work and Health Inequalities Network (Bywaters et al, 2009).

'Deviant' social work (Carey and Foster, 2011) entails social workers, particularly in statutory settings, pressed for time and resources, making space to stretch the accepted work boundaries and operate outside what might be considered their organisational remit to build good relationships with children and families. Tait and Wosu (2012) offer important suggestions for direct work with vulnerable children. Featherstone et al (2014) state that having the confidence to spend time with vulnerable children and their families is key to developing trust and overcoming 'othering' processes that lead to stigma and discrimination.

In addition, social workers need to be aware of social work as a control mechanism for society, and to acknowledge the difficulty of practising anti-oppressively.

Conclusion

Working from a critical stance is recognised as an important part of social work practice (Rutter and Brown, 2012). Practising in that way is increasingly difficult in settings that encourage the unquestioning acceptance of 'evidence-based practice' and the performance of interventions in order to meet managerial targets.

Cooper (2010) refers to evidence-based practice as 'politics-based evidence'. He argues that if the conditions for a certain type of practice are cultivated by social work organisations and political climates, then that is the only approach that practitioners can take; if there is no time and space to use relationship-based practice, it will not take place. Many therapies that have gathered a good evidence base are still disregarded by local authorities and statutory services as being too resource heavy, and thus not meeting the market-model criteria of being value for money.

The challenge for social workers is to argue the case for relationship-based work. They also have to fight to draw attention to the social and environmental pressures that weigh most heavily on the most vulnerable. Social action is a professional responsibility.

References

Adams, J. and Sheard, A. (2013) *Positive Social Work: The Essential Toolkit for NQSWs*, St Albans: Critical Publishing.

Adams, R., Dominelli, L. and Payne, M. (2008) *Social Work: Themes Issues and Critical Debates*, 3rd edn, London: Palgrave Macmillan.

Aynsley-Green, A. (2019) *The British Betrayal of Childhood*, Abingdon: Routledge.

Bamford, T. (2015) *Contemporary History of Social Work: Learning from the Past*, Bristol: Policy Press.

Barclay, P. (1982) *Social Workers: Their Role and Tasks*, London NISW.

BASW (2012) *The Code of Ethics for Social Work*, Birmingham: BASW.

BASW (2018) 'The 80–20 Campaign: how much "direct" time do social workers spend with children and families?', Birmingham: BASW.

BASW (2019) *The Anti-Poverty Practice Guide for Social Work*, Birmingham: BASW.

Brewer, C. and Lait, J. (1980) *Can Social Work Survive?*, London: Temple Smith.

Burke, B. and Harrison, P. (2002) 'Anti-oppressive practice', in R. Adams, L. Dominelli and M. Payne (eds), *Anti-Oppressive Practice*, Basingstoke: Palgrave Macmillan, pp 229–39.

Bywaters, P., McLeod, E. and Napier, L. (eds) (2009) *Social Work and Global Health Inequalities: Policy and Practice Developments*, Bristol: Policy Press.

Carey, M. and Foster, V. (2011) 'Introducing "deviant" social work: contextualising the limits of radical social work whilst understanding (fragmented) resistance within the social work labour process', *British Journal of Social Work*, vol 41, no 3, pp 576–93.

Community Care (1998) 'From the barricades to the boardroom', Viewpoint by Wally Harbert, *Community Care*, 7–13 May.

Community Care (2018) 'BASW to support social workers who take accreditation tests', 23 July.

Cooper, A. (2010) 'What future? Organisational forms, relationship-based social work practice and the changing world order', in G. Ruch, D. Turney and A. Ward (eds), *Relationship-Based Social Work. Getting to the Heart of Practice*, London: Jessica Kingsley, pp 229–43.

Diaz, C. and Alyward, T. (2019) 'A study on senior managers' views of participation in on local authority ... a case of wilful blindness?', *British Journal of Social Work*, vol 49, pp 1333–49.

Docx, E. (2019) 'The Translator', *New Statesman*, 19–25 July.

Elgot, J. and Walker, P. (2019) 'Party staff in GMB vote for motion condemning leadership response to whistleblowers', *Guardian*, 19 December.

Fairholm, M. and Fairholm, G. (2009) *Understanding Leadership Perspectives*, Springer: New York.

Featherstone, B., Broadhurst, K. and Holt, K. (2011) 'Thinking systemically – thinking politically: building strong partnerships with children and families in the context of rising inequality', *British Journal of Social Work*, vol 42, no 4, pp 1–16.

Featherstone, B., White, S. and Morris, K. (2014) *Re-imagining Child Protection: Towards Humane Social Work with Families*, Bristol: Policy Press.

Ferguson, H. (2011) *Child Protection Practice*, Basingstoke: Palgrave Macmillan.

Griffiths Report (1988) *Community Care: Agenda for Action*, London: HMSO.

Humphreys, C. and Thiara, R. (2003) 'Mental health and domestic violence: "I call it symptoms of abuse"', *British Journal of Social Work*, vol 33, no 2, pp 209–26.

Jones, M. (2018) 'National Assessment and Accreditation systems: where are we up to with NASS?', *Critical and Radical Social Work*, vol 6, no 3, pp 415–17.

McGhee, J. and Waterhouse, L. (2017) 'The lady and the pram: women in child protection', *The British Journal of Social Work*, vol 47, no 6, pp 1652–68.

Ravalier, J. and Boichat, C. (2018) *UK Social Workers: Working Conditions and Wellbeing*, Bath Spa University: Bath.

Rutter, L. and Brown, K. (2012) *Critical Thinking and Professional Judgement for Social Work*, London: Sage.

Seebohm Report (1968) *Report of the Committee on Local Authority and Allied Personal Social Services*, London: HMSO.

Sharland, E. (2006) 'Young people, risk taking and risk making: some thoughts for social work', *British Journal of Social Work*, vol 36, no 2, pp 247–65.

Sheedy, M. (2013) *Core Themes in Social Work: Power, Poverty, Politics and Values*, Maidenhead: Open University Press.

Shoesmith, S. (2016) *Learning from Baby P: The Politics of Blame, Fear and Denial*, London: Jessica Kingsley.

Singh, G. and Cowden, S. (2009) 'The social worker as intellectual', *European Journal of Social Work*, vol 12, no 4, pp 479–93.

SWAN (2019), 'Austerity-hit Bristol City's social care services – when "Better Care" is worse care', press release, 24 January.

Tait, A. and Wosu, H. (2012) *Direct Work with Vulnerable Children: Playful Activities and Strategies for Communication* (Practical Guides for Direct Work), London: Jessica Kingsley.

Thatcher, M. (1987) Interview with *Women's Own Magazine*, 23 September.

Thompson, N. (2012) *Anti-discriminatory Practice: Equality, Diversity and Social Justice*, Birmingham: BASW.

Thompson, N. (2019) *The Managing Stress Practice Manager*, Wrexham: Avenue Media Solutions.

Topping , A. and McIntyre, N. (2018) 'Abused women let down by "hostile environment" policy', *The Guardian*, 17 August.

Unwin, P. (2017) 'Poet Austeriate', following his participation in the 2017 BASW/SWU 100-mile walk.

Urwin, J. (2018) 'Imposter phenomena and experience levels in social work: an initial investigation', *British Journal of Social Work*, vol 48, no 5, pp 1432–46.

Utting, W. (2002) Speech to BASW Conference reported in *Professional Social Work*, June, pp 10–11.

Weinstein, J. (2011) '*Case Con* and radical social work in the 1970s: the impatient revolutionaries', in M. Lavalette (ed), *Radical Social Work Today: Social work at the crossroads*, Bristol: Policy Press, ch 1.

Wootton, B. (1959) *Social Science and Social Pathology*, Oxford: Macmillan.

8

From clients as fellow citizens to service users as co-producers of social work

Peter Beresford and Suzy Croft

Introduction

Social work has rarely been short on ambition. Now, with the major structural constraints that have been building on it, it demands serious re-evaluation if it is to have a real chance of serving the liberatory and social justice-based goals associated with it by progressive practitioners and theoreticians. That is the issue we want to explore in this chapter. Specifically, we want to explore it through the lens of user and carer involvement because we think that it both has been at the heart of the most progressive recent developments in social work and also offers particularly helpful insights if we want to challenge the reactionary neoliberal pressures that have been increasingly acting on social work, both statutory and non-statutory.

Social work's conflicted history

The shift to the right in mainstream formal politics and the emergence of service user movements have been parallel developments in the UK and beyond since the 1970s. Both put an emphasis on user/consumer involvement, although, as we shall see, there have been deep differences in service system and service user understandings of these. Equally important, both can be seen as a reaction to the top-down, state-led politics and social policy that, in the context of social work, was epitomised by the creation of social services departments in 1971 following the publication of the Seebohm Report in 1968. Harris has described these departments as 'Seebohm factories', degenerating into 'neoliberal production lines' during the second decade of the 21st century (Harris, 2019). Originally privileging children and family social work, because this was the most professionalised area of activity at the time, social services departments provided a new home for social work in large, formalised, hierarchical bureaucracies where workers were mostly women and senior managers mostly men. It has been a difficult inheritance to throw off.

Equally problematic for such state social work were the claims that were made for it by its advocates: that it could offer major solutions to increasingly evident problems of poverty. As an essentially individualised service, still largely based on psychodynamic theory, it clearly could not make serious inroads into the structural problems that it faced, creating a legacy of perceived inadequacy and political distrust through over-claiming.

But there was more that was progressive about such social work than the unsupported rhetoric of some of its leaders. It attracted many to its workforce who genuinely did want to work in different, more equal, social justice-based ways with disadvantaged people and groups. They created resistance that was reflected in the creation of the 'revolutionary' magazine *Case Con* and the development of the enduring tradition of radical social work in the 1970s (Bailey and Brake, 1975). New forms of social work, like 'community' and 'patch based' social work, were developed in the 1970s, and flowered in the 1980s, which self-consciously sought to return to work in more locally based, more equal and informal ways with communities and service users (Hadley, 1981). Social work's organisations with progressive goals, like CCETSW and NISW, were also pioneers in working to address diversity with equality and anti-discriminatory working. Social work was frequently ridiculed for this commitment, for being preoccupied with 'political correctness', yet this has since become the cultural, political and policy norm.

User involvement's competing origins

This is the highly conflicted historical context of social work. Again relatively early in this history, social work had its first brush with what has come to be called 'user involvement', our particular focus here. This came through the development of a distinct area of research, 'client studies', pioneered in the book *The Client Speaks* (Mayer and Timms, 1970). While there has been a tendency in social work to equate this development with a new commitment to clients' perspectives and participation, it may better be seen as a renewed focus on them as a data source for professional interpretation (Beresford and Croft, 1987). However, this publication is the first intimation of social work's particular interest in what its recipients had to say, and it must be said here, again, that social work was ahead of other policies and professions.

This is also reflected in its early recognition of the importance of service user perspectives in the development of professional practice. An early key expression of this was Mike Oliver's *Social Work with Disabled People*, published in 1983 with the support of BASW, and since running to several editions (Oliver, 1983). Mike was one of the pioneers of the international disabled people's movement. This, alongside other welfare service user movements – including those of older people, people with learning difficulties, people living with AIDS or long-term conditions and the mental health service users/ survivors movement – like other emerging new social movements, placed an emphasis on people reconceiving themselves in the light of their own definitions of their rights and needs and developing their own proposals for policy and change. At the heart of this was a concern with personal and political empowerment and people's direct and equal participation.

The impact of service users

Thus we can see the founding principles of user involvement emerging from disabled people's and service user movements. While each of these movements had its own history and particular problems and concerns, as well as ways of understanding and responding to them, some major common themes emerged. These included that:

- service users should have effective influence, control and choice over the services and support which impact on their lives;
- they should be recognised as having equal civil and human rights alongside other people in society;
- the social understandings of their situation and the difficulties that they develop need to be recognised, and medicalised individual interpretations of them, which tend to blame and pathologise, need to be reviewed;
- barriers restricting their lives and access to services, support and communities need to be removed;
- service users who face additional discriminations on grounds of gender, ethnicity, sexuality, belief and so on also need to be treated with equality;
- service users should be supported to develop their own user-led organisations and groups to advance individual and collective self-advocacy, instead of other people speaking on their behalf.

Such user involvement, as conceived by disabled people's and other service user movements, was essentially concerned with the redistribution of power and their having more effective say and control in their lives and over the policies and services that intervened in their lives and were meant to offer support. Thus we are talking about what has come to be called a democratic model of involvement, concerned with service users' emancipation, personal and political empowerment. Service users and their allies saw this as achievable through developing their own organisations that would provide a basis for increasing their skills, confidence and expectations and for reformulating their understandings of themselves and their worlds through developing their own ideas and narratives, and that would provide the framework for working together to achieve personal, social and political change (Beresford, 1999; Beresford and Campbell, 2004). Thus the social work advanced in Mike Oliver's ground-breaking book was one based on the social model of disability and the philosophy of 'independent living' developed by the disabled people's movement. The form of professional intervention advocated, as disabled people came to describe it, was one of 'professionals on tap, not on top'. This placed an emphasis on equalising relationships between service providers and service users, and on the latter defining what they wanted and how to achieve it with professional support, rather than vice versa. As can be seen, this liberatory approach to social work strongly echoed models advanced by progressive social justice-based practitioners around the same time, even if often the two had found their way to it independently.

We realise that, between the two of us, we had had a lot of experience at government level of social work (and social care) organisations. Thus we have been involved between us as trustees of the Social Care Institute for Excellence (SCIE), National Skills Academy for Social Care, Skills for Care, National Council for Palliative Care, Help the Hospices and The College of Social Work. We have also been members of ministerial, government and inquiry advisory groups and committees as well as of practitioner- and service user-led organisations. We have noticed that leadership organisations are increasingly controlled by people with backgrounds as social work and social care senior managers – a group frequently identified by face-to-face practitioners as one of the key problems they face in trying to undertake ethically and principle-based practice. Perhaps it is no surprise, then, that a lesson we have learned is that, generally speaking, we have been able to achieve little in these elevated roles in such important bodies. They mainly seem to have been self-censoring, and subordinated under ever-tightening neoliberal government. One important exception was being part of the move to effective user and carer involvement in social work education, under the committed leadership of Dame Denise Platt. On the other hand, we feel that it has been possible, despite all the problems and barriers, to make some real progress *bottom-up* through service user-led and practitioner organisations, changing how people relate to and work with each other, building trust and understanding.

Peter Beresford and Suzy Croft

A different ideological approach to involvement

However, this was not the only approach to user involvement that developed over this period, or that was associated with social work and health and welfare services more generally. The preference of the political New Right for the market, over state intervention, not only placed a fresh rhetorical emphasis on the new 'public consumer' in a transformed system of market-led public services, but was also firmly presented in these terms by Prime Minister Margaret Thatcher, her governments and her social policy theoreticians and policy makers.

As their organisations developed, service users began to articulate their view that they experienced welfare state services as patronising and paternalistic, limiting their opportunities and overlaying them with negative stereotypes that emphasised dependence and deviance. The New Right seized on the association of state services and welfare with paternalism; advocates of the New Right argued that state welfare reduced the choices open to people (Alcock, 2008, p 9). Instead, they advanced the market as offering freedom and efficiency. They emphasised the gains the market could bring people by extending to their dealings with public policy and services the choice and control it already offered them in their private lives (Pascall, 2012, p 271).

Reconceived as 'welfare consumers' and public service 'customers', people would be able to regain control of provision by owning or paying for it, and through enhanced opportunities to choose what services they wanted. From being passive clients and claimants, people would become active purchasing consumers. The 'say' service users were meant to have would be provided by the introduction of market research and consultation exercises along the same lines as operated in conventional market settings. Early inclusion of rights to comment and complaint in the 1989 Children Act and the 1990 NHS and

Community Care Act (Means et al, 2008) put social work in the vanguard of this development. But this model of 'consumerist' user involvement was very different from the democratic one advanced by service users and their allies. There was no suggestion that there would be any actual redistribution of power or control. Service users' views would be sought, but this did not mean that they would necessarily be listened to. Control remained where it was, but now those holding it would have added intelligence from service users to inform them and their political and market decision making.

The achievements of involvement

However, for a long time these competing interests and understandings of user involvement seemed to work to everyone's advantage. Service users and their allies wanted more say from democratisation, and the state and the service system seemed interested in offering this through hearing the voice of the consumer. User involvement opened windows of opportunity for service users, carers and their families. Some of the innovations and advances that this led to in social work include:

- the establishment of requirements, following the introduction of the social work degree, for the involvement of service users and carers in all aspects and stages of qualifying and post-qualifying social work courses, with financial support for providers offered by central government;
- the defeat by the Disability Rights Commission of the GSCC's attempt to exclude competent social workers with experience of using mental health services;
- the introduction of formal arrangements for the involvement of service users and carers into the governance of social work and social care organisations such as the SCIE and Skills for Care;
- recognition of the importance of user and carer involvement by successive social work regulators, and its extension to other health-related professions;
- the increasing recruitment of applicants with lived experience of using services, as well as other requirements, to become social workers;
- a growing recognition of the value of service users' experiential knowledge and their involvement in participatory, collaborative and user-led research;
- support from social workers for people to take greater control over their care, and support through personal budgets, direct payments and indirect payment schemes;

- a return to interest in more person-centred, relationship-based social work, engaging with service users.

While the service system has focused particularly on areas like complaints and comments procedures, planning and audit in its development of user involvement, service users have tended to focus their efforts in other directions to which they have attached more value. These include:

- research – to extend their knowledge base as a counter to traditional 'expert' knowledge;
- training – to improve occupational practice and provision;
- service development – advancing innovative, user-controlled services and support schemes particularly valued by service users.

These have all made ground-breaking progress, even if this has frequently been limited by a lack of political and financial support.

The exposure of ambiguity

However, there were tensions underlying the new enthusiasms for such user involvement, both within and beyond social work. Different stakeholders coming from different ideological positions were using the same terms to mean very different things. Different intentions and interpretations created increasing misunderstanding and frustration. Service providers, commissioners and researchers could find it difficult to respond to service users' views and proposals when they felt that they were just one of the stakeholders and interest groups to whom they were under pressure to respond. In turn, service users who were seeking more control over their lives raised serious concerns about tokenism and incorporation. They talked about 'consultation fatigue', being 'all consulted out', being expected just to rubber stamp decisions already taken. They increasingly began to feel that the gains they achieved were slight in return for the amount of sometimes diversionary effort involved (Beresford, 2002). They also increasingly raised questions about whom the involvement was for and who was actually benefiting from it. Thus, for example, why would it be helpful for mental health service users/survivors to get involved in research and other projects initiated by the pharmaceutical industry, when the primary aim would be to increase profits through the development of more psychotropic drugs, when already treatment responses were unhelpfully dominated by these?

Cracks in the participatory edifice were already opening up under New Labour, but when, from 2010 onwards, first the Coalition and then Conservative governments committed to making draconian cuts in public services and introducing radical welfare benefits reform designed to take very large numbers of service users off benefits, a clearer collision between competing interests and ideologies began to seem almost inevitable. It is difficult to see how user involvement could feel real any longer, when policy makers showed themselves committed to neoliberal policies that did not necessarily carry public support and certainly were strongly opposed by disabled people and other service users and their supporters.

The political Right's restructuring of social work

As a middle manager I go to meetings with the senior managers and it is quite clear that what you need to be doing is agreeing with them. Agreeing with them that cases should be closed that you don't think should be. What they are concerned about first and last is the bottom line, the budget. They collude in not mentioning that it is all to do with massive spending cuts. They don't challenge what is going on in any way. And generally, other middle managers know what's expected of them and toe the line. If you don't, you will be shouted at and told very clearly what you have to do. It is hopeless. All they seem interested in is crawling up the greasy pole. They bring in consultants at silly money and they do the same. Ofsted is everything and its rating all they care about, whatever it really means. Children and families don't have a seat at this table. I feel more powerless than I did as a team leader. I had a good team and they worked hard and well. Together we could do something. I don't know what I can usefully do in this role, although I do my best and I don't think I'm a pushover. They have lost the plot.

Anonymous middle manager, Children and Families service

The accelerating shift to the political Right and the influence of neoliberal ideology have been reflected in radical changes in the structures, nature and role of social work. These include:

- an increasing policy and political emphasis on the social control aspects of social work as its core 'role and tasks';
- a preoccupation with keeping costs down in family and children/child protection policy and services, at the expense of the child;

- government-supported reviews of social work education (Croisdale-Appleby and Narey reviews, the latter of which was an unevidenced polemic against social work education, in response to political attacks on its adequacy and effectiveness);
- the introduction, resourcing and expansion of so-called 'elite', 'fast-track', employer-based pathways into professional social work, like Frontline, to create a corps of disciplined future managers, in line with neoliberal ideology;
- the restructuring of social work's professional regulation, closing down New Labour's GSCC, initially replacing it with the HCPC and, when that proved insufficiently pliable, creating SWE;
- ongoing reductions in the resourcing of both children and families and adult social work, even as both needs and constituencies continued to increase in scale;
- a new emphasis on privatising children and families social work services;
- the 'McDonaldisation' of social work, that is to say, increasing surveillance and routinisation of practice and its micro-management;
- the appointment of a Chief Social Worker (CSW) for children, associated with the 'Hackney model' of social work supported by right-wing governments and reframing the CSW role as a government informant on social work, rather than a social work advocate in government;
- political support for a range of unevidenced, cost-cutting, individualising approaches to practice with service users, including 'motivational interviewing', 'strengths-based' work, 'personalisation', the 'three conversations' model and so on.

As neoliberalism has tightened its hold on formal politics in the UK and internationally (reflected in electoral successes for the hard Right in the US, parts of Europe and elsewhere), the fragile consensus over user involvement and broader participatory politics has been eroded. We now seem to have entered a new stage in what can be seen as a long history of working towards more inclusive and egalitarian democracy. If user involvement in social work can be seen as part of a broader phase of developing provision for participation in health, social care and other public services, then we now seem to have entered a stage of state and political reaction, with conflicts and competing agendas developing (Beresford, 2019a).

User involvement in services like health and social care (including social work) has been diminished, to become a cover for service cuts, privatisation and an emphasis on the individual taking personal and financial responsibility for themselves. What we have been seeing is the full-blown development, particularly visible in Brexit Britain and Trump's America, from its initial market consumerist origins in the late 20th century, of a new, right-wing demagogic populism. While this is currently dominating international political agendas, it is also dictating current dominant understandings of user and citizen involvement internationally. Consumerist involvement can now more clearly be seen as part of this right-wing populist project. It is ironic that the most extreme UK expression of this populism, the manipulation of the Brexit referendum by powerful right-wing ideological, political and financial interests, has been used both to advance that neoliberal agenda and also to make claims to be the true and majority voice of UK voters and citizens. We have seen similar developments elsewhere in Europe, but most notably in the US, where divisive, exclusionary and anti-egalitarian politics that privilege the economic and political elite have been advanced in the name of disaffiliated blue-collar workers, who are most likely ultimately to be disempowered even further.

I'm now working as a welfare rights worker after 30 years as a social worker. I visit older people aged 50 upwards and their families to sort out problems they are facing under 'welfare reform'. The situations I encounter are beyond belief. People living with dementia and their families, with no formal support to speak of. A county local authority that fails to offer such support. Adult social workers – where are they and what are they doing? The truth is, where they exist they mainly seem to be there to manage the rationing system and explain to people who get that far why they aren't going to get any help. I imagine that this is what it was like under the Poor Law. Manage on your own, and if you can't, tough. And it is tough. People old and with long-term conditions and impairments before their time, and the benefits system wanting to force them back to work for the last five or ten years left until their delayed retirement. Thank God the city local authority is progressive and even has a welfare rights department to help. But county social services, for adults, mental health service users and children are a disaster zone. You are on your own. I have to be honest, I still can't help feeling shocked when meeting people who haven't got family by how you can be left to 'cope'.

Suzy Croft

Meanwhile, returning to user involvement, as the anti-democratic thrust of neoliberal, market-led involvement has become more explicit, so service user movements have increasingly recognised this and strengthened their challenge against it. They have highlighted its phoneyness in anti-welfare-reform campaigns. They have increasingly evidenced and highlighted the way in which (i) the progress of user involvement in research has been undermined, (ii) its legitimacy and that of user researchers have been called into question and (iii) their place in research has been restricted and questioned (Carr, 2019). They have highlighted the way in which once-expanding opportunities and forums for involvement have been curtailed, restricting the chances of making it real.

The social work that has been developing in England under these ideological auspices is one that few of us are likely to see as having a helpful future. While the privatisation of probation fundamentally undermined that service, so we are seeing social work hollowed out – in different ways, but with the same destructive implications. It is no longer enough to fight for social work. We must now be clear about what kind of social work we should be fighting for. It is not enough that it is some 'care management' role that is primarily concerned with rationing social care services that are still essentially based on poor law principles of 'needs' and 'means' testing to match grossly inadequate budgets. The resulting social work is reactionary and will have little to offer most service users, although we should always be aware and supportive of those practitioners who, even under such dire conditions, continue to struggle, as Daphne Statham, then Director of NISW once put it, to 'smuggle in good practice'!

In our view social work, perhaps because of its own political significance and contentiousness, offers key insights in microcosm for the broader politics we are living under. We believe that service user pressures for involvement have radically shifted social work in a liberatory and useful direction, but formal politics have been pushing back in a quite different, regressive direction. We believe that this reflects a much bigger struggle that has been taking place between personal and formal politics in modern times. Hence the pressure from identity-based movements – including those of welfare service users – to be the definers of their own identities, for their experiential knowledge to be given equal value and to challenge the barriers, exclusions and discriminations that they have faced. They have challenged inequalities and demanded that their complex diversity be treated with equality and their shared rights be respected. A whole lexicon of discrimination can be seen to have been challenged by the enormous social and cultural changes driven by the new social movements. We no longer accept without question terms like 'illegitimate' child, 'unmarried mother', 'spinster', 'handicapped', 'family'. White privilege, institutionalised racism, hate crime, domestic violence, bullying, employment discrimination, sexual grooming, harassment and assault have all been dragged into the light as serious problems. As we have grown more used to living with each other, with more equal understandings of our diversity and with changed meanings for birth, marriage, ageing, death and disability, too often formal politics still seem committed to dragging us back to more prejudiced and divisive interpretations of each other, rather than respecting our right to be who we are.

Meanwhile these formal politics seem to have turned back to some notionally less complex past, while actually being characterised by xenophobia, selfishness, hate, divisiveness, inequality and disempowerment. While in some ways progress has been made, in others, formal politics seem to have been in retreat from the radical changes brought about by the modern revolution in personal politics. Of course the struggles to challenge inequalities on the basis of gender, ethnicity, sexuality, culture, belief and so on are far from over, but it would be wrong to ignore the massive progress that has been made through them. These are highly contradictory times. Looking at the demographics, processes, priorities and preoccupations of our formal political system, it can sometimes be difficult to reconcile the two: personal and formal politics. Indeed the conflict between the two seems to have been increasing, with the one, formal politics, in many key senses much more powerful than the other and able to impose enormous pressure on us, whatever our personal understandings, values and beliefs.

A future for social work

Social work is located at the heart of these changes and has played a disproportionately significant role in advancing them, with its fundamental commitments to social justice, human rights and the challenging of inequality and disadvantage. In our view that is why, of all professions, it has most often come under the heaviest right-wing attack. It has highlighted the relations between the personal and the political, just as neoliberal politics has sought to deny them and to create divisions between us through its culture of individualised blame.

That is why we, like the radical social work organisation the Social Work Action Network (SWAN), believe that social work is a profession worth fighting for. But we need to be clear about what social work, based on what principles, we are talking about, if social work is to be renewed and have a liberatory future. There is already good work going on to advance such social work, in both theory and practice, and it is important to support it (Lavalette, 2019; James et al, 2019). Here we offer some of the principles, building on this and our own work, that we believe offer ways forward for such empowering and liberatory social work. They include:

- developing social work as a universal service (not a marginal one confined to marginalised people), funded out of general taxation as part of a re-visioned social care system, free at the point of delivery, that recognises that we may all have needs that can benefit from social work support with its emphasis on a social approach and recognition of the importance of the intersection of the personal with the social and political;
- co-producing social work at every level, from direct practice jointly constructed between social worker and service user, through to policy and provision;
- prioritising the social work skills and qualities that service users repeatedly highlight that they value: treating people with equality, respect, warmth, reliability, listening, being non-judgemental;
- a true commitment to treating diversity with equality, and this reflected in social work's process, practice, theory, learning and knowledge development;
- advancing an inclusive and diverse knowledge base that gives equal value to service users' lived experience and experiential knowledge and challenges the conflicts between this and traditional medicalised and psychiatrised individualistic models and interpretations;
- drawing more on social models developed by service users, which value people in context rather than pathologising or victimising them;
- supporting user-led organisations and seeing them as an important home for social work;
- working for social work that is participatory in all its aspects and at every level, enabling effective user, family and worker participation (Beresford et al, 2011; Beresford, 2019b).

Together, these principles offer a basis for a sustainable, participatory social work committed to person-centred support and social justice, fit for the 21st century.

References

Alcock, P. (2008) *Social Policy in Britain* (3rd edn), Basingstoke: Palgrave/ Macmillan.

Bailey, R. and Brake, M. (1975) *Radical Social Work*, London: Hodder and Stoughton.

Beresford, P. (1999) 'Making participation possible: movements of disabled people and psychiatric system survivors', in T. Jordan and A. Lent (eds), *Storming the Millennium: The New Politics of Change*, London: Lawrence and Wishart, pp 34–50.

Beresford, P. (2002) 'User involvement in research and evaluation: liberation or regulation?', *Social Policy and Society*, vol 1, no 2, pp 93–103.

Beresford, P. (2019a) 'Public participation in health and social care: exploring the co-production of knowledge', *Frontiers in Sociology*, 4 January, https://www.frontiersin.org/articles/10.3389/fsoc.2018.00041/full.

Beresford, P. (2019b) 'Social work by and for all', in M. Lavalette (ed), *What is the Future of Social Work?*, Bristol: Policy Press, pp 83–97.

Beresford, P. and Campbell, P. (2004) 'Participation and protest: mental health service users/survivors', in M.J. Todd and G. Taylor (eds), *Democracy and Participation: Popular Protest and New Social Movements*, London: Merlin Press, pp 326–42.

Beresford, P. and Croft, S. (1987) 'Are we really listening? The Client Speaks, by John Meyer and Noel Timms', in T. Philpot (ed), *On Second Thoughts: Reassessments of the Literature of Social Work*, Surrey, Reed Business Publishing/Community Care, pp 50–55.

Beresford, P., Fleming, J., Glynn, M., Bewley, C., Croft, S., Branfield, F. and Postle, K. (2011) *Supporting People: Towards a Person-centred Approach*, Bristol: Policy Press.

Carr, S. (2019) '"I am not your nutter": a personal reflection on commodification and comradeship in service user and survivor research', *Disability & Society*, 17 May, https://www.tandfonline.com/doi/abs/10.1080/09687599.2019.1608424.

Hadley, R. (1981) *Going Local: Neighbourhood Social Services*, NCVO occasional paper, London: Bedford Square Press.

Harris, J. (2019) 'From Seebohm factories to neoliberal production lines? The social work labour process', in M. Lavalette (ed), *What is the Future of Social Work?*, Bristol: Policy Press, pp 123–42.

James, E., Mitchell, R., Morgan, H., Harvey, M. and Burgess, I. (2019) *Social Work, Cats and Rocket Science: Stories of Making a Difference in Social Work with Adults*, London: Jessica Kingsley Publishers.

Lavalette, M. (ed) (2019) *What is the Future of Social Work?*, Bristol: Policy Press.

Mayer, J.E. and Timms, N. (1970) *The Client Speaks: Working Class Impressions of Casework*, London: Routledge & Kegan Paul.

Means, R., Richards, S. and Smith, R. (2008) *Community Care: Policy and Practice*, Basingstoke: Palgrave Macmillan.

Oliver, M. (1983) *Social Work with Disabled People*, Practical Social Work Series, Basingstoke: BASW in association with Macmillan.

Pascall, G. (2012) 'Health and health policy', in J. Baldock, L. Mitton, N. Manning and S. Vickerstaff (eds), *Social Policy* (4th edn), Oxford: Oxford University Press, pp 260–84.

9

The 1989 England and Wales Children Act: the high-water mark of progressive reform?

Jane Tunstill and June Thoburn

Introduction

In the history of children's services a small number of Acts of Parliament can be identified as important exemplars of the dominant social and political eras within which they were framed. The 1834 Poor Law Amendment Act, the 1948 Children Act and the 1989 Children Act might all be seen as such signposts, as, more recently, can the 2017 Children and Social Work Act. In spite of the deficits that can be identified in the implementation of the 1989 Act, it stands in stark contrast to the patchwork of children's social services legislation across the preceding four decades and, indeed, since, with respect to broader child and family welfare provisions. It incorporates a clear vision for the delivery of child and family social work services, and of the nature of professional child and family social work. Thirty years on, although housing, health, education and social security Bills have come and gone, the 1989 Act remains barely changed. Moreover, it has consistently had an unusually high and very positive profile both in the child care policy literature and in the hearts and minds of social workers, past and present. Accounts of opposition to recent proposals to undermine it, as in the defeated 'exemption clauses' in the 2017 Children and Social Work Bill, describe it as 'carefully crafted' (Jones, 2019, p 55) and emphasise its evidence-informed design and implementation: 'the Act had an unusually empirical gestation period' (Tunstill and Willow, 2017, p 44). The Bill was, after all, first introduced in the House of Lords in the previous year by the Lord Chancellor as:

> the most comprehensive and far reaching reform of child care law which has come before Parliament in living

> memory. It brings together the public and private law concerning the care, protection and upbringing of children and the provision of services to them and their families. (*Hansard*, HL Deb, 6 December 1988, vol 502, col 488)

That is not to say that everything about its original design or likely implementation process was ever seen as entirely unproblematic. Its principles were in immediate conflict with the growing popularity among policy makers of a competitive-tendering/outsourcing approach to public service provision, a delivery model at complete variance with the collaborative approach and partnership principles (between agencies and with families) that were envisaged by the 1989 Act (DH, 1989, para 4.6; DH, 1991b; Stace and Tunstill, 1990; Tunnard and Ryan, 1991). This may in retrospect have been an epochal 'fork in the road' for the delivery of personal social services to adults and to children. The resource battles that followed implementation of the Act were accurately presaged in the Lords' debate, with Lord Mishcon, a robust supporter of the Bill, warning even then of the need for it to be adequately funded:

> I looked with fear and trembling at the commencement of the Bill ... where I read these words: 'the full annual cost of the Bill will be between £4m and £11m ... my plea to the Government is that of all measures being dealt with in the financial programme they should not stint on children ... (*Hansard*, HL Deb, 6 December 1988, vol 502, col 497)

Thirty years on, there is an increasingly anxious quality to much contemporary discussion. Delahunty (2019) asks whether the Act as a whole remains 'fit for purpose', and over the years other commentators have highlighted specific gaps between intention and execution. The Act's explicit commitment to both the promotion and protection of a child's welfare has been described as a possible 'bridge too far' (Tunstill et al, 2010). Featherstone et al (2014, p 78) even speculate that the Act's determination to generate a genuine *model of partnership working* between social workers and parents may have been a 'wolf in sheep's clothing'.

The wider social and economic context for child and family social services over the intervening 30 years has not, to put it too mildly, been a promising one. There are mixed views as to whether those sections of the 1989 Act and the values from which they emerged have proved resilient against the backdrop of a neoliberal policy trajectory that has introduced new managerialism, austerity and growing authoritarian and populist political values. This chapter considers whether the Act continues to influence contemporary child and family social work practice as its architects intended, or whether its aspirations for policy and practice have become little more than a footnote in the history of progressive child care policy. In other words, did 1989 mark a progressive high point after which, with respect to its intention to balance the rights of parents and children within the context of partnership-based services, the trajectory has been all downhill?

This chapter is divided into four sections. The first section outlines a brief social policy perspective on the 1989 Children Act, including its particular 'compact' with perennial tensions in child and family policy, and the values it explicitly incorporates. The next section provides a brief summary of its value base and the main intended implications for social work with children and families. This is followed by a section highlighting the political, social and economic *trends* that have dominated the period since the Act entered the statute book and have impacted on its influence: neoliberalism, austerity, new managerialism, aversion to risk. The final section explores 'progress' in respect of specific, quintessentially representative, aspects of the 1989 Act: (i) 'children in need', (ii) partnership working, (iii) the appropriate use of accommodation as a family support measure, and of court-mandated care only when necessary.

The 1989 Act in context: prior issues and debates

Specific initiatives towards children and families, whether at the legislative level or the policy/professional practice level can be fully understood only within a wider framework of social and political theory (Parker, 2010; Cummins, 2018). A transparent theoretical framework can help to enhance understanding of the rationale, design, delivery and, to some extent, outcomes of individual legislative interventions in respect of children and families. McGowan and Meezan (1983) identify a number of perennial tensions that, they argue, can be traced consistently through the history of child care policy, such as tension between parents' rights versus children's needs and child saving versus family support. These debates can be seen to have been resolved in different configurations across the chronology of UK child care policy. For example, the broad trend towards meeting family needs for assistance from state services, as seen in the 1948 Children Act and section 1 of the 1963 Children and Young Persons Act, was halted (or at least paused) through a focus on children's need for 'permanence' over other concerns in the design of the 1975

Children Act. The 1989 Act represents a clear exemplar of an explicit effort to resolve tensions between 'parents' rights and children's needs', between 'child saving and family support' and, crucially, to rebalance the relationship between community-based services for family support, for child protection and for the provision of out-of-home care. Fox Harding's (1991) UK-specific historical analysis of previous phases locates the 1989 Act within the post-Second World War 'modern defence of the birth family' paradigm – coming after the laissez-faire of the 19th century, the 'state paternalism' of the early welfare state period and before the more recent emphasis on children's rights.

In the UK context there is a particular difficulty involved in delineating and or evaluating legislation such as the 1989 Act – a complication for the aims of this chapter of course – because of the absence in the UK of an explicit 'children' policy, in spite of the appointment in 2005 of a Children's Commissioner. In reality *children policy* constitutes a subset of national welfare policies: children's lives are influenced from the very beginning by policies, resources and attitudes far beyond their immediate network, and over which they have no control (Hill and Tisdall, 1997). Such influences include parental income, access to child benefit, ante-natal care, the quality of housing, availability of early years services, the quality of education, health services, leisure and youth services. All of these *could*, and arguably *should*, form the content of a policy for children. Although it is a signatory to the UN Convention on the Rights of the Child and is required to make periodic submissions on which the Commissioners base their report (UNCRC, 2016), England has still not incorporated the Convention into domestic law (although Scotland has).

In summary, the UK had and, we argue, still has an uneasy mix of universal services such as education and health services, alongside a group of other services that, while explicitly deploying the term 'children' as in the 1989 Act, are in fact highly selective. They really impact on only a relatively small group of children – those assessed as 'in need' of additional services or with respect to whom social workers or the police seek a court order.

The 1989 Act was a brave attempt to improve on this, and to some extent succeeded in broadening out the remit to include court processes for separating and divorcing parents. Other 'broadening' changes required local authorities to be accountable for support and community-based child care services (including greater clarity about day care services), and for services for disabled children (including respite care), which were previously rather randomly scattered between social services, health and schools.

However, one area of disagreement during the planning stages of the Bill resulted in young offenders being removed from the remit of the family courts and child welfare services and the setting up of separate Youth Courts. This led to the loss of the innovative practice that had been developed by 'Intermediate treatment' teams and a loss of expertise in working with teenagers, which may be still apparent in the rising numbers of teenagers entering care.

The value base and key components of the Act

The evolution of the Act has been documented extensively, not least by its three key architects, Brenda Hale (2014), Rupert Hughes and Wendy Rose (Hughes and Rose, 2010). Their respective roles were of considerable significance to the Act's generation as well as to understanding its subsequent significance in social policy terms. Indeed the consultative strategy with stakeholders that was adopted by government in reviewing the proposed Bill before it even reached Parliament and became an Act reflects a broad set of inclusive values. These can be seen as anticipating the principles that underpinned the Act at an operational level. They were documented in additional detail in the Introduction to the Act (DH, 1989) and further spelled out by guidance documents, especially Volume 2 on *Family Support* (DH, 1991a) and Volume 3 on *Care Placements* (DH, 1991b), and by Jane Rowe as convenor of a DH working group (*Principles and Practice in Regulations and Guidance*: DH, 1990). The overarching principles are:

- the interests of the child are paramount;
- primary responsibility for the upbringing of children rests with parents;
- service providers should seek to work in partnership with parents.

Of the 26 principles described in respect of individual children, young people and their families, the following seven were central to overall policy.

- Children and young people and their parents should all be considered as individuals with particular needs and potentialities.
- Although some basic needs are universal, there can be a variety of ways of meeting them.
- Children are entitled to protection from neglect, abuse and exploitation.

- A child's age, sex, health, personality, race, culture and life experiences are all relevant to any consideration of needs and vulnerability and have to be taken into account when planning or providing help.
- There are unique advantages for children in experiencing normal family life in their own birth family and every effort should be made to preserve the child's home and family links.
- Time is a crucial element in child care and should be reckoned in days and months rather than years.
- Young people's wishes must be elicited and taken seriously. (DH, 1990, pp 7–12)

Wider trends impacting on implementation

It is only possible fully to understand the success or otherwise of the 1989 Act if account is taken of four political, social and economic *trends* which have dominated the period since it entered the statute book: neoliberalism, austerity, new public management and risk-averse policy and practice.

The architects of the 1989 Act could hardly have foreseen that in 2019 we would have incontrovertible evidence in official statistics of children living in food poverty – 1,959,431 in 2019. It can be argued from this that the number of children not meeting the threshold for social intervention totalled 1,959,431 (Children's Commissioner, 2019). These figures can be interrogated in a range of ways: there is clear evidence that the level of need assumed by the estimates of the cost of implementing Part III of the Act has greatly increased, and that those estimates were even then inadequate. Even then, some of the broader duties, such as reaching out to inform families who may need services, and assessing and providing services to any child 'unlikely to achieve a reasonable standard of health or development' without the provision of additional services (the section 17(10)(a) group), were vulnerable to being low in the priority list.

There was a short-lived attempt by the Labour government to have a more comprehensive approach, following the publication of *Every Child Matters* (DfES, 2003). Attempts at this time to introduce multi-agency Children's Trusts had little success, in part because the splitting of local authority social services departments into adults' and children's departments moved services for vulnerable parents (including addictions and disability services) away from services for children. In theory, combining children's social services with education services should have led to a more comprehensive service for all children, but such aims were in part thwarted by reducing the powers and resources of local authorities through the local management of schools policy.

The progress of the Act as exemplified in key provisions

In the period leading up to and after implementation of the Act, the Department of Health (DH) commissioned a broad programme of independent research studies. It followed these up with research overviews disseminated in a total of nine *Messages from Research* publications, sent out in multiple copies to all local authorities. The best-known of these (*Child Protection, Messages from Research*, DH, 1995) summarised 21 research studies that spanned the years before and after the Act. It was particularly influential in pointing to the ways in which the principles in the Act might be achieved at policy and practice level. The 24 studies contributing to *The Children Act Now: Messages from Research* (DH, 2001), on the ten years following 1989, form the background to our consideration of how these principles of the 1989 Act have fared over time with respect to specific, quintessentially representative, aspects of the Act: (i) 'children in need', (ii) partnership working (iii) the appropriate use of accommodation as a family support measure and court-mandated care.

Children in need

In order to persuade parliamentary business managers to find a space for their complex legislation, the DH team had to keep the number of clauses as low as possible. Detailed provisions about the services required to implement Part III (family support) provisions are to be found in Schedule 2. Together with section 17(3) of the Act, it is made clear that services may be provided to any family member if to do so is of benefit to the child assessed as 'in need'. Sections in the Act refer to 'care or supervised activities' for all ages, and specifically to day care for young children. Schedule 2, para 9 provides a definition of the family centres which every local authority must provide, but with the caveat 'as they consider appropriate in relation to children within their area'.

Family centres have traditionally delivered family support services across levels of need, and so provide a good example of the many implementation challenges that have confronted children and family services. They are unique in their identity as a family support agency, by virtue of being specifically named in the Act and thereby providing a 'case study' for the way that seamless, cross-tier services are or are not delivered. A family centre is defined in Schedule 2, para 9 of the Act as 'a centre at which any child, parent, carer or person with parental responsibility may attend for occupational, social, cultural or recreational activities; for advice, guidance or counselling, or to be provided with accommodation while [he or she] is receiving advice, guidance or counselling'. Research has documented both the usefulness and the practicability of family centres working simultaneously as the source of universal as well as targeted services. While the statutory definition is clear, identifying an accurate operational description has proved more challenging. As documented in research (Ghate et al, 2000; Smith, 1996; Tunstill et al, 2007), family centre work anticipated government policy towards children and families for 20 or so years after implementation. Research highlights: a stress on preventive rather than merely reactive work; partnership working; multidisciplinary working; a robust acknowledgement of the rights of those who use services to shape them; and the value of collaboration between statutory and voluntary sector agencies. Indeed, the Audit Commission (1994) recommended that family centres should become a one-stop shop for families to access family support services. A study by Tunstill and colleagues (2007) of 520 family centres explored the viability of this service model. The years 1999–2006 covered by this report include the roll-out of Sure Start local programmes (one of the Labour government's attempts to broaden the remit of child and family welfare services referred to above). This began in 2000 on a targeted area basis (but, importantly, inclusive of all young children and parents living in 'deprived neighbourhoods' and avoiding the stigma of 'targeting' individual (referred) families), and evolved quickly into national universal provision of Sure Start children's centres (Tunstill et al, 2005). The family centre study (Tunstill et al, 2007) identified several key characteristics of the core identity of family centres, of which a crucial aspect was the ability to respond to the wishes and needs of all living in the area. Centres offered a varied and flexible range of services. They were family focused as well as undertaking community work, but also encompassed formal child protection services. However, at each of the three points in time when the centres were surveyed, important changes had taken place that can be seen to link to wider national shifts in policy and service delivery. These undermined, if they did not fatally weaken, the aspirations of the Act to use the well-regarded family centres to provide supportive as well as protective services along a seamless continuum. Although the increase in multi-agency working was in line with the Act's family support provisions, the majority of centres can now be accessed only through referrals where there are concerns about children's care. The overall impact of such changes was a marked increase in reactive/crisis work. Of course, the introduction of a new national centre-based programme (Sure Start) for children under four years old was always likely to have consequences for the identity and service activity of family centres working with different ages and levels of need.

One negative consequence of the Sure Start centres being set up as a universal service was that, at the outset, many had weak links with children's social care and a less than whole-hearted engagement with local social workers. Tunstill and Allnock (2007) indicated that staff in many Sure Start programmes focused almost exclusively on 'straightforward' families. Over time, most moved on to welcome families with more complex problems to the non-stigmatised services that these families themselves chose to use. Since 2010, however, in the context of the Tory government's austerity policies there has been a move to referral-based services which has aggravated yet further the stigma and deterrence for families where safeguarding needs have been present. Yet again the intentions of the 1989 Act to maximise access to family support services have been subverted. In the face of the severe cuts to children's services budgets, many Sure Start centres have been closed or turned into social work 'hubs', attended only by appointment and by families at the higher ends of vulnerability (in the language of section 17(10)(b) of the Act, if a child's health or development is likely to be significantly impaired without such a service; or section 47, where the child is 'in need of protection').

Partnership working

Central to the philosophy of the 1989 Act was the principle of working in partnership with parents and young people and the provision of services on a voluntary basis whenever this could be achieved and was without detriment to the child's safety and wellbeing (Thoburn et al, 1995).

In the period between 1989 and 1991 the DH implementation team commissioned the Family Rights Group (FRG) to develop and disseminate explanatory leaflets and a video for parents and their advocates to explain the changes in the Act and assist them in exercising their right to be involved in decisions about what services they might expect and about new court services. With DH support, FRG convened a group of parents, voluntary sector support workers, social workers and researchers to publish more detailed guidance on partnership working, including guidance on working with families of minority heritage (DH, 1991c). Training materials, including a video, were also commissioned by DH to assist social services teams in working with the partnership principles in cases of child protection (Social Work Development Unit, 1991).

This emphasis is exemplified by the space provided for the use of discretion as to whether coercion was needed, even when there was a *prima facie* case that parental fault was contributing to 'significant harm'. Together with the requirement to provide evidence to the court that a care or supervision order was necessary, this led to a drop in the use of formal child protection procedures and care proceedings. That this was the result of a combination of social worker discretion and agency policy is demonstrated by the considerable variation between authorities in the extent to which they used formal child protection systems and care applications (Brandon et al, 1999; DH, 2001; Dickens et al, 2005). The 'refocusing initiative' (Rose, 1994; Hughes, 1996) further encouraged some authorities to make use of this discretion and to build up their family support services as the major vehicle for the delivery of 'safeguarding' services. In other local authorities with apparently similar levels of need and disadvantage, a *de facto* split opened up (and continues) between 'in need' services and 'child protection' services. Despite the stricture in guidance (DH, 1989) that support services should not be restricted to 'protection cases', locally determined thresholds moved these authorities a long way in that direction. This resulted in the unnecessary labelling of families seeking help as 'abusers' in order to receive a service they were asking for, and in professionals seeking help for families feeling obliged to use a 'child protection' label. The Common Assessment Framework (DH, 2000) followed on from the 'refocusing initiative' as another attempt by government to avoid this unhelpful and unnecessarily costly process, but the risk-averse climate following the Baby P case (Jones, 2014) has again resulted in heavy use of the formal child protection and court systems and a reduction of resources for support to families seeking help at an earlier stage of problem formation. The Troubled Families programme has had doubly negative consequences (Thoburn, 2013). It was welcomed by hard-pressed Directors of Children's Services as an additional source of funding, but risked fragmenting services to children in need by routing the funding through the Department for Communities and Local Government and not, as with most child and family social services funding, through the Department for Children. Schools and Families. More importantly, the need to label families as 'troubled' militated against the broadly inclusive aspects of the service.

The data on the ever-rising number of referrals responded to through the formal child protection route and the increasing number of care order applications demonstrates that these attempts failed (Bywaters, 2015). In the light of increased numbers of families living in circumstances of deprivation and acute housing stress, alongside the risk-averse social work climate, this is unsurprising.

The new vocabulary of 'looking after children'

Similar differences between authorities opened up with respect to the Act's intention that placement away from the parental home should, wherever possible, be part of the family support service. The new vocabulary of 'looked after' was another attempt to emphasise the partnership-based principles in the Act. In discussions around the terminology to be used it was argued by some that 'in care' had taken on a stigmatising meaning, and that if services for disabled children were to be included a different terminology was needed. In future all children in public out-of-home care were to be 'looked after', but only those entering care following a court order were to be known as 'in care'. Those looked after by voluntary arrangements (section 20) were to be referred to as 'accommodated', and the rights of parents and young people were strengthened.

The intention is clear in DH (1990) guidance. 'A wide variety of services, including short-term out of home placement, may need to be employed in order to sustain some families through particularly difficult periods. [...] If out-of-home placement is necessary, the least coercive legal status consistent with meeting the child's needs (including no order at all) should be the first choice' (p 8).

Looking first at planned periods of short-term accommodation, 'respite care' (provided under the section 20 short-term accommodation regulations) was intended to be available for the children of families coping with a range of stresses. These included families who had temporary stresses that might contribute to the risk of abuse or neglect, as well as children with disabilities. In the early stages, such schemes were developed and positively evaluated. Aldgate and Bradley (1999) reported on outcomes of four short-term schemes and found that parents and children had benefited in different ways. This early progress for non-disabled children has not been built upon. As reported by Greenfield and Statham (2004), short-break services for non-disabled children were not well developed in most local authorities.

Turning to more complex cases, the research by Packman and Hall (1998) and Brandon and colleagues (1999) demonstrated that in the early days of the Act some local authorities took the opportunity to move away from a 'keep them out of care at all costs' 'gate-keeping' approach and made greater use of section 20 accommodation for some children for whom there were child protection issues. The appropriate use of accommodation and care proceedings in 'significant harm' cases was carefully explored in the post-implementation research overview (DH, 2001).

After the initial drop, numbers in care rose, despite a commonly held view (especially among politicians) that those entering care did not do well. The research had shown up problems, especially around poor educational achievement and lack of stability in placement. A concerted effort was made in the 2000s, following the government's Care Matters initiative, to improve the service, resulting in improvements in stability, especially for younger children. However, the negative view of care persisted among the judiciary, as well as among politicians, and contributed to a policy to increase the numbers being placed for adoption from care. Most recently, numbers adopted from care have gone down as judges began to insist on the Act's 'no order' principle, with all alternatives being carefully balanced before it could be concluded that 'nothing else (other than adoption) will do' to secure the child's welfare. The drop in numbers leaving care via adoption has been more than balanced by those leaving care via Special Guardianship Orders – a welcome addition to children legislation to provide more security for those living with relatives.

Big differences are still apparent between local authorities in the extent to which they see out-of-home care as something to be avoided or, in appropriate cases, as part of the family support service. This is reflected in the differences between similar local authorities in the proportions starting to be looked after under section 20 accommodation provisions or following care proceedings (National Statistics and DfE, 2018).

Concerns about whether there is an appropriate balance between supporting children in their own homes, the use of the child protection system and court-ordered care or adoption have led to three voluntary sector-led inquiries involving family members and professionals. FRG coordinated a review of the way in which section 20 is being used, resulting in guidance on its appropriate (and inappropriate) use in different circumstances (FRG, 2018a). *The Care Inquiry* (Fostering Network, 2013) noted recent improvements in outcomes and emphasised the importance of continuity of relationships in placement, with birth families and with social workers. FRG (2018b) set in train a Care Crisis Review that pointed up the need for services to families and communities to be properly resourced if this trend is to be halted.

Conclusions

Our review of the implementation of the 1989 Children Act underlines how successive government policies have failed to consolidate the progressive framework it established. Rather, governments across the political spectrum have pursued a fragmented style of policy making, in many cases introducing 'new' provisions that have intentionally or unintentionally undermined the 'building blocks' laid down in the 1989 Act. In their desire to introduce yet another reorganisation or 'commissioning' paper or 'innovation' (the 'new broom' approach; Action for Children, 2008), each new administration has tended to ignore the existing knowledge base. For example, the overviews of the Children Act implementation (DH, 2001) and the Supporting Parents research (Quinton, 2004) had modest launches and minimal recognition in or impact on New Labour child welfare policy and planning. The overall picture of the implementation of the 1989 Act, in terms of safeguarding and promoting the welfare of children in need through supporting their families, is a gloomy one. However, some local authorities have succeeded in staying close to the original intentions of the Act (and the UN Convention on the Rights of the Child) to balance promoting and protection duties, demonstrating that this can be achieved without major change to the legislation. There have been some (mainly helpful) legislative changes following the publication of *Every Child Matters* and the 2004 Children Act, which strengthened the duty of all agencies to cooperate in the provision of services for children with additional needs. Attempts by government to use the 2017 Adoption and Children Act to remove certain sections of and weaken rights conferred by the 1989 Act were defeated (Tunstill and Willow, 2017).

There is much to be gained by paying close attention to the strategies employed by those local authorities that have succeeded in maintaining high-quality services for those children who need to be looked after, while increasing resources devoted to family support work. Essential to any major improvement is recognition at all levels that the increasingly high thresholds operating as barriers to families in accessing services result in greater harm to increasing numbers of children. The failure to fully implement Part III of the Act provides an example of the vulnerability of progressive, family-oriented policies to restricted funding for 'non-acute' services. It unfortunately strikes a major blow to the implementation of this very impressive piece of legislation, which uniquely addresses the dual task of both promoting *and* safeguarding the welfare of children. The 1989 Act remains on the statute books: it must be hoped that its time has yet to come to influence for the better policy and practice for all children.

References

Action for Children (2008) *As Long as it Takes: A New Politics for Children*, London: Action for Children.

Aldgate, J. and Bradley, M. (1999) *Supporting Families Through Short Term Accommodation*, London: The Stationery Office.

Audit Commission (1994) *Seen but Not Heard: Co-ordinating Community Child Health and Social Services for Children in Need*, London: HMSO.

Brandon, M., Lewis, A., Thoburn, J. and Way, A. (1999) *Safeguarding Children with the Children Act 1989*, London: The Stationery Office.

Bywaters, P. (2015) 'Inequalities in child welfare: towards a new policy, research and action agenda', *British Journal of Social Work*, vol 45, no 1, pp 6–23.

Children's Commissioner (2019) *Children's Vulnerability in Numbers*, https://www.childrenscommissioner.gov.uk/vulnerability-in-numbers/.

Cummins, I. (2018) *Poverty, Inequality and Social Work: The Impact of Neoliberalism and Austerity Politics on Welfare Provision*, Bristol: Policy Press.

Delahunty, J. (2019) 'The 30th anniversary of the Children Act 1989: is it still fit for purpose?', lecture given at Gresham College, London, 31 January, https://www.gresham.ac.uk/lectures-and-events/30-anniversary-children-act-1989.

DfES (Department for Education and Skills) (2003) *Every Child Matters*, Cm 5860, London: TSO.

DH (1989) *Introduction to the Children Act 1989*, London: HMSO.

DH (1990) *Principles and Practice in Regulations and Guidance*, London: HMSO.

DH (1991a) *The Children Act 1989 Guidance and Regulations Volume 2*, London: HMSO.

DH (1991b) *The Children Act 1989 Guidance and Regulations Volume 3*, London: HMSO.

DH (1991c) *The Challenge of Partnership in Child Protection*, London: HMSO.

DH (1995) *Child Protection: Messages from Research*, London: HMSO.

DH (2000) *Assessing Children in Need and their Families*, London: TSO.

DH (2001) *The Children Act Now: Messages from Research*, London: The Stationery Office.

Dickens, J., Howell, D., Thoburn, J. and Schofield, G. (2005) 'Children starting to be looked after by local authorities in England: an analysis of inter-authority variation and case-centred decision-making', *British Journal of Social Work*, vol 37, pp 597–617.

FRG (Family Rights Group) (2018a) *Children Looked After by Children's Services under a Voluntary Arrangement*, London: FRG.

FRG (2018b) *Care Crisis Review: Options for Change*, London: FRG.

Featherstone, B., White, S. and Morris, K. (2014) *Reimagining Child Protection*, Bristol: Policy Press.

Fostering Network (2013) *The Care Inquiry*, London: Fostering Network, https://www.thefosteringnetwork.org.uk/sites/www.fostering.net/files/resources/england/understanding-permanence-for-lac-janet-boddy.pdf.

Fox Harding, L. (1991) *Perspectives in Child Care Policy*, London: Longman.

Ghate, D., Shaw, C. and Neal, H. (2000) *Fathers and Family Centres: Engaging Fathers in Preventative Services*, York: Joseph Rowntree Foundation.

Greenfield, M. and Statham, J. (2004) *Support Foster Care*, London: University of London, Institute of Education.

Hale, Dame Brenda (2014) 'In defence of the Children Act', *Archives of Disease in Childhood*, vol 83, no 6, p 463.

Hansard (1988) House of Lords Debate: The Children Bill, 6 December, vol 502, cols 488 and 497.

Hill, M. and Tisdall, K. (1997) *Children and Society*, London: Longman.

Hughes, R. (1996) 'The Department of Health Studies in Child Protection – a response to Professor Parton', *Child and Family Social Work*, vol 1, no 2, pp 115–18.

Hughes, R. and Rose, W. (2010) 'Coming of age: has the Children Act 1989 lived up to its promise?', *Journal of Children's Services*, vol 5, no 2, pp 2–7.

Jones, R. (2014) *The Story of Baby P*, Bristol: Policy Press.

Jones, R. (2019) *In Whose Interest? The Privatisation of Child Protection and Social Work*, Bristol: Policy Press.

McGowan, B. and Meezan, W. (1983) *Welfare: Current Dilemmas, Future Directions*, New York: F.E. Peacock.

National Statistics and DfE (Department for Education) (2018) *Children Looked After in England including Adoption*, London: DfE.

Packman, J. and Hall, C. (1998) *From Care to Accommodation: Support, Protection and Care in Child Care Services*, London: The Stationery Office.

Parker, R. (2010) 'Change and continuity 1980–2010', *Adoption and Fostering*, vol 34, no 3, pp 4–12.

Quinton, D. (2004) *Supporting Parents: Messages from Research*, London: DfES.

Rose, W. (1994) 'An overview of the development of services – the relationship between protection and family support and the intentions of the Children Act 1989', paper for Seiff Conference, London: Department of Health.

Smith, T. (1996) *Family Centres and Bringing up Young Children*, London: HMSO.

Social Work Development Unit (1991) *Participation in Practice*, Norwich: University of East Anglia.

Stace, S. and Tunstill, J. (1990) *On Different Tracks: The Inconsistencies between the Children Act 1989 and the Community Care Act 1990*, London: FSU.

Thoburn, J. (2013) '"Troubled families", "troublesome families" and the trouble with payment-by-results', *Families, Relationships and Societies*, vol 2, no 3, pp 471–5.

Thoburn, J., Lewis, A. and Shemmings, D. (1995) *Paternalism or Partnership? Family Involvement in the Child Protection Process*, London: HMSO.

Tunnard, J. and Ryan, M. (1991) 'What does the Children Act mean for family members?', *Children and Society*, vol 5, no 1, pp 67–75.

Tunstill, J. and Allnock, D. (2007) *Understanding the Contribution of Sure Start Local Programmes to the Task of Safeguarding Children's Welfare*, London: DfE.

Tunstill, J., Aldgate, J. and Hughes, M. (2007) *Improving Children's Services Networks: Lessons from Family Centres*, London: Jessica Kingsley Publishers.

Tunstill, J. and Willow, C. (2018) 'Professional social work and the defence of children's and their families' rights in a period of austerity', *Social Work and Social Sciences Review*, vol 19, no 1, pp 40–65.

Tunstill, J., Allnock, D., Akhurst, S., Garbers, C. and the NESS Research Team (2005) 'Sure Start local programmes; implications of case study data from the National Evaluation of Sure Start', *Children and Society*, vol 19, pp 1–14.

Tunstill, J., Aldgate, J. and Thoburn, J. (2010) 'Promoting and safeguarding the welfare of children: a bridge too far?', *Journal of Children's Services*, vol 5, no 3, pp 14-25.

UNCRC (UN Committee on the Rights of the Child) (2016) *Concluding Observations on the Fifth Periodic Report of the United Kingdom of Great Britain and Northern Ireland*, Geneva: CRC.

10

Social work with offenders

Terry Bamford

I spent eight years in the probation service when the traditional duty to 'advise, assist and befriend' still applied. The words, taken from the 1907 Probation of Offenders Act, described the approach of probation for most of the 20th century. The Morison Committee (Morison, 1962) had reaffirmed the probation role as one of treatment, rehabilitation and reformation. Latterly, public protection, risk assessment and offender management have become the words used by government and the leaders of the service. This chapter traces that change and examines the place of social work in the modern service.

Although in a 1970 ballot the National Association of Probation Officers (NAPO) rejected the idea of joining the British Association of Social Workers (BASW), social work training remained the recognised route into the service until 1997, when specific training for probation was introduced by the Home Office. Yet social work methods are still used by many probation practitioners who have not wholly accepted the new culture.

Advise, assist and befriend

The service discharged its role through supervision and one-to-one contact with the offender. The nature of supervision was based on insights derived from psychology and psychiatry. In hindsight, it was naive to expect that weekly or less-frequent visits to the probation office for reporting sessions were likely in themselves to lead to rehabilitation.

The introduction of community service changed the focus of probation. The service became responsible for a range of non-custodial sentences, including day training centres, bail hostels and supervised suspended sentences. This greatly expanded the responsibilities of the service and widened the range of staff employed. While those on probation were supervised in the usual way, the responsibility for community sentences meant that social work skills were not the only approach in use.

The core role of the probation officer, the relationship with the offender, came under scrutiny after the IMPACT experiment (Intensive Matched Probation and After Care Treatment) (Folkard et al, 1976). This looked at the effectiveness of intensive supervision by officers with limited caseloads, and tested the long-standing claims of the service that more could be achieved if workloads were reduced. The results were disappointing, showing no significant differences between those subject to intensive supervision and those in the control group. Scepticism about the effectiveness of probation intervention was reinforced by Martinson's analysis of treatment programmes in the US, with its gloomy conclusion that Nothing Works (Martinson, 1974).

In the self-questioning that followed the IMPACT research, the traditional view of the service was challenged by those who argued that containment should be the 'unambiguous objective of supervision' (Griffiths, 1982). Mark Drakeford, then a humble probation officer and now the First Minister of Wales, argued that the core values still had merit (Drakeford, 1983). However, at a time of rising public and political concern about crime the tide was running towards a changed role for the service in the criminal justice system.

At this time management in the service was increasingly critical of the Central Council for Education and Training in Social Work (CCETSW), which was responsible for the training of probation officers. They argued that the generic social work training gave too little attention to the specific requirements of the role and that newly qualified workers were ill prepared for their full responsibilities. It is worth noting that similar complaints about social work training were made by the Association of Directors of Social Services (ADSS). Both critiques undervalued the importance of the probation period – a year for probation officers, six months for social workers – in equipping newly qualified staff for the full range of the role.

Law and order

The first explicit shift in the expectations of probation came in the Statement of National Objectives and Priorities in 1984. This set out national guidance for the probation service and saw its role as prioritising work with offenders at risk of imprisonment. These offenders were the ones regarded as presenting the greatest risk to the public, and the concept of risk was to become a dominant theme over the remainder of the 20th century. In future the rehabilitation model that had been the basis of probation practice had to sit alongside the move to surveillance and offender management.

The probation service was run by local committees composed of magistrates, and each local probation committee was encouraged to produce its own statement of objectives and priorities. The National Audit Office reported in 1989 that

> A few local probation services fundamentally disagree with the priorities expressed in the National Statement; and despite the intention of greater selectivity many areas were unwilling to designate any of their activities as lower priority, especially voluntary aftercare. Concern was also expressed that the statement took no account of recent developments in the probation service, such as bail information schemes and crime prevention initiatives. (NAO, 1989)

Divergence at local level was not welcome to the Home Office, which favoured greater alignment at national level, and the shift in opinion about the criminal justice system was reflected in the Home Office's redefinition of probation as 'punishment in the community' (Home Office, 1988). The Green Paper (*Punishment, Custody and the Community*) made it clear that community-based punishments were restrictions on liberty that enabled offenders to face up to the consequences of their crimes. Although the proportion of community sentences continued to rise, so too did the use of custody, while there was a marked decrease in the use of fines. The possibility of a national probation service was floated in another Green Paper, *Supervision and Punishment in the Community: A Framework for Action* (Home Office, 1990), with an emphasis on accountability and performance.

Seeing the successful results of the Intermediate Treatment programmes for juvenile offenders, the Home Office moved to apply a similar approach to adults in the 1991 Criminal Justice Act. NAPO bitterly opposed the proposals, seeing them as a change in focus and turning probation into a correctional service. In a scathing comment the civil servant responsible for probation attacked the service for 'its whingeing, doom-mongering, self-destructiveness, self-righteousness, arrogance and inwardness, with a belief that it was the only service with ethical standards' (Drew, 1992).

The 1991 Act introduced national standards for court reports and community sentences, and reiterated the intention that imprisonment should be limited to serious offenders, with supervision by probation officers being seen as a non-custodial punishment echoing the language of the 1988 Green Paper. The Act added new requirements for drug and alcohol treatment that could be added to a probation or combination order (up to 100 hours of community service and up to three years of probation supervision). The national standards extended to prescribing the frequency of contact between the probation officer and the probationer as 'in the first three months of an order there should be a minimum of 12 meetings (normally weekly) between offender and probation officer, followed by at least 6 appointments in the second three months, and at least one appointment a month thereafter'. How far these standards were followed varied from area to area, dependent on workload pressures.

Prison works

The neoliberal approach of the government encouraged greater individual responsibility and was less tolerant of indiscipline. Social attitudes were shifting, and there was extensive press coverage of youth crime, presenting a picture of feral young people. The highly publicised murder of two-year-old Jamie Bulger by two young boys in 1993 intensified the pressure for firm action. This led to the tightening of sentencing policy, notably through the 1994 Criminal Justice and Public Order Act, which increased the range of offences referred to the Crown Court and doubled the length of the detention period available. Youth courts were empowered to use new custodial sentences for 12- to 14-year-old persistent offenders, and in the Bulger case the Home Secretary responded to calls in the tabloid press by increasing the minimum sentence for the killers from the eight years ordered by the judge to 15 years.

The Home Secretary, Michael Howard, moved away from the previous consensus that too many people were sent to prison and that the emphasis should be on strengthening community sentences. He told the 1993 Conservative Party conference that 'prison works'. A much harder line on crime brought immediate results in the form of a 50% increase in the numbers in prison between 1992 and 1997. The earlier emphasis on keeping people out of prison was abandoned, and punishment and retribution were securely established as the primary response to crime.

The decision by Michael Howard in 1995 to change the pattern of training by establishing specific training for probation rather than a social work qualification, which had been the established route for 25 years, was part of a populist reaction against 'soft' social work approaches. The result was that 'the combined effect of political populism, prescriptive managerialism and the end of the benign world of political consensus which probation had inhabited throughout its history was to make probation a criminal justice service rather than a social work agency' (Raynor and Vanstone, 2016).

The national training scheme for probation officers was scrapped, the probation budget was cut and, with the proposals in the 1995 Green Paper *Strengthening Punishment in the Community* (HMSO, 1995), the very future of the service as an independent agency within the criminal justice system was at risk.

Modernisation

The 1997 general election saw an incoming Labour government committed to being 'tough on crime and tough on the causes of crime'. Its election slogan 'things can only get better' was welcomed in the probation service after the emphasis of its predecessor on custody and containment. The modernisation agenda wanted to drive efficiency and effectiveness, and probation embraced the What Works initiative with enthusiasm at managerial level. Measures that had proved effective with certain groups of offenders were replicated, often using cognitive behavioural techniques. The national prescription of methodology was echoed in the effective nationalisation of the service, with a national director and local operational areas coterminous with police authorities. Localism was represented by a probation board, but this had limited authority over the national service.

The National Probation Service formally came into being in 2001, but within a year of its inception the government appointed Lord Carter to review correctional services. His radical recommendation was the establishment of a National Offender Management Service (NOMS) providing 'end to end' management of offenders by bringing prisons and probation together in a single service (Carter, 2003). His recommendations were swiftly accepted, and by 2004 the National Probation Service came to an end. It became part of NOMS, with a national director and ten regional offender managers – nine of whom were drawn from the prison service.

The Carter Report's concept of 'end to end' management envisaged an integrated process from admission to prison through to discharge support. Unfortunately, the overcrowded prison system did not readily lend itself to integration and continuity of care, as offenders were placed many miles from their home and sustained contact with family and friends was difficult.

Carter also favoured what he termed 'contestability' – commercial competition that would allow public sector, private and voluntary agencies to bid against existing providers. The tenor of the New Labour government is captured in the title of a Home Office consultative paper *Rebalancing the Criminal Justice System in favour of the Law-abiding Majority* (Home Office, 2006). The Prime Minister, Tony Blair, invoked populist language to attack the failures of criminal justice – a recurrent theme of successive governments. This was despite a fall in the numbers of reported crimes and a sharp decline in the likelihood of being a victim of crime. The government was determined not to be outflanked on law and order issues.

The advent of the Coalition government

In 2010 the incoming Coalition government launched a Green Paper (Ministry of Justice, 2010a) that was described as an *Evidence Report*, although remarkably thin on evidence. This introduced the concept of desistance – how and why offenders stop offending. It encouraged prevention, early intervention, diversion and resettlement initiatives, and floated the idea of payment by results in criminal justice, with rehabilitation programmes run by independent providers potentially on a for-profit basis.

Another Green Paper, *Breaking the Cycle: Effective Punishment, Rehabilitation and Sentencing of Offenders* (Ministry of Justice, 2010b), asserted that 'the fundamental failing of policy has been the lack of a firm focus on reform and rehabilitation'. It welcomed the payment-by-results approach that was being trialled in Peterborough prison and announced at least six new rehabilitation programmes, to be delivered on a payment-by-results basis. This was described somewhat grandiloquently as a rehabilitation revolution.

The untested model using private providers was rapidly developed, with pilots in prisons and in two probation areas. It was attractive to government in its involvement of the private and voluntary sectors and the clear market mechanism whereby the efficacy of the model could be tested. This represented a 'shift of focus from processes to outcomes, intended to drive innovation and creativity by enabling providers to explore new ways of reducing reoffending, free from process-based targets prescribed by central government' (Collins, 2011).

At the same time the future structure of probation was again called into question. A consultation document (Ministry of Justice, 2012) proposed strengthening the punitive element of community sentences, and a clear division between the commissioners and providers of services. It suggested opening to the market the management of lower-risk offenders, with much greater involvement of voluntary and private providers.

A very different approach was taken in Scotland. 'In comparison with the market-based approach in England and Wales, the Scottish government is placing state and public bodies at the heart of the planning and delivery of community supervision. This is very much in keeping with the Scottish government's current commitment to placing the state, not the market, at the heart of public service planning and delivery' (Garside, 2015).

The contrast between England and Scotland was rendered more acute by the decision to proceed in advance of results from the pilots. Under its strategy of *Transforming Rehabilitation* (Ministry of Justice, 2013) the government aimed to extend statutory rehabilitation to offenders serving custodial sentences of less than 12 months by:

- introducing nationwide 'Through the Gate' resettlement services for those leaving prison;
- opening up the market to new rehabilitation providers to get the best out of the public, voluntary and private sectors;
- introducing new payment incentives for market providers to focus relentlessly on reforming offenders;
- splitting the delivery of probation services between the National Probation Service (offenders at high risk of harm) and Community Rehabilitation Companies (low and medium-risk offenders); and
- reducing reoffending.

Supervision was extended to the extra 45,000 prisoners in England and Wales released from short-term prison sentences of less than 12 months who were not routinely provided with post-sentence support and supervision. It was expected that opening up the market of rehabilitation providers to partners from the private, voluntary and social sectors would not only introduce private sector investment into this extension of supervision but would also enable more flexible and innovative forms of service delivery. The majority of offenders would be dealt with by providers contracted on a payment-by-results basis. A new public sector probation service would be established with the focus on public protection. The service would carry out risk assessments of all offenders and be responsible for the direct management of those offenders who posed the highest risk of serious harm to the public and who had committed the most serious offences.

This ambitious programme meant that 35 Probation Trusts, the local link for probation, were dissolved. After a speedy bidding process, 21 Community Rehabilitation Companies (CRCs) were approved to manage offenders who posed a low or medium risk of harm. Of these,

20 were led by the private sector with 6 going to Sodexo and 5 to Interserve, both companies with a record of delivering outsourcing. The two major companies in the field – Capita and Serco – were barred from bidding because of evidence of previous failures in criminal justice.

There were numerous warnings of the risks of dividing the probation service in this way and, in particular, of the risks associated with a payment-by-results approach. The Institute of Government (Gash, 2013) warned that contracts should not 'be let all in one go in summer 2014'. This approach, staggering the letting of contracts, would both encourage new providers of probation services to get up to speed quickly so they could win future contracts and allow the Ministry of Justice (MoJ) to improve the contracting model after its first round. The report encouraged the MoJ to ensure that it contracted with different types of organisation. While private sector providers would probably win the bulk of contracts, the MoJ should ensure that some non-profit providers were involved. This would allow government to test whether a profit motivation had a positive impact on performance or simply created an additional cost for government. Matthew Taylor (Taylor, 2013) warned that the de facto exclusion of voluntary sector providers heightened the risk, as 'charities lacked the contract planning and negotiation capacity of the private sector'. The structure of the contracts, the exacting compliance regime and low margins made it a 'costly and unattractive option'.

The first signs that all was not going as planned came from a National Audit Office report (NAO, 2016). This was critical of the lack of performance data available and noted some tensions between the CRCs and the National Probation Service. By 2017 the tone had changed. The Annual Report of the Probation Inspectorate referred to deep-seated problems and noted that CRCs were struggling. In a scathing comment the Chief Inspector concluded:

> I question whether the current model for probation can deliver sufficiently well … in some CRCs, individuals meet with their probation worker in places that lack privacy, when sensitive and difficult conversations must take place. Some do not meet with their probation worker face-to face. Instead, they are supervised by telephone calls every six weeks or so from junior professional staff carrying 200 cases or more. (HM Inspectorate of Probation, 2017)

The report concluded that none of the aspirations for Transforming Rehabilitation had been met in any meaningful way.

The government attempted to shore up CRCs by changing the terms of the contracts and releasing providers from some of the onerous conditions. The much-trumpeted payment by results was dropped.

The Public Accounts Committee concluded in 2018 that '[i]n its haste to rush through its reforms at breakneck speed the Ministry of Justice not only failed to deliver its "rehabilitation revolution" but left probation services underfunded, fragile, and lacking the confidence of the courts. Inexcusably, probation services have been left in a worse position than they were in before the Ministry embarked on its reforms' (House of Commons Public Accounts Committee, 2018). It was backed in June 2018 by the Justice Committee (House of Commons Justice Committee, 2018), which concluded that 'we are unconvinced that the TR [Transforming Rehabilitation] model can ever deliver an effective or viable probation service'.

The pressure on the MoJ was reinforced by the Chief Inspector of Probation. In her Annual Report she said bluntly: 'The probation model delivered by Transforming Rehabilitation is irredeemably flawed. Above all, it has proved well-nigh impossible to reduce probation services to a set of contractual requirements. Professional probation work is so much more than simply a series of transactions, and when treated in that way it is distorted and diminished' (HM Inspectorate of Probation, 2019).

Faced with sustained criticism from the National Audit Office, the Probation Inspectorate, the Public Accounts Committee and the Justice Committee, the MoJ under new leadership changed its previous commitment to the split between the National Probation Service and the CRCs. It accepted that 'the split in responsibility for offender management on the basis of risk would not be retained under future probation arrangements. In future the National Probation Service will have responsibility for managing all offenders on a community order or on licence following release from prison' (House of Commons Justice Committee, 2019).

This was a remarkable volte-face, which was immediately represented as the renationalisation of the probation service. It was certainly a victory for NAPO and those who had consistently warned against the haste with which the changes were introduced. But the most profound challenge to the approach taken by the MoJ came from the Chief Inspector's warning against reducing probation to a series of contractual requirements. It remains to be seen whether those lessons have been learned and the new model for rehabilitation activities will offer greater flexibility.

The Through the Gate plans to offer consistent support to offenders had also failed to deliver. A joint inspection found that if Through the Gate services 'were removed tomorrow … the impact on the resettlement of prisoners would be negligible' (Criminal Justice Joint Inspection, 2017).

Why did the plans go so wrong, so swiftly? First, an evangelically enthusiastic minister did not wait for the results of the pilots before a national roll-out of the plans. Second, the MoJ set up the contracts in a way that discouraged a voluntary sector that was unable to match the scale of parent-company guarantees demanded. Third, the paucity of bidders, once Capita and Serco had withdrawn, meant that the MoJ cheerfully accepted the projections of the bidders even where they were over-optimistic. Fourth, there were serious IT problems throughout the duration of the CRC contracts that also affected the National Probation Service. Fifth, and probably most important, the financial viability of CRC providers was undermined by a lower volume of work than predicted by the MoJ when letting the contracts – a reduction of up to one third for some companies.

The consistent failure of criminal justice to prevent reoffending was a theme of Green and White Papers throughout the decade. There are significant variations in reoffending rates across the UK. Northern Ireland has the lowest, at 18% within 12 months of discharge, while England has 25% and Scotland has 28%. Northern Ireland also has the lowest rate of imprisonment in the UK. The difference is striking, and inevitably poses the question whether the reoffending rate is correlated to a high rate of imprisonment, with its consequent effect on prison standards. Without work in prisons on accommodation, family support, alcohol issues, employment and education the prospects for changing the pattern of reoffending are bleak.

Addressing reoffending is likely to be a major task facing the reconfigured National Probation Service, with its wide-ranging commissioning responsibilities. After the turmoil of the last 20 years, since 2000, with numerous changes in organisational structure, a period of stability for probation would be welcome. It is not likely to happen. Governments feel obliged to respond to public pressure both to create new offences and to toughen punishments. The dilemma was neatly exposed in *The Times* (Winsor, 2019), when the Home Secretary signalled life sentences that would mean life for child murderers, a tightening of the existing early release from prison conditions and increased minimum tariffs for some offences. On the same day the Chief Inspector of Constabulary said that 'very high proportions of people in prison are unwell, uneducated, undervalued, and justifiably angry. In childhood many have suffered domestic violence or abuse. Many more have severe and chronic mental ill health, intensified by years without diagnosis or treatment' (Winsor, 2019).

Young offenders

It is instructive to contrast the approach to adults with that for young offenders. The 1969 Children and Young Persons Act set the framework for juveniles. It was not popular with probation, as it placed most of the responsibility for young offenders with social services. While the tension between the rehabilitation ideal and the protection of the public was also evident in thinking about how to handle young offenders, the balance has more consistently been in favour of rehabilitation. The aim has been to limit custody to a last resort, with the emphasis being on treatment in the community. This was clear in funding priorities.

The DHSS, which was responsible for children's services, made substantial investment in Intermediate Treatment (IT). The initial thinking after the 1969 Children and Young Persons Act had been to focus these programmes on offenders, but in practice they were most used for children defined as at risk. The intention of IT was to divert young people from antisocial behaviour by means of programmes of activity. Courts could require juveniles to take part in activity programmes – both residential and non-residential – for a period of up to 90 days. With a few notable exceptions, activities copied the youth club model of hobbies, sports and outdoor pursuits.

Under the Intermediate Treatment Initiative 110 projects were funded by the DHSS to refocus IT on offenders. The results were dramatic. Custody figures in project areas fell from 6,135 in 1983 to 1,835 in 1989, and care orders for offending from 1,796 to 146 (NACRO, 1991).

The incoming New Labour government introduced the 1998 Crime and Disorder Act. This established 'a new youth justice system, replete with multi-agency teams in every local authority dedicated to working with "young offenders" and with central oversight for both community and custodial regimes provided by the Youth Justice Board (YJB). While youth justice services continued to be delivered through local structures these were significantly shaped by national policy and practice direction, the conditions of central government grants, and enhanced National Standards and inspection regimes' (Byrne and Brooks, 2015). The teams included social workers, youth workers, police officers and education staff. Multi-agency partnerships figured in a number of New

Labour's modernisation initiatives, with varying success. In a changing political and policy environment the Youth Offending Team (YOT) model has now been operational for over 20 years.

While YOTs had the ambition to be connected to other specialist and mainstream services for vulnerable young people, the model developed a discrete set of services for young people who had offended or were at risk of offending. Their structural separation marked their clientele apart from their peers (Gray, 2005, cited by Byrne and Brooks, 2015, p 4).

The Youth Justice Board introduced national standards in 2000, following the introduction of minimum standards for probation supervision. The Youth Crime Action Plan (Home Office, 2008) took a triple-track approach of enforcement and punishment where behaviour is unacceptable, non-negotiable support and challenge where it is most needed and better and earlier prevention. This emphasised early intervention in order to target universal services such as Sure Start at families that needed them most. It called for intensive support in schools through Safer Schools Partnerships and an expansion of Family Nurse Partnerships. These universal services were subsequently badly affected by the years of austerity, with many Sure Start centres and Family Nurse Partnerships being closed. While reoffending remains an issue for the Youth Justice Board, the numbers in custodial settings have been reduced to under 1,000.

What role for social work?

As the responsibilities of probation increased, the quality of the interaction between offender and supervisor came under examination. The development of national standards and key performance indicators measured what could be measured, but, as the National Audit Office commented 'Eighteen per cent of the Integrated Probation Performance Framework targets focus on completions of individual requirements and 20 per cent on timeliness, whereas only 11 per cent measure quality and these tend to focus on the quality of risk of serious harm assessments [...] There are no targets assessing the quality of engagement with offenders' (NAO, 2008).

Desistance – the diversion of offenders from reoffending – was a focus of research. In a major study (Shetland et al, 2012) the following themes were identified.

• Approaches to supervision must accommodate and exploit issues of identity and diversity. One-size-fits-all interventions will not work.

- The development and maintenance not just of motivation but also of hope become key tasks for probation officers.
- Desistance can be understood only within the context of human relationships; not just relationships between staff and offenders (although these matter a great deal) but also between offenders and those who matter to them.
- Although in England and Wales there is a tendency to focus on offenders' risk and needs, offenders also have strengths and resources that they can use to overcome obstacles to desistance – both personal strengths and resources, and strengths and resources in their social networks.
- Since desistance is about discovering agency, interventions need to encourage and respect self-determination; this means working with offenders, not on them.
- Interventions based only on human capital (or developing offenders' capacities and skills) will not be enough. Probation needs to work on social capital issues with communities and offenders.

The authors indicate the need to work on the accommodation, family support, alcohol, employment and education issues that link to offending histories.

It could be argued that this is the usual stock-in-trade of probation officers. It is essentially social work with the family, social environment and personal problems. The increased prescription of probation methodology may have militated against this holistic approach to the problems of the offender.

There are lessons for the service from youth justice, which stresses that 'establishing an identity which is not reliant upon offending requires young people to be able to acquire a steady and adequate income. Thus access to education, training and ultimately reliable employment should be central to any service which works with young people who are offending' (Prince's Trust, 2007).

Each reform, each new sentence, reflected the tension between the welfare approach and the justice approach. The former stressed the need to look at the whole of the background of the young person and to seek alternatives to custody. The latter was concerned to ensure that the youth justice process was more transparent, with sentences that reflected public concern, were seen as fair and contained elements of reparation. The youth justice approach described above enjoyed considerable success. The number of first-time entrants into the criminal justice system fell by 72% between December 2006 and December 2012 and has continued to fall. The rate of reoffending remains high. That, and the increase in knife crime and the increasing proportion of black and minority ethnic young people being drawn into the system, are major concerns for the Youth Justice Board.

Looking ahead

The change of government in 2010 did not lead to a dramatic shift in priorities, which remained the diversion of offenders from custody, the development of a wider range of community sentences and strengthening educational and family support for the minority who required custody. The language of rehabilitation is still used and figures prominently in Home Office and MoJ documents, but is used as a synonym for supervision. Rehabilitation in such documents is an expression of hope rather of than experience.

Throughout the criminal justice system we see shifts in the balance of the system between rehabilitation and reform with a commitment to community sentences, and the contrasting emphasis on punishment, 'just deserts' and reparation. But the division is not as clear cut as it seems. Even the proponents of tougher sentences accept the futility of short prison sentences. Even the advocates of rehabilitation accept that a minority of offenders will need detention possibly for a very long period. The probation service stands at the intersection and has to demonstrate its ability to tailor its methods to the background of the offender. Its range of interventions has broadened, although the reconfiguration of the National Probation Service will test its ability to commission effective services from third-party providers.

The current recruitment material for probation officers emphasises risk management as a central role: 'They use their expertise in risk assessment and management … they assess the risk the offender may pose to the public and their risk of reoffending … You will be assessing risk, implementing plans, and liaising with a range of partner agencies to protect the public' (HM Prisons and Probation Service, 2019). The absence of any mention of the importance of the personal relationship with the offender is striking. Without putting the relationship with the offender at its heart, and the values in social work of acceptance and starting where the client is, little will be achieved through surveillance, risk assessment and supervision alone.

The collapse of Transforming Rehabilitation offers an opportunity to rethink the role of probation in contemporary society. The service needs to reconnect with its social work heritage in order to deliver its full potential in rehabilitation.

References

Byrne, B. and Brooks, K. (2015) *Post-YOT Youth Justice*, Howard League What is Justice? Re-imagining Penal Policy Working Papers No 19/2015, London: The Howard League for Penal Reform.

Carter, P. (2003) *Managing Offenders, Reducing Crime: A New Approach*, London: Home Office Strategy Unit.

Collins, J. (2011) 'Payment by results in the criminal justice system', https://www.crimeandjustice.org.uk/sites/crimeandjustice.org.uk/files/09627251.2011.599617.pdf.

Criminal Justice Joint Inspection (2017) *An Inspection of Through the Gate Resettlement Services for Prisoners serving 12 Months or More*, Manchester: HM Inspectorate of Probation.

Drakeford, M. (1983) 'Probation: containment or liberty', *Probation Journal*, vol 30, no 1, pp 7–10.

Drew, P. (1992) 'The probation service: a few valedictory comments', *Probation Journal*, vol 39/2, pp 92–4.

Folkard, S., Lyon, K., Carver, M.M. and O'Leary, E. (1976) *IMPACT, vol 2, The Result of the Experiment*, Home Office Research Study 36, London: HMSO.

Garside, R. (2015) *Criminal Justice: What Happened since 2010 and Why*, Centre for Crime and Justice Studies: London.

Gash, T. (2013) 'Probation reform: doing it all', Institute of Government, 9 May, https://www.instituteforgovernment.org.uk/blog/probation-reform-doing-it-all.

Gray, P. (2005) 'Community interventions' in T. Bateman, and J. Pitts (eds) *RHP Companion to Youth Justice*, Lyme Regis: Russell House, pp 130–6.

Griffiths, W.A. (1982) 'Supervision in the community', *Justice of the Peace*, 22 August.

HM Inspectorate of Probation (2017) *Annual Report*, Manchester: HM Inspectorate.

HM Inspectorate of Probation (2019) *Annual Report*, Manchester: HM Inspectorate.

HM Prisons and Probation Service (2019). Available from: https://www.traintobeaprobationofficer.com/.

HMSO (1995) *Strengthening Punishment in the Community*, London: Her Majesty's Stationery Office. Available from: https://assets.publishing.service.gov.uk/government/uploads/system/uploads/attachment_data/file/272037/2780.pdf.

Home Office (1988) *Punishment, Custody and the Community*, London: Home Office.

Home Office (1990) *Supervision and Punishment in the Community: A framework for action*, London: Home Office.

Home Office (2006) *Rebalancing the Criminal Justice System in favour of the Law-abiding Majority*, London: Home Office.

Home Office (2008) *Youth Crime Action Plan*, London: Home Office.

House of Commons Justice Committee (2018) *Ninth Report of Session 2017–19*, London: House of Commons.

House of Commons Justice Committee (2019) *Government Response to Ninth Report*, London: House of Commons.

House of Commons Public Accounts Committee (2018) *Ninety-fourth Report of Session 2017–19, Transforming Rehabilitation: Progress Report*, London: House of Commons.

Martinson, R. (1974) 'What works in prison reform: questions and answers', *The Public Interest*, vol 35, pp 22–54.

Ministry of Justice (2010a) *Green Paper Evidence Report, Breaking the Cycle: Effective Punishment, Rehabilitation and Sentencing of Offenders*, London: the Stationery Office.

Ministry of Justice (2010b) *Breaking the Cycle: Effective Punishment, Rehabilitation and Sentencing of Offenders*, London: The Stationery Office.

Ministry of Justice (2012) *Punishment and Reform: Effective Probation Services*, London: Ministry of Justice.

Ministry of Justice (2013) *Transforming Rehabilitation: A Strategy for Reform*, London: The Stationery Office.

Morison, R. (1962) *Report of the Departmental Committee on the Probation Service*, Cmnd 1650, London: HMSO.

NACRO (1991) *Seizing the Initiative: NACRO's Final report on the DHSS Intermediate Treatment Initiative to Divert Juvenile Offenders from Care and Custody, 1983–89*, London: NACRO.

NAO (1989) *Home Office: Control and Management of Probation Services in England and Wales*, London: HMSO.

NAO (2008) *National Probation Service: The Supervision of Community Orders in England and Wales*, London: TSO.

NAO (2016) *Transforming Rehabilitation*, HC-951, London: House of Commons.

Prince's Trust (2007) *The Cost of Exclusion: Counting the Cost of Youth Disadvantage in the UK*, London: Prince's Trust.

Raynor, P. and Vanstone, M. (2016) 'Moving away from social work and half way back again: new research on skills in probation', *British Journal of Social Work*, vol 46, pp 1131–47.

Shetland, J., Bottoms, A., Farrall, S., McNeill, F., Priede, C., Robinson, R. (2012) 'The quality of probation supervision – a literature review', Sheffield: University of Sheffield Centre for Criminological Research.

Taylor, M. (2013) 'Probation-PBR – (a lot) more questions than answers', London: Royal Society for the encouragement of Arts, Manufactures and Commerce. Available from: https://www.thersa.org/discover/publications-and-articles/matthew-taylor-blog/2013/05/probation-pbr---a-lot-more-questions-than-answers

Winsor, Sir T. (2019) 'We are paying for failure to prevent crime', *The Times*, 16 September.

11

The impact of scandal and inquiries on social work and the personal social services

Ray Jones

Over the 50 years since 1970 there have been several step changes in the personal social services. This chapter considers what has led to these changes in legislation, in organisational arrangements, and in policy and practice. As is noted below, it has been commented and assumed, in particular, that the major inquiries following public and political concern prompted by the press – especially following the deaths of children – have been at the root of legislation that has reshaped and reset local authority social services, but this is too simplistic, and indeed misleading, as an explanation for the legislative changes that have occurred.

What *has* happened, however, is that the focus of social work practice and of the personal social services over the last 50 years has been shaped and skewed by inquiries, as well as by media coverage, that have often followed an awful event such as the killing of a child or a killing by someone with a mental disorder. This has generated an overwhelming focus on risk and on actions to minimise and manage risk, and this has trumped in importance the provision of help and assistance to people in difficulty.

The impact of scandal and concern on legislation

It has been assumed (Hopkins, 2007; International Centre for Therapeutic Child Care, 2011) that it was the death of Dennis O'Neill and the subsequent inquiry (Monckton, 1945) that led to the government setting up the Curtis Committee (Care of Children Committee, 1946), which in turn spawned the 1948 Children Act. Roy Parker (Parker, 1983), however, noted that the Act's genesis was in the government's concerns, which had started to arise as early as 1943, about what care should be provided for children who had been evacuated during the war and who were now unable to return, for whatever reasons, to the care of their parents. Parker commented:

> It is understandable – and perhaps comforting – to maintain, as many accounts of the evolution of child care legislation do, that Dennis O'Neill's death led to the Curtis Committee and thereby to major reforms. The imperatives for change, however, were by then already in existence and had been building since at least 1943. (Parker, 1983, p 205)

The Maria Colwell Inquiry and the 1975 Children Act

Using the death of a child to explain the advent of major legislation impacting on the personal social services may be convenient, but it is erroneous – or, at least, not an adequate and full account of the roots of subsequent legislation. This was also illustrated in the early 1970s shortly after the formation of social services departments by the 1970 Local Authority Social Services Act (LASSA).

The 1970 LASSA and the family social service that it promoted reflected changes in social work practice, away from an overwhelming focus on caring for children away from their families (which had been central to the 1948 Children Act) and towards how to assist families to care well for their children (Donnison, 1975; Packman, 1975), which were enabled in legislation by the 1963 and 1969 Children and Young Persons Acts. The focus on assisting people within their homes, families and communities also underlay the 1970 Chronically Sick and Disabled Persons Act, which gave the new social services departments the tasks of identifying within their area disabled people to be informed of the range of services that were available and being developed (Topless and Gould, 1981).

These aspirations were soon to be thwarted by a national economic crisis that was generated by a significant international rise in oil prices following the Arab oil-producing countries' restricting the supply and increasing the cost of oil to those countries that had supported Israel in its Six Day War with neighbouring Arab states (Sandbrook, 2011). The value of sterling fell, and the Conservative government fell too, and the incoming Labour government negotiated a loan from the International Monetary Fund that then, as now (Klein, 2017), demanded as a condition of the loan that public expenditure be reduced (Timmins, 1996).

But it was the death of a child in 1973 that possibly had the biggest and longest-lasting impact on how local authority personal social services were to develop, with a legacy that is still in place today. Seven-year-old Maria Colwell was killed by her stepfather in Brighton. She had previously for many years been well cared for by foster carers, but when her mother asked that she be returned to her care this was agreed. She subsequently experienced awful neglect and physical abuse.

Following coverage and campaigning, in particular by the local newspaper and with the local MP lending his support, the government ordered an inquiry (Department of Health and Social Security, 1974). Unlike the Monckton Inquiry following the death of Dennis O'Neill, which was undertaken and completed in four days, the Maria Colwell Inquiry was to last 41 days and was held in public amid a febrile atmosphere, with hostility and hatred targeted at the social worker who had supervised Maria's return to her mother (Butler and Drakeford, 2003, 2011).

It has been assumed and stated (Hayden et al, 1999) that the Maria Colwell Inquiry led to, or at least was a significant spur for, the 1975 Children Act, with children in care to be given greater security through adoption or custodianship.

However, as in the case of the Monckton Inquiry in 1945, changes were already in stream before the setting up and reporting of the Maria Colwell Inquiry and had not been promoted by the child's death (albeit the Act did, as noted by Parker, 1980, introduce the principle that the child's needs are paramount when deciding between the claims of different parent figures, and this was directly related to the Maria Colwell case and inquiry). As with Dennis O'Neill and the 1948 Children Act, and later the death of Victoria Climbié and the 2004 Children Act, a child's death did come to be seen as the generator of legislative and policy changes on permanency arrangements for children in care that were already partly in train.

In the early 1970s the Departmental Committee on the Adoption of Children (Home Office and Scottish Education Department, 1972) was already under way (see Packman, 1975, pp 96–100); the *Children Who Wait* research study (Rowe and Lambert, 1973) on children who were languishing in care with no plans or actions for securing their future care and stability was published in 1973; Rutter (1972) had reviewed and refined Bowlby's concept of maternal deprivation and concluded that what was important was for children to have a consistent and stable relationship with a primary care giver who need not necessarily be the child's mother; and there was the American import of concern about the 'battered child' (Kempe and Helfer, 1972).

This was the time of the battle of ideas about the cycle of deprivation (Rutter and Madge, 1976), about what was argued to be the over-stated importance of the 'blood tie' for children (Goldstein et al, 1973; Kellmer Pringle, 1974), and about whether natural parents should continue to have close involvement with their children when they were in care (Holman, 1975). The Colwell Inquiry reported in the midst of this maelstrom of ideas, at a time when the ground had already been set for the 1975 Act.

As will be explored in more detail below, what did more explicitly occur as a response to the Maria Colwell Inquiry was a resetting of social work practice and procedures and a refocusing of the work of social services departments, changes that have been confirmed and reinforced over the subsequent years in response to further inquiries following the deaths of children.

The Cleveland Inquiry and the 1989 Children Act and the 1990 NHS and Community Care Act

The 1987 Cleveland Inquiry (Secretary of State for Social Services, 1988), led by Lady Butler-Sloss, changed the direction of the press and public concerns about child abuse away from children's being left unprotected and towards their being inaccurately and inappropriately identified as being abused. Professionals and the courts were viewed as too energetic and evangelical in assessing children as having been abused (Bell, 1988; Waterhouse, 1994).

In Cleveland between February and July 1987 120 children were diagnosed as having been sexually abused, in part following an anal dilation test used by two paediatricians. Social workers and the police acted on the basis of the medical assessments. The Inquiry criticised the paediatricians 'for the certainty and over-confidence with which they pursued the detection of sexual abuse in children referred to them' and stated that 'the presence of the physical signs was elevated from grounds of "strong suspicion" to an unequivocal "diagnosis" of sexual abuse' (Secretary of State for Social Services, 1988, p 243).

This turning of press, public and political attention away from children's not being protected from abuse to children's being abused by the child protection system arose not only in Cleveland. In Orkney, Rochdale and elsewhere there were concerns that children had been wrongly assessed as being subjected to ritualised satanic sexual abuse and had been placed in local authority care by the courts (Waterhouse, 1994; La Fontaine, 1998). The debates about whether, and to what extent, children had been inaccurately assessed as having been abused[1] continue, and some 30 years on there are still polarised views (Tonkin, 2014; Richardson and Bacon, 2018; Campbell, 2018).

It has been assumed (Rains, 1991) that it was the Cleveland Inquiry that resulted in the 1989 Children Act. The Act sought to reset the attention of social workers and others to helping 'children in need' within their families by working in partnership with parents to assist them to care for their children, rather than the great majority of actions and activities being to protect children through applying child protection processes and procedures.

But, as in the cases of the 1948 and 1975 Acts noted above, the roots of the 1989 Act were already well established before the Cleveland scandal arose and the Butler-Sloss Inquiry report was produced (Pragnell, 2002). First, there was a review of child law (Department of Health and Social Security, 1985a) that considered both public and private law related to children. Second, there was a collection of research commissioned by the Department of Health, the results of which were collated and published in 1985 (Department of Health and Social Security, 1985b). Third, there were political, civil service and academic champions (Harris, 2006) who remained consistent and determined to rebalance the focus of the law and of social work practice to promote more engagement with, and help for, children and families, as recommended by the research, rather than the predominant narrower focus on child protection.

The 1989 Children Act was accompanied by ten volumes of statutory guidance totalling over 1,000 pages. This in itself pushed specialisation in children's social work within social services departments, with separate divisions for children's and adults' social services. This was also promoted by the 1990 NHS and Community Care Act, which was implemented at the same time as the 1989 Children Act. The 1990 Act and subsequent guidance promoted a purchaser–provider separation within adult services, whereas the thrust of the 1989 Act was towards integration and inter-agency and inter-professional working. The differing organisational and management requirements generated the divisional separation of children's and adults' services, albeit still within one department of social services with a social services director.

Every Child Matters, the Climbié Inquiry and the 2004 Children Act

The specialisation in children's social work and the separation from adult services was taken further by the 2004 Children Act, which required that within local authorities services for schools and education were brought together within a children's services department under the leadership of a director of children's services, while adult services were to be led by a director of adult services. This was the demise, after 30 years, of social services departments and Directors of Social Services.

It is often assumed that the Laming Inquiry (Laming, 2003) into the death of 8-year-old Victoria Climbié in Haringey was the major precipitator of the 2004 Children Act. But, as with the previous children's legislation, the road to the creation of the 2004 Act was longer and more convoluted than a straightforward response to an inquiry report.

Victoria was neglected, abused, and died in February 2000 while in the care of an aunt and her boyfriend. The Laming Inquiry, which reported in 2003, found failings in social work and police practice and in the leadership and coordination of services (Laming, 2003, p 3). The Inquiry Report had 108 recommendations, 25 of which were particularly and explicitly about the role and responsibilities of Directors of Social Services. There are no recommendations in the Laming Report about abandoning and abolishing social services departments.

But there were other factors and dynamics shaping the route to the 2004 Act (Batty, 2005). The first was that New Labour, elected in 1997, were committed to 'joined up' government and 'joined up' public services (Ling, 2002; Caulkin, 2006). Second, the children's minister was Margaret Hodge. She had been the leader of Islington Council from 1982 until 1992 and had introduced the integration of council services based on neighbourhood offices (Boddy and Fudge, 1984, p 203). Third, there was experience in the delivery of newly initiated programmes such as Sure Start that raised issues about the complexity and lack of integration of services, as noted by Sure Start's first national director:

> Many of the principles of Sure Start, the need to integrate service delivery, the need to work with parents and children and particularly the need to work to outcomes rather than inputs were highly influential in the emerging Every Child Matters agenda. The Every Child Matters agenda also began to address some of the main barriers that Sure Start had been experiencing at local level: the difficulties in information sharing between agencies, the absence at local level of a single senior-level responsibility for all children and the struggle in many areas to get agencies to work together. (Eisenstadt, 2007)

As with the 1948, 1975 and 1989 Acts, the 2004 Children Act was not the exclusive or even the direct consequence of a preceding media, public and political child abuse scandal. In each instance there were already factors and forces in play that were heading in the direction of, and leading the development of, the new legislation. The scandals – each of which led to an official inquiry – became attached to and symbolic of the legislation that followed and could be and were used to support the need for the new legislation, but they occurred later within the processes that were already shaping the legislative change. These processes included law reviews that had already been initiated, changing government policy frameworks and also the interests and commitments of key players, including politicians.

The impact of scandal and concern on practice, policy and procedures

If the relationship between scandal, inquiries and changed legislation seems rather more complex than might have been assumed, the impact on practice of media, public and political concerns about – in particular – the deaths of children from neglect and abuse is clearer and more immediate.

The contemporary framework for child protection largely has its genesis in the mid-1970s and is directly related to the death of Maria Colwell and the subsequent inquiry. It was at that time that the government first issued a circular (LASSL 74/13; Department of Health and Social Security, 1974) on inter-agency and inter-professional working to protect children, with Area Review Committees (ARCs) to be established in each local authority area to 'formulate local practice and procedures to be followed in the detailed management of cases', to 'review the work of case conferences in the area' and to 'provide education and training programmes to heighten awareness of the problem [of non-accidental injury to children]'. The circular also noted that 'A case conference is recommended for every case involving non-accidental injury' and that 'A central record of information is essential to good communication between the many disciplines involved in the management of these cases'.

The 1974 circular explicitly noted that it was 'recent cases', which would certainly have included the death of Maria Colwell, that 'underlined the need for regular joint reviews of these measures [to prevent, diagnose, and manage cases of non-accidental injury to children] by all the agencies concerned'. The requirements for a local multi-agency and senior-level coordinating and oversight committee

(ARCs), for multi-agency and multi-professional case conferences and for a register of children deemed to have been abused or at risk of abuse were all expanded upon in more detail in a further circular (LASSL 76/2) in 1976.

This was the child protection infrastructure that was put in place in 1974, which has remained largely intact and has shaped and determined the focus of much social work practice with children and families over the subsequent period of almost 50 years. It is a framework that has been expanded (and also adopted and adapted within more recent adult protection procedures and processes) following subsequent child (and adult) abuse scandals and inquiries, but even this framework had a long gestation that predated the Maria Colwell Inquiry, as was noted by Olive Stevenson, who was a member of the Colwell Inquiry team:

> An analysis of the period demonstrates, first, that the notion of interprofessional activity in child abuse was established well ahead of the Colwell inquiry. Second, there were complex forces propelling work in that direction in which central government administration played a significant, but not the only part. The direct interplay of politicians with the professionals, with doctors in a lead role, further confirmed interagency and interprofessional activity at different levels and in different ways. (Stevenson, 1999, p 103)

The 1980s saw a flurry of child abuse public inquiries following the deaths of children, including Jasmine Beckford (London Borough of Brent, 1985), Tyra Henry (London Borough of Lambeth, 1987) and Kimberley Carlile (London Borough of Greenwich, 1987). Writing in 2004, Stanley and Manthorpe coined the phrase 'the age of the inquiry' (Stanley and Manthorpe, 2004). It was an age that started in the 1970s, gathered momentum in the 1980s and has not slowed down since, and the impact has been selective and negative, as noted by Eileen Munro:

> Approximately 40 more inquiries [after the 1973–74 Maria Colwell Inquiry] were published up to 1990, providing a constant reminder to the public of the existence of child abuse and the apparent failure of professionals to protect children. A review of inquiry reports found that 25 per cent of the reports were not critical of any professional group and social workers escaped censure in 42 per cent. Media coverage, however, varied, with more attention being paid to inquiries that castigated professionals and less

to the ones that exonerated them, fostering an image of all deaths being, in principle, preventable if only professionals acted competently. In this coverage, social workers were repeatedly singled out for blame even when other professional groups had played a major role. (Munro, 2004)

It was in this context of inquiries that the Department of Health prepared further guidance on inter-agency working in child protection. Drafted in 1986, this was revised and published in 1991 under the title *Working Together: A Guide to Arrangements for Inter-agency Co-operation for the Protection of Children from Abuse* (Home Office et al, 1991). It had 126 pages. It subsequently went through several iterations, and in 2010 *Working Together to Safeguard Children* (HM Government, 2010) ran to 390 pages.

The increase in statutory and non-statutory policy, procedural and practice guidance, along with the increased scrutiny, when a child dies, through serious case reviews – which were introduced in 1988, with the requirement expanded upon in the 1991 guidance – has had three implications.

First, social work practice with children and families where there might be concerns about a child's welfare or safety has become more proceduralised and bureaucratised, skewing how social workers spend their time – with more time committed to recording, data inputting and report writing (see, for example, White et al, 2009; Munro, 2011). Second, more attention has been given to scrutinising practice through case auditing and performance management where the cult of managerialism (Harris, 2003; Harris and Unwin, 2009) – which became more prevalent in the 1990s and beyond – has now been further layered by an audit and procedural compliance culture. Third, how social workers approach their work with families has also changed, with greater attention being given to the monitoring and surveillance of families while there is less time for direct work and advocacy to assist families (Featherstone et al, 2018).

The impact of the media's story of 'Baby P'

How this changed approach is a consequence of policy and practice responding to scandal is well illustrated by the changes that occurred immediately following the media shaping and selling of the 'Baby P' story in 2008.

Peter Connelly was 17 months old when he died in August 2007. In November 2008 his mother, her boyfriend and the boyfriend's brother were each found guilty of 'causing or allowing' Peter's death. The media coverage, led by *The Sun* newspaper and its then editor, Rebekah Brooks, focused not on those who had abused Peter (who, because of a still-to-be-held separate criminal trial into the sexual abuse of another child, was known through the media only as 'Baby P') but on the social worker who had sought to help the Connelly family, and her managers, along with a community paediatrician. They and their families were placed in danger of violence and attack by the press coverage, in which *The Sun* claimed that they had 'BLOOD ON THEIR HANDS' (Jones, 2014).

There was an immediate step change across the country in local authority social work and legal decision-making. Care proceedings applications to the courts to seek removal of children from their families increased from 482 in September and 496 in October 2008 to 716 in December 2008 (Children and Families Courts Advisory Service, 2009) when the media's 'Baby P' story was launched.

Following previous child abuse media scandals, after an initial increase in child protection activity there would be some reduction towards the pre-scandal level of activity. For example, following the death of Jasmine Beckford in 1985 there was sharp rise in the numbers of children in care in the next two years, but then the numbers fell back (Schorr, 1992, p 33).

But just as the 'Baby P' story continues to be referenced in the media, the defensive practice and decision-making that it promoted in 2008 still continues. Child protection inquiries undertaken under section 47 of the 1989 Act have increased year on year from 89,300 in 2009/10 to 198,090 in 2017/18 (+122%); child protection plans have increased from 29,200 as at 31 March 2008 to 53,790 in 2018 (+84%); from 2007/08 to 2016/17 care proceedings increased by 130%; and the number of children looked after by local authorities in England has risen from 60,000 in March 2008 to 75,420 in March 2018 (+26%).

The blame tree

What has generated what is now an overwhelming focus on risk assessment, risk management and risk avoidance? It is a combination of blaming, naming and shaming; and the blame tree (Figure 11.1) has its roots in key developments that have occurred since the 1990s. These include the requirement that serious case reviews are now published in full and that they should allocate accountability; inspection reports from the national inspectorates; and national league tables based on

Figure 11.1: The blame tree

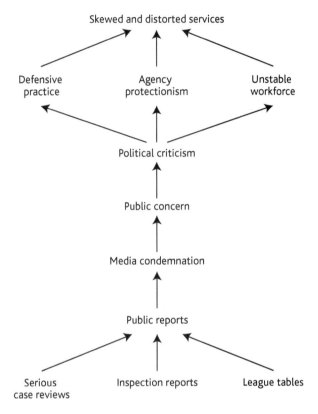

bar graphs publicly reporting comparisons between local authorities on nationally collected and collated key performance indicators.

The reality and experience is that what is then given attention by the local media – and sometimes also more widely – is any criticism or concerns about performance and practice. This has been assisted by Ofsted, for example, even front-loading reports about services that it has assessed as being good with recommendations about what could still be improved, and changing its grading terminology from 'adequate' to 'requires improvement'. The negative coverage then generates a public concern, with politicians 'playing to the gallery' and assuming that there must have been *failures* by social workers if a child has been killed, and demanding that further public inquiries should be held (BBC, 2016) or that workers and senior managers should lose their jobs and be hounded (Coventry Live, 2013).

A high-profile example, and possibly most shocking because she was subsequently appointed as chair of the fast-track, foreshortened Frontline children's social work training programme, was Camilla

Cavendish, a *Times* journalist, who became Prime Minister David Cameron's strategy advisor. She wrote in *The Times* that the death of Elsie Scully-Hicks, an 18-month-old child killed by one of her adoptive parents, was due to 'failures by social workers' (Cavendish, 2017) – a view not supported by the subsequent serious case review, nor by the evidence at the criminal trial of the adoptive parent.

This is all a recipe that cooks up more defensive practice and less stable and more distorted services at the same time that the menu of help to families has been cut and curtailed. Children and families who might have received help when in difficulty are now caught in the child protection monitoring and surveillance net. The public probably think that children within the child protection system have mainly experienced physical or sexual abuse, but 86% of child protection plans in England are because of concerns about the impact on children of chronic neglect and emotional abuse. These are concerns that previously would have been responded to through family support services to tackle family poverty and parental stress, or through the work of Sure Start, family centres and parenting programmes to tackle lack of competence – the very services that have experienced big cuts since 2010.

Scandal and adult abuse

In the 20 years since 2000 there have been similar practice trends in adult social services, albeit these are more likely to be the consequence of the recognition of and response to adults' being abused in residential and larger institutional care. This is not new. For example, in 1967 *Sans Everything* (Robb, 1967), a book about poor and institutionalised care in six long-stay hospitals, was published, and in 1969 an inquiry report was published into the lack of care and the abuse of patients with learning disabilities at Ely Hospital, a former Poor Law workhouse in Cardiff (Butler and Drakeford, 2003, pp 33–60).

This focus on abuse within institutions has largely continued to dominate concerns about the care of adults. In 1998 the Longcare Report (Buckinghamshire County Council, 1998) about the abuse of people with learning disabilities in private care homes in Buckinghamshire was published. More recent examples include the exposure by an undercover reporter in 2011 of abuse at Winterbourne View, a private hospital in South Gloucestershire for people with learning disabilities (BBC, 2011); abuse of older people in a private care home in Essex (Holt, 2014); and abuse at Whorlton Hall in County Durham, a private learning disability hospital (Triggle, 2019).

When there have been infrequent publicly reported inquiries into the abuse of disabled adults, as in Cornwall in 2006 following the killing of Stephen Hoskins (Quarmby, 2011; Morris, 2007), a man with a learning disability, the media coverage has been limited and short-lasting. As Fyson and colleagues have argued (Fyson et al, 2004), 'People with a learning disability are not generally perceived as being of interest to the public at large. Unlike children, adults with learning disabilities do not offer photogenic images of innocence; unlike people with mental health problems, they seldom pose a threat to public safety' (Fyson et al, 2004, p 216). Quarmby noted that 'Right-minded people did not believe ... that disabled people were being targeted. It was an invisible crime' (Quarmby, 2011, p 110).

However, in 2000 the government published *No Secrets* (Home Office and Department of Health, 2000), with 'guidance on developing and implementing multi-agency policies and procedures to protect vulnerable adults from abuse'; and in 2001 the White Paper *Valuing People* (Department of Health, 2001) referred to the abuse of people with learning disabilities. But, as with much of the discussion and ambition at that time, the emphasis in the White Paper was on the ability and right of people to be self-determining, to have choice and control within their lives, and to live independently.

Mental disorder and the impact of inquiries

Greater significance in terms of the impact of scandal and concern has been the attention that has been given to killings *by* someone with a mental disorder and that has led to more controlling mental health legislation and practice, such as assertive outreach teams and services. For example, in 1984 Isabel Schwarz, a social worker at Bexley Psychiatric Hospital, was killed by a former client, Sharon Campbell. An inquiry was belatedly ordered by the Secretary of State for Social Services, but only after campaigning by Isabel's father. It reported in 1988 and gave particular attention to the training, supervision and safety of social workers. It made recommendations about discharge planning, but, although it discussed the possibility of compulsory community treatment orders, it did not argue for the introduction of compulsory orders, commenting that 'We limit ourselves to the comment that we see it as important to guard against the possibility that compulsory treatment in the community might be adopted to some extent as an alternative to providing an adequate range of after-care services' (Department of Health and Social Security, 1988, p 69).

The Inquiry also warned against replicating child protection procedures and processes in mental health services. While recommending that (as with child protection registers) District Health Authorities 'should be required to maintain a register of those patients who are designated as vulnerable in the community', it added:

> Although the analogy with systems operating in the field of child abuse will be obvious enough to many readers of this Report (and as we have made clear, we fully support the concept of multi-disciplinary working), we do not see this proposal as necessarily involving a burdensome amount of 'conferencing' time. (Department of Health and Social Security, 1988, p 70)

The Sharon Campbell Inquiry was followed by a spate of further inquiries after killings by someone with a mental disorder; or in a smaller number of instances there was media reporting of someone with a mental disorder who had themselves died (such as Ben Silcock, who died in 1992 after climbing into the lions' den at London Zoo; see Oxford, 1993).

Notable among these inquiries was the media, and therefore public, attention given to the killing by Christopher Clunis of Jonathan Zito at Finsbury Park underground station. Butler and Drakeford described it as a 'landmark scandal' (Butler and Drakeford, 2003, p 147) and stated that it was influential in creating a concern that care in the community was failing and leading to danger.

The Clunis Inquiry was one of 14 mental health homicide inquiries in the 1990s reviewed by McCulloch and Parker, who reflected that:

> A few inquiries have demonstrably influenced policy – for example the inquiry into the care and treatment of Sharon Campbell led to the Care Programme Approach. However, while the report into the care and treatment of Christopher Clunis brought some policy changes (such as the introduction of section 117 registers), the major policy changes were announced in August 1993 six months before the panel's report was published. Most inquiries have had few direct policy implications. The policy analysis in inquiries is usually weak and naïve, and the influence is mediated by media driven anxiety around the incident leading to a policy response generated by the Department of Health rather than borrowed for the policy team. Thus,

inquiries are therefore only one factor in the political landscape leading to mental health policy. (McCulloch and Parker, 2004, p 147)

Sheppard (2004) gives information about 158 independent mental health inquiries held and reported between 1985 and 2003. Cumulatively, the impact of the media's reporting and coverage of mental health homicides, even if not the outcome of conclusions and recommendations from inquiries, was a more robust, rigorous and reactionary response from the government, with the introduction of compulsory community treatment orders, supervised discharge orders, assertive outreach services and the requirement that health authorities should commission a publicly reported inquiry (as with serious case reviews in child protection) every time there is a mental health homicide.

What was and has been given less attention by governments, however, is the conclusion of the Clunis Inquiry that '[it] is abundantly clear that South East London has insufficient beds for the patients who need secure facilities' (Ritchie, 1994, p 59). Among the criticism of workers and the plethora of more guidance and procedures that usually follow, the issue of resources is rarely addressed in inquiries.

The 2005 Mental Capacity Act and deprivation of liberty safeguards

Legislation that has had a particular and noticeable impact on the workloads of adult social services and social workers was introduced in the early 2000s. The 2005 Mental Capacity Act had a long gestation. Its history goes back at least as far as 1991 and a legal case that was finally decided by the House of Lords as to whether a person who was assessed as lacking capacity to decide for herself could be sterilised (House of Lords, 1989). Subsequent work by the Law Commission throughout the 1990s, with consultative Green (Lord Chancellor, 1997) and White Papers (Lord Chancellor, 1999) led to draft legislation that was passed as the 2005 Mental Capacity Act in 2005 and implemented in 2007.

At the time of its implementation it was expanded by a section in the 2007 Mental Health Act that added Deprivation of Liberty Safeguards (DOLS) to the legislation. DOLS were a consequence of concerns that a man with autism and a severe learning disability was being held at Bournewood Hospital (House of Lords, 1997). He had been living in an adult fostering placement but the carers had been prevented from removing him from the hospital and returning him to their care. The High Court determined that he was being held in the hospital illegally and that being apparently compliant with arrangements that were made (in this case by the hospital) was not the same as giving agreement and consent to the arrangements. In 2014 the Supreme Court (Supreme Court, 2014) upheld a judgment about Cheshire West Council that confirmed that residents in care homes who did not have the capacity to decide to leave the home were covered by DOLS, greatly extending the coverage of, and workloads related to, DOLS.

The 2005 Mental Capacity Act and the DOLS have led to skews in workloads and attention within adult social services and social work, albeit more recently than in children's services. Alongside the increasing emphasis on rationing assistance and services in the context of government funding cuts imposed on local authorities, the adult protection workloads of adult social services have escalated. In 2012/13, for example, 176,000 adult safeguarding concerns were referred to adult social services and by 2017/18 this had increased to 394,655 (+124%). DOLS applications increased from 13,715 in 2013/14 to 227,400 in 2017/18 (+1,558%).[2]

This mirroring in adult social services of the capture of children's services to focus on abuse, protection and risk assessments and risk management is also reflected in the nature of the abuse that dominates adult protection activity, with the most prevalent category of abuse (as in child protection) being neglect (32%).

Summary and concluding comments

The impact of scandal and inquiries on legislation is not as influential or impactful as has often been assumed. Legislative change may be seen and badged as an immediate response to the media's coverage and public concern about, for example, the death of a child, but the legislative change was often already being shaped and promoted prior to the story and scandal about something awful having happened.

A more obvious and clear response to scandal and concern has been change in practice in both children's and adults' services. Attention and activity have been skewed away from direct work to provide assistance and help and towards risk assessment and risk management, with the consequent emphasis being on the monitoring and surveillance of families and individuals. Alvin Schorr, writing in 1992, anticipated that this would happen, noting that 'an early effect of a swelling child abuse caseload is to reduce and eventually wipe out work with parents and preventive work' (Schorr, 1992, p 33).

This has distorted the role of social workers and others, how they are perceived and even how they define and describe their remit. It would be timely to reflect and review whether the direction of travel over recent years and decades has been positive and constructive, or whether it has neutralised and negated the role of providing help and assistance to those who are in difficulty and in crisis.

Notes

[1] At this time the concern was largely about assessments of sexual abuse, which had previously hardly been a major feature within child protection, although it was to have a growing significance in the 1980s and 1990s inquiries into the abuse of children in children's homes and boarding schools, and in the early 2010s inquiries into the sexual exploitation and abuse of children within communities.

[2] Calculated from the Digital.NHS.UK annual statistical reports on Safeguarding Adults and on DOLS Assessments.

References

Batty, D. (2005) 'Climbié Inquiry: the issue explained', *Guardian*, 5 August, https://www.theguardian.com/society/2005/aug/05/ Climbié .

BBC (2011) 'Four arrests after patient abuse caught on film', 11 June, https://www.bbc.co.uk/news/uk-13548222.

BBC (2016) 'Ayeeshia Jane Smith murder: Burton MP Andrew Griffiths calls for inquiry', 9 April, https://www.bbc.co.uk/news/ uk-england-stoke-staffordshire-36006198 .

Bell, S. (1988) *When Salem Came to the Boro: True Story of the Cleveland Child Abuse Case*, London: Pan.

Boddy, M. and Fudge, C. (eds) (1984) *Local Socialism? Labour Councils and New Left Alternatives*, London: Palgrave Macmillan.

Buckinghamshire County Council (1998) *Independent Longcare Inquiry*, Buckingham: Buckinghamshire County Council.

Butler, I. and Drakeford, M. (2003) *Scandal, Social Policy and Social Welfare*, Bristol: Policy Press.

Butler, I. and Drakeford, M. (2011) *Social Work on Trial: The Colwell Inquiry and the State of Welfare*, Bristol: Policy Press.

Campbell, B. (2018) *Official Secrets: Child Sex Abuse from Cleveland to Savile*, Chicago, University of Chicago Press.

Care of Children Committee (1946) *Report of the Care of Children Committee*, Cmd 6922, London: HMSO.

Caulkin, S. (2006) 'Why things fell apart for joined-up thinking', *Guardian*, 26 February, https://www.theguardian.com/society/2006/ feb/26/publicservices.politics.

Cavendish, C. (2017) 'To avoid more deaths like little Elsie's, we need to ask tough questions: a toddler's murder by her adopter reveals a failure by social workers to challenge each other's decisions. They must be trained to do so', *The Times*, 12 November, https://www.thetimes.co.uk/article/camilla-cavendish-to-avoid-more-deaths-like-little-elsie-s-we-need-to-ask-tough-questions-nwj2lh97z.

Children and Families Courts Advisory Service (2009) *CAFCASS Care Demand*, London: CAFCASS.

Coventry Live (2013) 'Coventry MP blasts former head of Coventry's children's services new job after Daniel Pelka case', 19 September, https://www.coventrytelegraph.net/news/coventry-news/coventry-mp-blasts-former-head-6064660.

Department of Health (2001) *Valuing People: A New Strategy for Learning Disability for the 21st Century*, Cm 5086, London: Department of Health.

Department of Health and Social Security (1974) *Report of the Committee into the Care and Supervision Provided in Relation to Maria Colwell*, London: HMSO.

Department of Health and Social Security (1985a) *Review of Child Care Law*, London: HMSO.

Department of Health and Social Security (1985b) *Social Work Decisions in Child Care: Recent Research Findings and Their Implications*, London: HMSO.

Department of Health and Social Security (1988) *Report of the Inquiry into the Care and After-Care of Miss Sharon Campbell*, Cm 440, London: HMSO.

Donnison, D. (1975) 'The development of casework in a Children's Department', in D. Donnison, V. Chapman, M. Meacher, A. Sears and K. Urwin (eds), *Social Policy and Administration Revisited*, London: George Allen and Unwin, pp 103–32.

Eisenstadt, N. (2007) 'Foreword', in J. Belsky, N. Barnes and E. Melhuish (eds), *The National Evaluation of Sure Start: Does Area-Based Early Intervention Work?*, Bristol: Policy Press.

Featherstone, B., Gupta, A., Morris, W. and White, S. (2018) *Protecting Children: A Social Model*, Bristol: Policy Press.

Fyson, R., Kitson, D. and Corbett, A. (2004) 'Learning disability, abuse and inquiry', in N. Stanley and J. Manthorpe (eds), *The Age of the Inquiry: Learning and Blaming in Health and Social Care*, London: Routledge, pp 215–30.

Goldstein, J., Freud, A. and Solnit, J. (1973) *Beyond the Best Interest of the Child*, New York, The Free Press.

Harris, J. (2003) *The Social Work Business*, London: Routledge.

Harris, P. (2006) 'The making of the Children Act: a private history', *Family Law*, December, pp 1054–9.

Harris, J. and Unwin, P. (2009) 'Performance management in modernised social work', in J. Harris and V. White (eds), *Modernising Social Work: Critical Considerations*, Bristol: Policy Press, pp 9–30.

Hayden, C., Goddard, J., Gorin, S. and Van Der Spek, N. (1999) *State Child Care: Looking After Children*, London: Jessica Kingsley.

HM Government (2010) *Working Together to Safeguard Children*, London: Department for Children, Schools and Families.

Holman, R. (1975) 'The place of fostering in social work', *British Journal of Social Work*, vol 5, no 1, pp 3–29.

Holt, A. (2014) 'Staff sacking and suspensions over poor elderly care', 30 April, https://www.bbc.co.uk/news/uk-27128011.

Home Office and Scottish Education Department (1972) *Report of the Departmental Committee on the Adoption of Children*, Cmnd 5107, London: HMSO.

Home Office and Department of Health (2000) *No Secrets: Guidance on Developing and Implementing Multi-agency Policies and Procedures to Protect Vulnerable Adults from Abuse*, London: Department of Health.

Home Office, Department of Health, Department of Education and Science, and Welsh Office (1991) *Working Together Under the Children Act 1989*, London: HMSO.

Hopkins, G. (2007) 'What have we learned? Child death scandals since 1944', https://www.communitycare.co.uk/2007/01/10/what-have-we-learned-child-death-scandals-since-1944/.

House of Lords (1989) *In Re F (Mental Patient Sterilisation)*, May, www.bailii.org/uk/cases/UKHL/1991/1.html.

House of Lords (1997) *R. v Bournewood Community and Mental Health NHS Trust ex p. L* [1997] EWCA Civ 2879.

International Centre for Therapeutic Child Care (2011) '"The Monckton Report" by Sir William Monckton', https://www.thetcj.org/child-care-history-policy/the-monckton-report-by-sir-william-monckton.

Jones, R. (2014) *The Story of Baby P: Setting the Record Straight*, Bristol: Policy Press.

Kellmer Pringle, M. (1974) *The Needs of Children*, London: Hutchinson.

Kempe, C. and Helfer, R. (1972) *Helping the Battered Child and His Family*, Philadelphia: J.B. Lippincott Company.

Klein, N. (2017) *No Is Not Enough: Defeating the New Shock Politics*, London: Allen Lane.

La Fontaine, J. (1998) *Speak of the Devil: Tales of Satanic Abuse in Contemporary England*, Cambridge: Cambridge University Press.

Laming, Lord (2003) *Independent Report: The Victoria Climbié Inquiry: Report of an Inquiry by Lord Laming*, Cm 5730, London: The Stationery Office.

Ling, T. (2002) 'Delivering joined-up government in the UK: dimensions, issues and problems', *Public Administration*, vol 80, no 4, pp 615–42.

London Borough of Brent (1985) *A Child in Trust: The Report of the Panel of Inquiry into the Circumstances Surrounding the Death of Jasmine Beckford*, London: London Borough of Brent.

London Borough of Greenwich (1987) *A Child in Mind: Protection of Children in a Responsible Society: The Report of the Commission of Inquiry into the Circumstances Surrounding the Death of Kimberley Carlile*, London: London Borough of Greenwich.

London Borough of Lambeth (1987) *Whose Child? The Report of the Public Inquiry into the Death of Tyra Henry*, London: London Borough of Lambeth.

Lord Chancellor (1997) *Who Decides*, Cm 3803, London: Lord Chancellor's Department.

Lord Chancellor (1999) *Making Decisions*, Cm 4465, London: Lord Chancellor's Department.

McCulloch, A. and Parker, C. (2004) 'Mental health inquiries, assertive outreach and compliance: is there a relationship?', in N. Stanley and J. Manthorpe (eds), *The Age of the Inquiry: Learning and Blaming in Health and Social Care*, London: Routledge, pp 133–50.

Monckton, Sir W. (1945) *Report on the Circumstances which led to the Boarding-Out of Dennis and Terence O'Neill at Bank Farm, Minsterly, and the Steps taken to Supervise their Welfare*, Cmd 6636, London: HMSO.

Morris, S. (2007) 'Tortured, drugged and killed, a month after the care visits were stopped: social workers and police face criticism for failing to spot abuse of vulnerable man', *Guardian*, 4 August, https://www.theguardian.com/society/2007/aug/04/socialcare.crime.

Munro, E. (2004) 'The impact of child abuse inquiries since 1990', in N. Stanley and J. Manthorpe (eds), *The Age of Inquiry: Learning and Blaming in Health and Social Care*, London: Routledge, pp 75–91.

Munro, E. (2011) *The Munro Review of Child Protection: Final Report*, Cm 6802, London: Department for Education.

Oxford, E. (1993) 'London Zoo lion's victim has eight hours of surgery', *Independent*, https://www.independent.co.uk/news/london-zoo-lions-victim-has-eight-hours-of-surgery-1475989.html.

Packman, J. (1975) *The Child's Generation: Child Care Policy from Curtis to Houghton*, London: Basil Blackwell.

Pragnell, C. (2002) 'The Cleveland child sexual abuse scandal: an abuse and misuse of professional power', www.davidlane.org/children/choct2002/choct2002/pragnell%20cleveland%20abuse.html.

Parker, R. (1980) *Caring for Separated Children: A report of a working party established by the National Children's Bureau*, London: Macmillan, p 66.

Parker, R. (1983) 'The gestation of reform: the Children Act 1948', in P. Bean and S. MacPherson (eds), *Approaches to Welfare*, London: Routledge and Kegan Paul, pp 196–217.

Quarmby, K. (2011) *Scapegoat: Why We Are Failing Disabled People*, London: Portobello Books.

Rains, R. (1991) 'The Cleveland crisis and England's Children Act 1989', https://scholarlycommons.law.case.edu/cgi/viewcontent.

Richardson, S. and Bacon, H. (2018) *Child Sexual Abuse: Whose Problem*, Bristol: Policy Press.

Ritchie, J. (1994) *Report of the Inquiry into the Circumstances leading to the death of Christopher Clunis*, London: HMSO.

Robb, B. (1967) *Sans Everything: A Case to Answer*, London: Nelson.

Rowe, J. and Lambert, L. (1973) *Children Who Wait: A Study of Children Needing Substitute Parents*, London: Association of British Adoption Agencies.

Rutter, M. (1972) *Maternal Deprivation Reassessed*, Harmondsworth: Penguin.

Rutter, M. and Madge, N. (1976) *Cycles of Disadvantage*, London: Heinemann Educational Books.

Sandbrook, D. (2011) *State of Emergency: The Way We Were: Britain 1970–74*, London: Penguin, p 612.

Schorr, A. (1992) *The Personal Social Services: An Outside View*, York: Joseph Rowntree Foundation.

Secretary of State for Social Services (1988) *Report of the Inquiry into Child Abuse in Cleveland 1987*, Cm 412, London: HMSO.

Sheppard, D. (2004) 'Mental health inquiries 1985–2003', in N. Stanley and J. Manthorpe (eds), *The Age of the Inquiry: Learning and Blaming in Health and Social Care*, London: Routledge, pp 175–212.

Stanley, N. and Manthorpe, J. (2004) *The Age of the Inquiry: Learning and Blaming in Health and Social Care*, London: Routledge.

Stevenson, O. (1999) 'Children in need and abused: interprofessional and interagency responses', in O. Stevenson (ed), *Child Welfare in the UK 1948–1998*, Oxford: Blackwell Science, pp 100–20.

Supreme Court (2014) *P v Cheshire West and Chester Council and P&Q v Surrey County Council*, https://www.supremecourt.uk/cases/docs/uksc-2012-0068-judgment.pdf.

Timmins, N. (1996) *The Five Giants: A Biography of the Welfare State*, London: Fontana, p 314.

Tonkin, B. (2014) 'The "moral entrepreneurs" who cash in on child abuse: instead of listening to manipulative zealots, we need an inquiry into how we can make sure children are kept safe', *Independent*, https://www.independent.co.uk/voices/comment/the-moral-entrepreneurs-who-cash-in-on-child-abuse-9600692.html.

Topless, E. and Gould, B. (1981) *A Charter for the Disabled*, Oxford: Basil Blackwell and Martin Robertson.

Triggle, N. (2019) 'Whorlton Hall: hospital abuse missed despite at least 100 official visits', 23 May, https://www.bbc.co.uk/news/health-48388430.

Waterhouse, R. (1994) 'Satanic abuse dismissed as "myth" by government inquiry: report blames Evangelical Christians and "specialists" for the scare which led to investigations', *Independent*, https://www.independent.co.uk/news/uk/satanic-abuse-dismissed-as-myth-by-government-inquiry-report-blames-evangelical-christians-and-1420013.html.

White, S., Hall, C. and Peckover, S. (2009) 'The descriptive tyranny of the Common Assessment Framework: technologies of categorization and professional practice in child welfare', *British Journal of Social Work*, vol 39, no 7, pp 1197–217.

12

British social work: international context and perspectives

Karen Lyons

Introduction

Social work is essentially a local activity, shaped in accordance with the nation-state's historical factors, prevailing political philosophy and socioeconomic conditions and the cultural norms of a particular society, with special reference to the recognised needs of vulnerable individuals, marginalised communities and/or excluded groups. However, such activity is also affected by international geopolitical and economic factors, and social work itself is now recognised as a 'global profession', so it is important to understand social work developments in an international context. Consideration of the global context and taking an international perspective are increasingly relevant to British social work developments, the education and training of social workers, and to their employment, practices and research.

The UK was an early initiator of social work as a recognised activity in the late 19th century. Similar initiatives in response to social problems, and then the establishment of education programmes, were occurring in the US and some European countries (notably Germany and the Netherlands) (Kendall, 2000). British social work developments also influenced the establishment and form of social work in various other countries around the world in the 20th century, although such developments were frequently not suited to these very different societies and have been the basis for challenge and change from the 1960s on. It is not possible to discuss this aspect of the international context further in this chapter for reasons of space (for some 21st-century examples of 'indigenisation' see, for instance, Grey et al, 2008). Climate change, a current issue of international concern, is giving rise to developments in environmental social work that also cannot be addressed here (see, for instance, McKinnon, 2012).

British social workers played a part in the establishment of three international associations, the International Council on Social Welfare

(ICSW, www.icsw.org); the International Association of Schools of Social Work (IASSW, www.iassw-aiets.org) and the International Federation of Social Workers (IFSW, www.ifsw.org). These had their origins in the Paris Conference of 1928 and have all since also developed regional bodies and activities. They currently serve a worldwide membership, aiming to provide opportunities for shared learning and actions addressing local and global social problems. However, despite the fact that BASW took over membership of the IFSW from the Standing Conference of its constituent bodies, it is reasonable to presume that, for the majority of social workers in the UK around 1970, international perspectives were lacking, given the considerable uncertainties about impending changes at home.

I focus here on the international context and perspectives, rather than giving a comparative account of social work in other countries, although reference will be made to national examples as relevant. Some of the material presented relates to Europe (rather than being international): countries across the Channel are our neighbours (a relationship cemented when the UK joined what is now the European Union in 1973) and the UK's exit from the European Union (EU) will have profound implications for the UK population, not least those who are most likely to be the recipients of current social work and welfare services. The chapter comprises three main sections: an outline of selected developments in the international context during the period 1970 to the present; discussion of some issues and controversies related to international engagement and perspectives; and consideration of the changes and challenges for UK social work in the current international context. A concluding summary reiterates the need for developing increased understanding of international contexts and perspectives throughout the profession.

Selected developments in international context from 1970

Naming social work as a global profession might be seen as a 21st-century phenomenon, but, since its inception, a few 'internationalists' have been active at supra-national level in promoting the exchange of ideas and cooperative policy actions that could be to the benefit of social workers and service users nationally. Since 1970 senior figures in BASW have taken significant roles in IFSW. At this time several schools of social work were in membership of IASSW and some large third sector organisations (for example, the Salvation Army) were in membership of ICSW. British social workers and educators had access to international conferences and other ways of gaining international perspectives and participating in international social work. This was a period when the latter term often meant working abroad, usually in countries where social work services and community development activities were limited, leading to a lingering association of international social work (education and practices) with cultural imperialism (Hockenstad, 2012).

Throughout the late 20th century and into the present, some social workers have been directly involved in international social work (or transnational social work) through working for specialist agencies such as the London-based branch of International Social Services (renamed nationally as Children and Families Across Borders, CFAB, see below). However, national/local social workers can also be drawn into such work by chance, as the following case study illustrates. The 1970s followed a period when ties with Commonwealth countries were strong and a long-established practice of voluntary agencies (primarily Barnardos) of sending children in care to orphanages or farms in former colonies (mainly Australia) had only just come to an end.[1] In 1986 an Australian woman ('deported' when she was four years old) contacted Nottinghamshire social services department requesting help to trace her relatives. This led the social worker Margaret Humphries to found the Child Migrants' Trust, which has since campaigned for rights, reparation and recognition for this group of children. Services have been developed for individual former child migrants (for example, family tracing, legal advice and counselling here and in Australia) and a users' group was established in 1997 (International Association of Child Migrants and their Families; IACMF). Official inquiries have been held and apologies have been received (one from the British government as recently as 2010) for a policy that was belatedly recognised as 'misguided' and for the maltreatment of some of the children in the receiving country.[2]

Notwithstanding this example, for many, international social work came onto their radar in the European context. The 1970s–1980s was a period when US literature and theories of practice underpinned the training of British social workers (see Chapter 4). However, this influence began to shift, not only with the growth of more domestic research and literature, but also in line with European policy initiatives from the mid-1980s that favoured professional mobility and links between higher education institutions. The extension of bilateral relationships to multilateral networks was encouraged by the establishment of the Erasmus (European Region Action Scheme for the Mobility of University Students) programme from 1987, based on competitive funding awards. A small but increasing number of social work students benefited from this initiative due to the early formation of networks that expanded or were newly formed after 1990 when former Soviet Union countries became eligible for funding. Further network changes occurred in the present century with the establishment of the Erasmus Mundus programme (2009–13), extending 'membership' to third countries (countries outside Europe).[3]

Network activities included teaching exchanges and international (European) seminars and conferences, some of which resulted in publications (for example, Chytil and Seibel, 1999; Littlechild et al, 2005) adding to the emerging body of literature about social work and Europe (Hill, 1991; Cannan et al, 1992; Lorenz, 1994). They also prompted (from the 1990s) the development of some European or international social work courses (mostly at postgraduate level), including at a few universities in the UK (Lyons and Lawrence, 2006). These have given opportunities for shared learning (formal and informal) about, for example, comparative social work, cross-cultural differences and the wide range of contexts within which social work is practised. Other funding streams aimed at women or youth enabled a wider range of people who might be involved in social work, including service users, to benefit from international – or at least regional – opportunities and perspectives.

The growth of expertise among social work staff may also have had some influence on the teaching of all students on professional courses in the 1990s and into the 21st century, although the particularities and churn in the British system around the turn of the century (see Chapter 5) militated against a more determined effort to embrace international perspectives. It also seems likely that the eventual establishment of a social work degree from 2003 onwards owed more to British preoccupations about domestic social work than to the efforts of some staff to argue for this over a decade or more. Certainly, the Department of Health had been immune to arguments from CCETSW regarding the comparability of British qualifications in 1990, just before the Maastricht Treaty (1992) ruled on free movement of goods, services, capital and *labour* within the European Union (Barr, 1990). At this time many British social workers qualified on shorter courses than the three years stipulated in the 1989 EEC Directive for 'recognition of higher education diplomas awarded on completion of professional education and training'.

Notwithstanding this lack of influence on the Department of Health, CCETSW played a positive role in encouraging efforts to include European perspectives and participation in European programmes, although its main international responsibility was the assessment of equivalence of the overseas qualifications of people wanting to take up social work posts in the UK. Many such applicants might have been judged to hold superior qualifications (for example, most Australian social workers would have graduated from four-year degrees as well as holding a professional award). However, some would have had qualifications based on educational programmes lacking particular elements deemed essential for the award of a Diploma in Social Work (see below and Chapter 5). The need for overseas recruitment increased in the late 1990s, when the majority of social workers applying for approval to work in the UK were coming from Anglophone countries whose education and training programmes (and indeed social welfare systems) were seen as being similar to the UK's.

As staffing problems continued into the 21st century, international recruitment intensified, and in 2005 the head of the GSCC England contributed to a JUC–SWEC conference looking specifically at international labour mobility (Littlechild and Lyons, 2006). A subsequent analysis of GSCC (England) statistics demonstrated that, while the number of overseas social workers remained a very small proportion of the total workforce, there had been a shift in recruiting relatively more people from the EU in line with EU free movement of labour rules and UK immigration policy (Lyons and Hanna, 2011). At the time of writing it is unclear whether this recruitment trend will be reversed when the UK leaves the EU. Meanwhile, recruiting social workers whose mother tongue is not English could potentially affect communication with service users, as well as adding to the workers' learning and transition needs (Kornbeck, 2003; and see later).

Selected issues and controversies

From the late 1990s globalisation was recognised by some international social workers as having a universal (but variable) economic impact and affecting the political philosophy and policy choices of national governments, including in the UK, and thus having relevance for social workers (Lyons, 1999; Khan and Dominelli, 2000; Healy, 2001). This was also signalled in the IASSW/IFSW world conference in Canada in 2000 (Special Issue, 2000). Trends related to globalisation were already evident in UK policies affecting the financing and provision of public services, including in the social welfare field (Pollitt, 1990, 1993). Outsourcing, 'the bottom line' and managerialism increasingly became driving forces underpinning legislation and the reorganisation of social services – no less than other aspects of the welfare state (see below). Globalisation thus impacted on people's lives – negatively in the case of those most likely to be in need of welfare benefits and social services, as could be seen in the financial crash of 2008, leading in the UK to a prolonged period of austerity and the restructuring of various welfare benefits and social services However, the exact way that global events and trends impact on domestic provisions and practices, and the perceived relevance of international conventions and perspectives, varies greatly between countries and has led to an increasing interest in the notion of 'glocal' practice. This means developing interventions and services appropriate to local populations while acknowledging the impact of global issues and events and utilising international knowledge and perspectives.

A more fundamental and ongoing controversy concerns the perennial question about the nature – and reach or 'boundaries' – of social work itself. This in turn leads to associated questions about the appropriate form(s) of education and training for workers in a wide range of organisations concerned with, for example, material needs, family breakdown, alternative care for children, elders or people with disabilities, or community action and social development programmes. In the European context, the editors of a new journal (Otto and Lorenz, 1998) publicised the inclusive term 'Social Professionals' to recognise the diversity of qualifications, titles, roles and settings of the likely readership and to distinguish those whose primary focus is 'the social' from, for example, health workers or educators. European networks introduced British participants to many new terms, including those relating to the naming of their counterparts on the other side of the Channel, for example, *Sozial Arbeit* (statutory social work, including social/financial assistance, in Germany) and social pedagogy (Germany, and also, for example, Spain, Denmark); *animateurs* (for example, France and the Netherlands) or *assistantes de services sociales* (France) (Cannan et al, 1992). At the time, youth and community workers from the UK participated in various networks, although these occupational groups had been separated from the training and, ultimately, the registration of social workers in Britain: English social workers seem to have a very specific remit and rather narrow roles when viewed from an international perspective.

The international definition of social work, agreed in 2000 and revised in 2014 by IFSW and IASSW, presents a 'principles' based view of social work, to be amplified and implemented according to each national context. Some national examples have been illustrated in a series of publications (Social Work Around the World) produced by IFSW (for example, Hall, 2012). In addition, the more recent inclusion of 'social development' in the title of world conferences and in the Global Agenda promoted by IFSW and IASSW[4] recognises the role of social workers in contributing to policy and practical efforts to improve the living conditions of whole populations, rather than the more individualistically focused 'social work' familiar to many in the West. Other documents approved in 2004 have also been revised[5] or are currently undergoing revision (www.ifsw.org/iassw-ifsw-to-update-global-standards-for-social-work-education-and-training/).[6] Yip (2004) had previously critiqued the 'educational standards' as reflecting 'western ideas' about social work, without due regard for differences in cultural norms and the political, socioeconomic and demographic contexts affecting the expectations of social workers. However, these (revised) statements represent important initiatives relevant to national developments, whether social work is a long-established profession, newly emerging or taking new directions, such as being reinvented in the post-communist era.

The IFSW/IASSW Global Agenda chimes with the UN Global Development Goals (signed up to by 190 world leaders in 2015) aiming for sustainable development through ending extreme poverty, tackling climate change and reducing inequality by 2030. While poverty in the Global North is a relative concept rather than being absolute (as it is for some populations in countries of the Global South), inequalities within and between societies are pervasive and not just to be assessed or addressed on economic grounds. The different bases for inequalities recognised in the UK, and in Europe from the 1980s on, led to a shift in focus from European 'anti-poverty programmes' (1975–80; 1985–89; 1990–94) to recognition of the marginalisation of particular populations and strategies to address social exclusion and promote inclusion (Lyons and Huegler, 2012). These unfamiliar terms might have been seen as not relevant to social work in the UK, but they identified that some individuals and minority groups faced not necessarily or exclusively poverty, but discrimination such that they had limited or no opportunities for participation in all aspects of community life and society. They were thus important concepts for addressing divisive aspects evident in many societies, including racism.

Racism was a topic that had received varying amounts of attention in British society in the 1980s and 1990s. Government initiatives and some legislation during that period were aimed at establishing 'multi-cultural' attitudes and behaviour towards minority groups who had settled in Britain (from the 1950s on) from various former colonial territories. From the late 1980s there was a questioning of the accessibility of services, including social work, to the 'black' population (widely defined by some as anyone not included in the white majority population, and more recently renamed Black and Minority Ethnic (BME) groups). This prompted CCETSW's requirement regarding anti-racist training on social work courses, and, although not without its controversies domestically, it was initially regarded as something of a 'British concern', for example in Erasmus networks. However, racism was increasingly identified as a matter for professional concern across Europe (for example, Aluffi-Pentini and Lorenz, 1996; Hazenkamp and Popple, 1997) and perhaps contributed to the emerging awareness in Brussels that 'Fortress Europe' was not a monochrome entity and that all member states had minority groups discriminated against on the grounds of race or ethnicity.

Another social issue seen as peculiarly British by European neighbours related to child abuse and child protection work. Anecdotal evidence in the early 1990s suggested that child abuse was 'not an issue' elsewhere in Europe, although it was well recognised by this stage in the US (where it had first been identified) and in other Anglophone countries. A bilateral research project between English and French partners in the 1990s comparing British and French practices in this field of work, and extending to a comparison of child protection work in seven countries, illustrated the different conceptions of family and community responsibilities towards the child and the varied relationships between the social worker, the child, the family and the state (Hetherington et al, 1997). These differences have continuing relevance in relation to transnational work currently (see below). The wider issue of abuse of women in domestic situations (and the impact on children) has yet to be addressed in the policies of some countries – for example, Russia (Hawkins and Knox, 2014), where the situation is likely to have worsened since the decriminalisation of domestic abuse in 2017 on 'cultural grounds' (Roche, 2018). While attitudes towards elders in Asian and other societies where 'traditional values' prevail are reputedly more respectful and caring than in the West, elder abuse can also be found in many societies (for example, Lopez Borghalo de Carvalho, 2012) but is not yet universally recognised as a focus for public education and intervention by social workers.

Into the 21st century: some changes and challenges

Factors related to the global economy alongside the prevailing political ideology have had a bearing on British social work developments over recent decades. This includes the roles of social workers, the majority of whom have previously been employed in local authority social services departments (Lyons and Manion, 2004). Social work has continued to be seen as a first sector activity, although increasingly statutory work is carried out by social workers employed by third sector/non-governmental organisations under contract to local authorities. However, employment patterns vary across the (western) world and have been closely tied to the existence (or not) of a welfare state.

Welfare states vary widely in terms of their origins, scope and coverage and how services are funded; and, as the case of the US demonstrates, welfare provisions are related at least as much to political and cultural factors as to the economic means to support such provisions, even on a very selective basis. Policy analysts' descriptions of welfare regimes (Esping-Andersen, 1990; Ginsburg, 1992; Abrahamson, 1993) have provided a useful framework for social work analysts as well, for example in recognising the differences in employment bases and responsibilities in different countries.

However, welfare states have come under increasing attack on the grounds of cost and disincentives to individual effort. By 2000, US social workers were warning their UK counterparts about the implications of US welfare reform for UK policy (Link et al, 2000) – predictions which were well founded in terms of a shift to more conditionality in welfare benefits eligibility. This change in the basis and processes for meeting needs as well as in specific social security benefits, now apparent in the UK, is also evident in countries such as Finland, following a brief experiment there with awarding unemployed people a Universal Basic Income (Goodman, 2018). Such changes in the wider social welfare system have a knock-on effect for the expectations of social work and have prompted the re-emergence in the UK of a campaigning and lobbying role for BASW in relation to poverty.[7]

Regarding the charge of 'disincentives', an alternative framing has become prevalent based on individual responsibility and 'consumer choice', these being the rationale for the 'personalisation' policies promoted in the UK (see Chapter 7). Back in 1984, Mishra identified the welfare state as being 'in crisis', and this was a recurring theme into the present century (also referred to as the hollowing-out or dismantling of the welfare state). The welfare state in the UK and elsewhere continues to be under threat as various aspects of provisions are sold off. Some, including many social workers, fear that these processes will be exacerbated by the impending Brexit increasing Britain's vulnerability to US economic and political influence – extending to patterns of employment and roles of social workers.

In 'the age of migration' (Castles and De Haan, 2013) the extent to which migration has featured on the domestic social work agenda (whether in practice, education or research) is variable between countries, despite its being recognised as an important concept and process by those teaching international social work. Immigration to the UK continued through the 20th century, with more diversity of countries of origin and reasons for migrating in the 1990s and into the 21st century, when immigration from the Middle East became a focus of national and European policy concerns (Marshall, 2015). In addition to pre-existing myths and prejudices about immigration and particular groups of migrants, migration has also become conflated with concerns about national and international security fuelled by the 9/11 attacks in New York in 2001, by ongoing conflicts in the Middle East and by periodic localised terrorist attacks in various countries. These are generally attributed to the activities of radical Islamic movements and have had the effect of throwing suspicion on minority Muslim populations in many societies, leading to increased tensions and hate crimes, including in Britain (Weaver, 2018).

Overall, therefore, the 21st century has seen a hardening of policies relating to migration on the part of policy makers and bodies such as the EU, and there have been significant efforts by the UK government to create a 'hostile environment' through legislation and immigration policies and practices since before 2010. Such policies have affected public attitudes to migrants, and anti-immigrant sentiments were a factor in the decisions of some voters in the 2016 referendum on British membership of the EU. The long drawn-out process of leaving the EU has contributed to overt hostility towards immigrants, including many (white) Europeans who have established homes and families in the UK (for example, Duda-Mikulin, 2019).

It has also fed into attitudes that label migrants as 'good' (asylum seekers) or 'bad' (economic migrants), although the latter includes groups of people whose skills and qualifications enable them to participate in international labour mobility on a privileged basis, including social workers (Bartley and Beddoe, 2018) and others whose services are needed in the social care sector. In general, consideration of push and pull factors in the motivations to migrate and of forced migration is more useful, including in assessment processes. The recognition of some migrants as refugees (according to the UN 1951 Refugee Convention) enables some people to seek asylum in countries where they feel safe and can secure a livelihood, and brings human rights into sharp focus, giving a basis for social work activities in this field in some countries. But, although international human rights conventions relating to various populations were developed by the UN during the latter half of the 20th century and 'promotion of human rights' is included in the international definition of social work and in the Global Agenda for social work, human rights have not been well recognised as the basis for much British social work. Some have seen the UK's 1998 Human Rights Act as leading to 'defensive practice' rather than enabling social workers to utilise a rights-based approach in their work, while the Act itself has been perceived as 'foisted' on the UK government by the EU and may therefore be vulnerable to repeal.

Exceptions to the above generalisation about British social workers' role in relation to migrants are evident in the work of some voluntary agencies providing services to selected groups of migrants (for example, Freedom from Torture). Social workers in statutory agencies may have responsibility for migrant children (under 18 years), particularly if they enter the UK as unaccompanied minors; and child migrants are the focus of work for some long-established international non-governmental organisations. The reasons why separated children travel to and across Europe were identified by a Save the Children report (Ayotte, 2000) and include trafficking for exploitation, a situation that had just started to come onto the social work research radar (Barrett et al, 2000) and that is now receiving more attention in both research and practice. It is one of the issues being addressed by social workers in, for instance, the Salvation Army, and also by national agencies such as Barnardos in the UK.[8]

UK immigration policies have put pressure on public service workers and providers of jobs and housing to assess the eligibility of applicants for access to resources. Earlier in the 21st century social workers in local authority departments were encouraged to avoid being drawn into 'the work of immigration authorities' in deciding whether or not applicants were eligible for their services, with the expectation that children in particular should be assessed on the basis of need for services rather than their nationality or immigration status (Hayes and Humphries, 2004), and this is still a contested issue (Wroe, 2019). However, following an audit of cases that identified various issues related to children crossing national borders (www.cfab.org.uk/news/research), CFAB ran a campaign in 2019 to promote the importance of social workers identifying the nationality of service users or children already in care (some of whom might be technically 'stateless') in order that their status can be regularised and they can secure their rights (including to citizenship and family reunification). CFAB is also working closely with partner agencies to address variations in assessment practices relating to such children and (at the time of writing) is hosting a working party of stakeholders in the policy field partly to address the implications of Brexit for this particular minority group. This provides an example of the way in which a specialist agency involved in transnational social work can contribute research and specialist knowledge relating to domestic policies and practices.

Concluding comments

Social work can reasonably be described as a global profession, but for most social workers it remains an activity shaped by national contexts, with variable recognition as to the relevance of international conventions and global events and trends. Globalisation itself consists of a number of interrelated processes, spreading beyond the economic effects of big business and finance, although these clearly play a major role in the huge disparities in wealth and inequalities between and within countries worldwide. These processes have included the spread of political ideologies which affect ideas about the welfare state and the role of social workers. This has been evident in UK social work in (re-emerging) concerns about poverty and the need for more attention by social workers to the policy environment.

Globalisation forces are also a driver of migration, posing challenges to many societies (whether they are sending or receiving countries), including having implications for the policies and practices of social workers. Nationally, social workers may be involved in addressing hostile attitudes of local populations as well as in working with new immigrant groups to develop culturally relevant services. Strengths-based approaches underpinned by human rights principles are evident in some of this work and in some countries, including those where a wider definition of social work (as allied with social development) prevails. At a time when it seems that social work itself is under threat and needs to 'reinvent itself' in the UK, international perspectives and reference to the work of the three international professional associations could encourage national social workers and assist in 'learning from abroad'.

International social work takes different forms and may be the focus of specialist agencies where workers develop specialist knowledge. As such, they can highlight areas where changes are needed in (national) policies and practices. They may also be involved in comparative/cross-national research, in addition to that carried out by academics and specialist research institutes and networks: this may take a comparative form, but can also illustrate how processes at supra-national level affect the practice contexts of, and requirements placed on, national social workers. Not all social workers will become involved in international social work as specialists, but, given the cross-national nature of many families and communities and the negative impact of globalisation processes on the most vulnerable members of societies, having some international awareness and perspectives is now essential for development of professional practice and services. And, even if most social workers are not themselves participants in the transnational workforce, increased numbers of social workers will find themselves drawn into some form of transnational social work.

Finally, development of international social work and perspectives does not mean a drive to uniformity or imposition of particular ways of professional thinking and working. The Brexit vote and subsequent processes and events have highlighted deep divisions within British society, but also the extent to which individual countries are (inextricably?) involved in regional as well as international trading and other interdependent relationships. While social workers – along with the rest of the British population – may be divided in their views as to the advisability or otherwise of leaving the EU, a close association with colleagues in Europe and beyond has illustrated the need for understanding of, and respect for, difference both across and within national borders. Such respect provides a necessary basis not only for positive developments in social work nationally but also for participation in ethical international policy work and transnational practices.

Notes

[1]   www.barnardos.org.uk/former-barnardos-children.
[2]   www.childmigrantstrust.com/our-work/about-us.
[3]   https://eacea.ec.europa.eu/sites/2007–13/erasmus-mundus-porgramme_en.
[4]   www.ifsw.org/social-work-action/the-global-agenda.
[5]   *Ethics and values* (2018), www.ifsw/global-social-work-statement-of-ethical-principles/.
[6]   www.ifsw.org/iassw-ifsw-to-update-global-standards-for-social-work-education-and-training/.
[7]   www.basw.co.uk/resources/psw-magazine/psw-online/basw-launches-anti-poverty-practice-guide-socialwork.
[8]   www.barnardos.org.uk/what-we-do/protecting-children/trafficked-children.

References

Abrahamson, P. (1993) 'Welfare pluralism: towards a new consensus for a European Social Policy', *Cross National Research Papers*, vol 2, no 6, pp 5–22.

Aluffi-Pentini, A. and Lorenz, W. (eds) (1996) *Anti-Racist Work with Young People: European Experiences and Approaches*, Lyme Regis: Russell House Publishing.

Ayotte, W. (2000) *Separated Children coming to Western Europe: Why they Travel and How they Arrive*, London: Save the Children.

Barr, H. (1990) *Social Work Education and 1992*, London: CCETSW In Europe 1.

Barrett, D. with Barrett, E. and Mullenger, N. (eds) (2000) *Youth Prostitution in the New Europe: The Growth in Sex Work*, Lyme Regis: Russell House Publishing.

Bartley, A. and Beddoe, L. (eds) (2018) *Transnational Social Work: Opportunities and Challenges of a Global Profession*, Bristol: Policy Press.

Cannan, C., Berry, L. and Lyons, K. (1992) *Social Work and Europe*, Basingstoke: Macmillan.

Castles, S. and De Haan, H. (2013) *The Age of Migration: International Population Movements in the Modern World* (5th edn), London: Sage.

Chytil, O. and Seibel, F. (eds) (1999) *European Dimensions in Training and Practice of Social Professions*, Boskovice: ALBERT.

Duda-Mikulin, E.A. (2019) *EU Migrant Workers, Brexit and Precarity: Polish Women's Perspectives from inside the UK*, Bristol: Policy Press.

Esping-Andersen, G. (1990) *The Three Worlds of Welfare Capitalism*, Cambridge: Polity Press.

Ginsburg, N. (1992) *Divisions of Welfare: A Critical Introduction to Comparative Social Policy*, London: Sage Publications.

Goodman, P.S. (2018) 'Finland has second thoughts about giving free money to jobless people', *New York Times*, 24 April, www.nytimes.com/2018/04/24/business/finland-universal-basic-income.html).

Grey, M., Coates, J. and Yellow Bird, M. (eds) (2008) *Indigenous Social Work Around the World: Towards Culturally Relevant Education and Practice*, Aldershot: Ashgate.

Hall, N. (ed) (2012) *Building the Global Agenda for Social Work and Social Development*, Geneva: IFSW.

Hawkins, C. and Knox, K. (2014) 'Gender violence and discrimination in Russia: learning from an American Russian partnership', *ISW*, vol 57, no 5, https://doi.org/10.1177/0020872814536416.

Hayes, D. and Humphries, B. (2004) *Social Work, Immigration and Asylum: Debates, Dilemmas, and Ethical Issues for Social Work and Social Care Practice*, London: Jessica Kingsley.

Hazenkamp, J.L. and Popple, K. (eds) (1997) *Racism in Europe: A Challenge for Youth Policy and Youth Work*, London: UCL Press.

Healy, L. (2001) *International Social Work: Professional Action in an Interdependent World*, New York: Oxford University Press.

Hetherington, R., Cooper, A., Smith, P. and Wilford, G. (1997) *Protecting Children, Messages from Europe*, Lyme Regis: Russell House Publishing.

Hill, M. (ed) (1991) *Social Work and the European Community: The Social Policy and Practice Contexts*, London: Jessica Kingsley.

Hockenstad, T. (2012) 'Social work education: the international dimension', in K. Lyons, T. Hokenstad, M. Pawar, N. Huegler and N. Hall (eds), *The SAGE Handbook of International Social Work*, London: Sage, pp 37–43.

Kendall, K. (2000) *Social Work Education: Its Origins in Europe*, Alexandria, VA: Council on Social Work Education.

Khan, P. and Dominelli, L. (2000) 'The impact of globalisation on social work in the UK', *European Journal of Social Work*, vol 3, no 2, pp 95–8.

Kornbeck, J. (ed) (2003) *Teaching Language in the Social Work Curriculum*, Mainz: Logophon.

Link, R. and Bibus, A. with Lyons, K. (2000) *When Children Pay: US Welfare Reform and its Implications for UK Policy*, London: CPAG.

Littlechild, B. and Lyons, K. (eds) (2006) *International Labour Mobility in Social Work*, BASW monograph, Birmingham: Venture Press.

Littlechild, B., Erath, P. and Keller, J. (eds) (2005) *De- and Reconstruction of European Social Work*, Stassfurt: ALBERT.

Lopez Borghalo de Carvalho, M.I. (2012) 'Violence against the elderly: challenges for social workers', in N. Hall (ed), *Building the Global Agenda for Social Work and Social Development*, Geneva: IFSW.

Lorenz, W. (1994) *Social Work in a Changing Europe*, London: Routledge.

Lyons, K. (1999) *International Social Work: Themes and Perspectives*, Aldershot: Ashgate.

Lyons, K. and Hanna, S. (2011) 'European social workers in England: exploring international labour mobility', *Social Work Review*, vol 3, pp 185–96.

Lyons, K. and Huegler, N. (2012) 'Social exclusion and inclusion', in L. Healy and R. Link (eds), *Handbook on International Social Work*, New York: Oxford University Press, pp 37–43.

Lyons, K. and Lawrence, S. (eds) (2006) *Social Work in Europe: Educating for Change*, Birmingham: Venture Press.

Lyons, K. and Manion, K. (2004) 'Goodbye DipSW: trends in student satisfaction and employment outcomes', *Social Work Education*, vol 23, no 2, pp 133–48.

Marshall, T. (2015) *Prisoners of Geography: Ten Maps that Tell you All you Need to Know about Global Politics*, London: Elliott and Thompson Ltd.

McKinnon, J. (2012) 'Social work and changing environments', in K. Lyons, T. Hokenstad, M. Pawar, N. Huegler and N. Hall (eds), *The SAGE Handbook of International Social Work*, London: Sage, pp 265–78.

Mishra, R. (1984) *The Welfare State in Crisis*, Brighton: Wheatsheaf Books.

Otto, H-U. and Lorenz, W. (1998) 'Editorial: the new journal for the social professions in Europe', *European Journal of Social Work*, vol 1, no 1, pp 1–4.

Pollitt, C. (1990, 1993 2nd edn) *Managerialism and the Public Services*, Oxford: Blackwell Publishers.

Roche, M. (2018) 'What happened after Russia decriminalised domestic abuse', www.newhumanist.org.uk/articles/5326/what-happened-after-Russia-decriminalised-domestic-abuse.

Special Issue (2000) *Social Work and Globalization*, Special Issue of *Canadian Social Work*, vol 2, no 1.

Weaver, M. (2018) 'Hate crime surge linked to Brexit and 2017 terrorist attacks', *Guardian*, 16 October, www.theguardian.com/society/2018/oct16/hate-crime-brexit-terrorist-attacks-england-wales.

Wroe, L. (2019) 'We are not border police', *Professional Social Work*, July/August, pp 24–5.

Yip, K. (2004) 'A Chinese cultural critique of the global qualifying standards for social work education', *Social Work Education*, vol 23, no 5, pp 597–612.

Afterword

Terry Bamford and Keith Bilton

The overall picture emerging from the preceding chapters is one of social work survival in a cold climate. The halcyon days of the early 1970s with double-digit growth rates have never been repeated. Even when the Blair/Brown government was investing heavily in the NHS during years of plenty, social care was the poor relation. (And in the British system social work is regarded as being subsumed within social care.) It was not before about 2010 that government came to realise that the effects on the NHS of a failing social care system will be disastrous.

But the impact of years of austerity goes far beyond the looming collapse of social care. It has reawakened social workers to the impact on the poor and vulnerable of decisions made in Whitehall. Social workers do not have to go to watch a Ken Loach movie to see families forced into poverty by the cumulative consequences of frozen benefit levels, the two child policy, the bedroom tax and benefit sanctions. Those least able to cope are punished most harshly. The mushrooming growth of food banks tells its own story. But austerity has also had an impact on the daily practice of social workers. This should be a rewarding experience, but for too many it clearly is not. In the decade of austerity it has been social workers' misfortune to have been employed (or otherwise paid for) by local authorities, whose budgets have been cut more severely than those of other public services.

The 'Boot Out Austerity' march led by one of our contributors had a real impact on social workers. While social workers have to see social action as part of their professional responsibility, how to do so in a constrained local authority context remains a dilemma.

Tompsett, in Chapter 5 on social work education, draws attention to the relatively short time social workers spend in practice compared with other professions. She observes that 'an over-focus on recruitment rather than retention risks wasting recruitment costs and reducing practitioner experience and continuity in the workplace'. But there is a yawning gap between social work as taught on most courses and the reality of daily practice in both adult and children's services. Too often practice consists of following procedures rather than providing opportunities for creativity and imagination. Care management has the potential to deliver personalised services co-designed with the recipient, but preoccupation with controlling budgets has stifled that potential. It will not be recovered until care management is freed from its false association with the purchaser/provider split.

It is no easy matter to combine appropriate space for the individual exercise of professional discretion and judgement with the necessary accountability of public service organisations. An excess of procedures is usually a sign that professional discretion is being unduly restricted. The classic definition of the purpose of bureaucracy is that it exists to ensure that like cases are treated alike, and in this form it provides a necessary safeguard against favouritism, discrimination (in its negative sense) and corruption. But social work practises discrimination in its positive sense, that of discerning critical differences between apparently like cases, and over-prescriptive procedures can get in the way of this. In the application of the three Es – economy, efficiency and effectiveness – economy (reducing input) has been to the forefront in the decade of austerity. Excessive proceduralisation, however, has been with us for longer, and is a sign of a misguided pursuit of effectiveness (the extent to which output achieves objectives), which, ironically, serves only to reduce efficiency (the input–output relationship). It is misguided if it seeks to achieve by organisational means objectives that depend largely on professional competence; and it is inefficient when it imposes time-consuming requirements. It happens because there is insufficient public and political confidence in the competence of social workers (and here the relatively short shelf-life of social workers does not help) and because the profession has in consequence been denied an adequate say in its regulation.

In adult social services the problems of financing residential and domiciliary social care grow ever greater, and are of greater public and political concern than the future health of social work. In children's social services the dominance of child protection work, 'another social issue seen as peculiarly British by European neighbours', as Lyons observes in Chapter 12, has had most unfortunate consequences. Child protection work needs to be undertaken by an agency whose primary role is family support, within an adequately functioning welfare state. Ray Jones, in Chapter 11, observes that '86% of child protection plans in England are because of concerns about the impact on children of chronic neglect and emotional abuse'. It is likely that a hostile social security system contributes to this, as does the stripping out of family support services, with the role ascribed to social workers in child protection increasingly that of surveillance and risk management. The unhappy history of probation serves a as warning of the consequences if those tasks assume primacy over relationship building. There are risks in this approach. When a child dies when the family is under supervision, the all-too-predictable 'this must never happen again' reaction overrides normal recognition of the difficulties of predicting and preventing crime.

Children's services social work is now dominated by child protection. Preventive work and family support are a luxury that local authorities can no longer afford, although in reality the cost to society of our failure to do so will be greater in the long run. Lyons observes in Chapter 12 that 'English social workers seem to have a very specific remit and rather narrow roles when viewed from an international perspective'. The classic US terminology divides social work into casework, group work and community organisation. (Barack Obama was a community organiser in Chicago Southside.) In France le travail social includes assistants de service social, éducateurs spécialisés and animateurs socioculturels. In this country, social work has become synonymous with social casework, and is defined by agency function. Local authority social care settings are taken for granted as the normal environment for social work, despite the Children and Family Court Advisory and Support Service employing more than 1,400 social workers, and many social workers working in Youth Offending Teams. While protection of title was seen as a step forward in limiting the designation 'social worker' to those with a qualification and registered as such, has it cut out many engaged in undertaking good caring work based on relationships, from Samaritans to the Trussell Trust? Is the political impotence of social work due to our failure to mobilise with the much larger group of social carers to challenge an unfair and inhumane welfare system?

The question powerfully posed by a number of contributors is whether good social work is possible in the constraints of local government. In Chapter 8 Beresford and Croft offer one solution: social work as a universal service; but if the cost of free social care makes government hesitate, one wonders if this is realistic. Another option tried was the experiment with social work group practices funded by contracts with the local authority but organising themselves to offer a social work service, but this never really took off. The practices were caught between the accusations that they were privatising social care and the requirement to comply with local authority procedures constraining their freedom to act.

Through this review of the last half century runs the conviction of all the authors that the enterprise of social work is worth undertaking. Its professional voice, BASW, has played an important role in demanding that social work clients be viewed as fellow citizens long before it was accepted practice; in campaigning for registration, again 20 years ahead of its coming to fruition; in promoting an ethical code; and latterly in campaigning against austerity and the poverty it has created. Yet BASW still speaks for a minority of registered social workers. Its challenge, and that of the social work profession as a whole, is to engage all social workers in campaigning for social justice and for a working environment that promotes good practice. As Emma Gant notes at the end of Chapter 7, social action is a professional responsibility.

Index

Lightning Source UK Ltd.
Milton Keynes UK
UKHW021533150620
364974UK00003B/47